A MANUAL OF

HINDU LAW

ON THE BASIS OF

SIR THOMAS STRANGE

A MANUAL OF
HINDU LAW

ON THE BASIS OF

SIR THOMAS STRANGE

REGINALD THOMSON

GYAN

Published by

Gyan Publishing House
5, Ansari Road
Daryaganj, New Delhi-110002
Phone: 011-47034999, 9811692060
E-mail: books@gyanbooks.com

Distribution Network
gyanbooks.com
India, USA, Canada, UK, Australia

ISBN: 978-93-6920-970-5 (PB)

First Published, 1881

2nd Impression 2025

Printed at: Gyan Press, Delhi.

A MANUAL OF HINDU LAW ON THE BASIS OF SIR THOMAS STRANGE
Author: REGINALD THOMSON

A
MANUAL OF HINDU LAW.

A MANUAL OF HINDU LAW

ON THE BASIS OF

SIR THOMAS STRANGE,

LATE CHIEF JUSTICE OF MADRAS,

AND ILLUSTRATED

BY THE DECISIONS OF THE COURTS

OF ALL THE PRESIDENCIES,
AND OF THE PRIVY COUNCIL,

BY

REGINALD THOMSON, LL.B.,
OF THE MIDDLE TEMPLE, BARRISTER-AT-LAW, AND AN
ADVOCATE OF THE HIGH COURT OF MADRAS.

Let him (the king) establish the laws of the conquered nation, *as declared in their Books.*
MENU, ch. vii, v. 203.

SECOND EDITION.
(Revised and Enlarged.)

MADRAS:
HIGGINBOTHAM AND CO.
By special Appointment to H. R. H. The Prince of Wales,
and Publishers to the Madras University.
1878.

To

The Honorable

SIR ROBERT STUART, KT., Q.C.,

Chief Justice of the North West Provinces.

MY LORD CHIEF JUSTICE,

I need hardly say it gives me much pleasure to be allowed to dedicate this Book to you.

As a Member of the Bar, I cannot but feel a high respect for your Lordship's attainments, and judicial capacity, but apart from this, your Lordship has laid me under obligations, for which, I trust, I shall always feel grateful.

Without holding your Lordship responsible for any of the opinions herein expressed, I am,

My Lord Chief Justice,

Your Lordship's much

obliged and faithful servant,

REGINALD THOMSON.

MADRAS, *November* 1878.

PREFACE.

THE publication of the Second edition of this work requires no studied preface. It is a thorough recast of the first edition. Several hundreds of new sections have been added; numerous references to the decisions of the different Courts in India and of the Privy Council have been affixed; and various alterations, also, have been otherwise made. Appendices, too, have been attached to the work.

The object in view has been to make this Manual a handy book of reference to the practical, work-a-day lawyer, as well as useful to others, by presenting a summary of the law, as administered at the present day, without encumbering it with unnecessary matter. The attainment of this object is my earnest hope.

Hindu law is a many-sided subject, and various have been the views that have been propounded on some of its most important questions. There is certainly a want of uniformity, not only amongst text writers, but also in the decisions of the Courts. And there are also several points that are still involved in doubt. Different remedies have been proposed for this state of things; most prominent among which is the inauguration of a general code of Hindu law, which, it is said, will once and for ever settle the difficulties that are daily met with. But codification, although it may settle the law, might make matters worse than they are at present.

Before making a code, the law should, at least first, be ascertained. There are many people who think, and apparently with reason, that several portions of Hindu law are misinterpreted. Take the case, for instance, of *Stridhanum*. *Sanskrit* scholars, such as MR. JUSTICE WEST and Drs. BURNELL and BUHLER affirm that, if the *Mitakshara* be correctly interpreted, *all* property inherited by a woman forms her *Stridhanum*. Yet, except in Bombay, from the Privy Council downwards, it has been solemnly declared to be otherwise. And the question naturally suggests itself, who is right? One cannot help feeling instinctively that the scholars are right, and the Courts are wrong. In a case of this sort, resting as it does on the interpretation of *Sanskrit Slokas*, how can it possibly be otherwise. And if this be so, we shall only commit untold mischief, if we were to codify doctrines which Hindu lawyers declare to be unsound. As to *Stridhanum*, indeed, so far as the widow is concerned, it seems to be pretty well settled, at any rate in Bengal and Madras, that what she inherits from her husband, she cannot take as *Stridhanum*. It would be urged, therefore, by way of example, that the law should not be unsettled. There may be something in this, so far, at least, as the widow is concerned. But then there are other relationships besides that of widowhood. There is that of the daughter, as well as that of the sister. And the law at any rate, in Southern India, on the inheritances of these persons, does not seem as clearly defined as that which relates to the inheritance of the widow. These and other matters require determination before they are embodied in a code. A code, therefore, in the present state of the law would, by no means, be a *desideratum*. The remedy would probably be worse than the disease, and the result would be that the last state of the Hindu law would be even worse than the first.

There can be no doubt that the cause of the evil is the ignorance of the *Sanskrit* language that almost universally prevails. It would of course be simply absurd to expect the Judges of our Courts to be *Sanskrit* scholars. However desirable this might be, it would be simply impossible. One of two plans therefore seems to suggest itself. Either that a conclave of *Sanskrit* scholars should assemble, (as seems to have been done in the time of *Warren Hastings*), and, by a comparison of the various law books, authoritatively declare what the law *really is*, or else that there should be attached to each Court a *Sanskrit* scholar or more of some eminence, who will be able *thoroughly* to sift the language of any disputed text and to inform the Court of the precise meaning of the *Sloka*. Where of course any of the Judges happens to be a skilled *Sanskritist*, there would be no necessity for the arrangement, but otherwise it seems absolutely necessary for the right understanding of the law that some such an arrangement should be made. The old *Sudder* plan of having *Pundits* was not a bad one, but their *futwahs* were so often contradictory, that latterly their utterances were almost entirely disregarded. It appears doubtful also, whether they were thoroughly versed in the *Sanskrit* language.

It seems indeed anomalous that the expounders of the Hindu law should be Englishmen generally ignorant of the customs of the people, of their language, and of their literature.[a] This is sufficient to account for the diverse views, often expressed by the same Judges at different times on the same topic of the law. As English lawyers, too, they have insensibly allowed ideas borrowed from the English and the Continental laws to be engrafted on the Hindu system. The consequence is that, the Hindu law of the present day consists of a medley, which, perhaps, the ancient Hindu sages themselves would hardly be able to recognise. This state of things has lasted long enough. It is time that a reform should be initiated. We seem to be drifting into a sea of confusion and uncertainty, from which it is proposed to save us by the more than questionable remedy of a code. The evil lies in the system under which the law is administered.

Attention is drawn to Appendix A, a discussion of the recently decided *Shivagungah* case in the *Madura* District,

[a] See *Mr. Justice Pontifix's* remarks, 14 Bengal Reports, 237.

as involving important points of Hindu inheritance, and as illustrating to a great extent the preceding remarks.

For any errors that may be found in the Book I ask the indulgence of the Profession. Those, who know the labor involved in wading through a mass of legal matter, will be the most ready to grant me the indulgence. I regret also that I have not had more time at my disposal for revision.

I must apologise for the Book not having appeared earlier, but this is owing to professional engagements, proofs sometimes being obliged to follow me over the country.

REGINALD THOMSON.

MADRAS, 18*th* *Nov.* 1878.

CONTENTS.

A MANUAL
OF
HINDU LAW.

CHAPTER I.

THE SCHOOLS AND AUTHORITIES OF HINDU LAW.

Sruti and Smriti.

1. THE laws of the Hindoos, civil and religious, are by them believed to be alike founded on revelation. They consist of the *Sruti* (revealed law), which includes the *Vedas,* and the *Smriti* (remembered law), which comprises forensic law, or the *Dharma Sastra.* [a]

Authorities of Hindu law.

2. Forensic law is to be sought primarily in the Institutes (*Smritis* or *Text-books*) attributed to holy sages under the assumed names of *Menu, Yajnyawalkya* and others. But *Glosses* and *Commentaries* published under successive dynasties have been written upon these, which together with the *Digests,* are now regarded as conclusive authorities, and are preferred to the *Text-books.*

Schools of law.

3. There are five distinct schools of law which differ more or less from each other. They may be termed the schools of *Bengal,* of *Benares,* of *Mithila,* of the *Dekhan*

a 1 Strange's Hindu Law, 315, Colebrooke.

(*Dravida*), and of the *Mahrattas* (Western India). The original *Smritis* are of course common to all, but they each assign the preference to particular Commentators and Scholiasts. [a]

4. There are, however, but two principal schools of law—that of Southern India which follows the *Mimansa* (the rules of the interpretation of precepts or logic) : while in the East (Bengal and Behar) the *Nyáyá* (dialectics) is followed. These are divided into sects of jurisprudence, which altogether form five. [b]

5. These schools differ but slightly from each other, except the school of Bengal, which differs from the others on several points relating especially to the law of inheritance. The doctrines of the Bengal school are somewhat in advance too of those of the others, and tend towards the separation of law from religion.

The *Dharmasastra.*

6. The *Manava Dharma Sastra,* or Institutes of Menu, the highest authority of memorial law, is admittedly not only the oldest work, but also the holiest after the Vedas, and is considered the basis of the present system of Hindu Jurisprudence. It is divided into three classes: first, the *Smritis* or *Text-books*, which are the foundation of all Hindu law. Second, *Vyakhyana* or *Glosses* and *Commentaries* upon the *Smritis,* many of which partake of the nature of Digests. Third, the *Nibandhana Grandha,* or Digests properly so called, either of the whole body of the law, or

a Morley's Digest.

b 1 Strange's Hindu Law, App.

of particular portions thereof collected from the Text-books and their Commentators. [a]

Commentaries.

7. Among the numerous commentaries on the Institutes of Menu, the most esteemed are a commentary of *Medhatithi:* another by *Govinda Raja:* a third by *Dharanidhera:* and the celebrated gloss of *Kullakabhatta,* entitled *Menuvurtha Muctavali.* [b]

8. There are other legislators of repute besides Menu. The principal are *Yajnyawalkya, Apastamba, Katyayana, Vrihàspati, Parasara, Vyasa,* son of *Parasara,* and the reputed author of the *Puranas, Sancha* and *Lichita, Gautama* and *Vasishtha.* [c]

9. These heroic personages are reputed to be the authors of Institutes similar to Menu's. Some of these have well known Commentaries, such as the *Mitakshara* of *Vijnyaeswara* on the text of *Yajnyawalkya,* and the *Madhavya* of *Vidjanarayanaswami* on the text of *Parasara.* Other important Commentaries are the *Smriti Chandrika* by *Devandabhatta:* the *Vivada Chintamani,* the *Vyavahara Mayukha* and the *Viramitrodaya:* also the *Saraswati Vilasa.* To these may be added the works of *Sri Rama Pundita,* the *Subodhini* by *Viseswara* and the work of *Balambhattà,* the two latter on the *Mitakshara,* and much relied on by Colebrooke in his translation of that work. [d]

a Introduction, Morley's Digest.

b Preface, Colebrooke's Digest.

c Ibid.

d Introduction, Morley's Digest.

Digests.

10. Among the Digests the following are some of the principal. The *Dharma Ratna* of *Jimuta Vahana*: the Chapter on Inheritance being the celebrated *Daya Bhaga* on which there is a remarkable Commentary by *Sri Krishna Taikalankara*. The latter has written an epitome of the Law of Inheritance called *Dayakraya Sangraha*, translated by Mr. Wynch; the *Smriti Tatwa* of *Raghunandana*; the *Vivada Ratnakara*, the *Nirnaya Sindhu* and others. Of modern Digests, the *Vivada Bhangarnava* by *Jagannatha*, translated by Colebrooke, is the most important, especially on the Law of Contracts. [a]

Bengal Authorities.

11. (i.) The authorities last cited except the *Vivada Ratnakara* and the *Nirnaya Sindhu* are standard in the Gauriya or Bengal school, particularly the *Daya Bhaga*, translated by Colebrooke, which is almost on every disputed point opposed to the *Mitakshara*, and the *Smriti Tatwa*, the greatest authority of all, a complete Digest in twenty-seven volumes. The portion on inheritance is called the *Daya Tatwa*, and is highly praised by Colebrooke.

Benares.

(ii.) The leading authorities of the Benares school, to which the Madras school belongs, are the *Mitakshara*, *Viramitrodaya*, *Madhavya*, and *Nirnaya Sindhu*.

Mithila.

(iii.) Of Mithila: the *Mitakshara*, *Vivada Ratnakara*, *Vivada Chintamani*, translated by the late Honorable Prossonno Tagore. *Vyavahara Chintamani*, *Smriti Tara* and others.

a Introduction, Morley's Digest.

(iv.) Of the Dravidian or Madras school: the *Mitakshara* of *Vijnyaneswara,* treating of inheritance, on which subject it is a standard work of reference. The portion on inheritance has been translated by Colebrooke. Madras.

The *Smriti Chandrika,* a treatise on judicature by *Devandabhatta,* considered by Colebrooke to be a work of uncommon excellence. A reliable translation has been published by *T. Krishnasamy Iyer,* lately a Principal Sudr Ameen in the Madras Presidency.

The *Madhavya* by *Vidjanarayanswami* on the text of *Pareswara,* a work of extensive research and copious disquisition.

The *Saraswati Vilasa* by *Pratapuradradeva,* a prince of the Telingana country, the next authority to the Mitakshara in Southern India.

The *Vyavahara Mayukha,* a treatise on civil and criminal jurisprudence, by Nilakantha, translated by Borrodaile. The above five works are considered of great authority and are generally referred to as the *Puncha Grandha.*

The *Nirnaya Sindhu* by *Kamalakara Bhat,* treating of social and religious duties: the *Varadarajaya* similar to the *Smriti Chandrika* and others.

(v.) Of the Mahratta school (Western India): The *Mitakshara, Mayukha, Nirnaya Sindhu, Madhavya* and others. [a] Maharastra or Western India.

a As to above authorities generally, see Introduction, Morley's Digest. As to Madras authorities, see also 2 Madras Reports, 206. Strange's Manual, Chapter 1.

Dattaka Mimansa and Dattaka Chandrika.

12. There are also two treatises on adoption of standard excellence and acknowledged by all the schools, namely, the *Dattaka Mimansa* by *Nanda Pandita*, the most celebrated work extant on this subject, and a more concise treatise, the *Dattaka Chandrika* by *Devandabhatta*, the author of the *Smriti Chandrika*, and supposed to be the basis of the former.[a]

Duty of Judge.

13. The duty of the Judge is not so much to inquire whether a disputed doctrine is fairly deducible from the ancient authorities, as to ascertain whether it has been received by the particular school which governs a particular district and has there been sanctioned by usage.[b]

Alterations of the law by legislative enactments.

14. Some portions of Hindu law have become obsolete, and others have been altered by legislative enactments. Primogeniture as a general rule of inheritance has ceased to exist : slavery has been abolished by Act V of 1843 : Act XV of 1856 authorizes the re-marriage of widows, divesting them in such a case, however, of all right to maintenance out of the property of their deceased husbands, as well as of all right of inheritance to them : *Suttee* no longer exists under Regulation I of 1830 : under Act XXI of 1850 apostacy and exclusion from caste cannot now affect the right of inheritance : Act XXI of 1866 provides for the dissolution of marriage of Native Converts, whilst the wills of Hindoos are recognised by Regulation V of 1829, Act

a Introduction, Morley's Digest.

b 12 Moore's Indian Appeals, 397.

XXVII of 1860, and Act XXI of 1870, the Hindoo Wills Act for Presidency Towns; and lastly, the Madras Civil Courts Act of 1873 regulates the trial of suits in which Hindoos and others are concerned.

15. The *status* of Christian Converts has also been decided upon by the Privy Council to the effect that upon the conversion of a Hindoo to Christianity, the Hindu law ceases to have any continuing obligatory force upon the Convert—that the Convert may renounce the old law of which he was bound as he has renounced the old religion, or, if he thinks fit that he may abide by the old law, notwithstanding he has renounced the old religion, that the Convert, though not bound as to his rights and interest in property, either by the Hindu law or by any other positive law, may by his course of conduct after his conversion have shown by what law he intended his rights to be governed—that the *lex loci* Act XXI of 1850 does not apply where the parties have ceased to be Hindoos in religion—and that the conversion of a Hindoo to Christianity amounts by the Hindu law to a severance of parcenership. [a] Christian Converts.

16. The Hindu law is also held applicable to *Maravars* and others of the very lowest caste. The absurdity of this has impressed itself upon the Courts, but it is considered too late to alter this condition of things. Others again are governed by custom and usage for enforcing Maravars.

a 9 Moore's Indian Appeals, 195.

which provision is made in the Madras Civil Courts Act of 1873.[a]

Custody of Converts' children.

17. A Hindoo father is not deprived of his right to the custody of his children by reason of his conversion to Christianity.[b]

Law of Hindoos migrating.

18. A family of Hindoos on migrating may adopt the precepts and customs of the country they migrate to, and may abandon those of their own country. The law of a Hindoo family is presumed to be that of its origin, and not that of its new domicile.[c]

Malabar and Canara Law.

19. In Malabar "the rule of nephews," or the *Marumakkatayum* law prevails as to property which will be noticed in a separate Chapter. In Canara also a similar law called *Aliya Santana* exists. It differs only from that of Malabar in more consistently carrying out the doctrine that all rights to property are derived from females.[d]

CHAPTER II.

ON PROPERTY AND ITS ALIENATION.

Kinds of property.

20. PROPERTY, according to Hindu law, is of four descriptions—*real, personal, ancestral* and *self-acquired.* Under the first head is included not only what is ordinarily consi-

a 6 Madras Reports, 310.
b 5 Sutherland's Weekly Reporter, 235; Weekly Reporter, 1864, 56.
c 2 Moore's Indian Appeals, 132.
d 1 Madras Reports, 380.

dered immovable property, such as land but also assignments thereon corresponding to *corodies* under English law. [a]

Descent of real and personal property.

21. Real and personal property under Hindu law do not descend in the same way as they do under English law. Under the latter realty goes to the heir, while personalty passes under a will, or according to the statute of distributions. Among Hindoos they descend to the same persons alike.

Definition of ancestral property.

22. Ancestral property besides what is strictly termed the family property, includes also the acquisition of a coparcener, when such acquisition has been made with the aid of the family funds. [b]

23. The ordinary gains of science, therefore when made by one who has received a family maintenance are partible. [c]

Definition of self-acquired property.

24. Self-acquired property, in its widest sense, includes everything that has been obtained *without the aid of the family property*, as well as ordinary and nuptial gifts, the former not having been made in return for something previously given, the latter being such as a man receives with his wife, as also the presents made to the father or kinsmen

a W. H. Macnaghten's Hindu Law, 1, 2d ed. A *corody* is an incorporeal heriditament (a right of maintenance) charged on the *person* of an owner of an inheritance in respect of such inheritance.

b 1 Strange's Hindu Law, 213, 214, 215.

c 2 Madras Reports, 56; 4 Ibid., 5.

of the bride, in the *Asura* form of marriage, but these must be exclusive to the donee. [a]

Recovered property.

25. Lost ancestral property recovered without the aid of the family funds and with the privity of the co-heirs ranks also as self-acquisition. [b]

Presumption as to ancestral property.

26. A Hindoo's property is presumed to be ancestral and not self-acquired.

Inchoate rights of son.

27. According to the *Mitakshara* a son has by birth a co-ordinate interest in ancestral property and can compel a partition in his father's lifetime. He has however only an interest in property which belonged to his father at the time of his birth, and has no legal claim to property of which a *bonâ fide* disposition effectual as against his father, had been made long before he was born. [c] In Bengal birth is not considered as a means of acquisition, and heritage arises only upon the death of the father, natural or civil.

Alienations.

28. Ancestral property (real) cannot be alienated without the consent, express or implied, of the co-heirs, except when they are minors and the alienation is for their benefit, in which case their consent will be always implied; while ancestral property (personal) may be so alienated only for purposes warranted by texts of law. This applies to joint property beyond the share of the actual alienor. [d]

a 1 Strange's Hindu Law, 215-217.

b Ibid.

c Ibid., 57; 4 Madras Reports, 307.

d 1 Strange's Hindu Law, 19-21, 25, 200, 201; 2 Ibid., 340, 348, 436, Colebrooke; 1 Madras Reports, 412; 6 Sutherland's Weekly Reporter, 71; 10 Ibid., 287; 1 Bombay Reports A. C., 27.

29. Personal property, however, ancestral or self-acquired, and self-acquired real property may be alienated by a co-parcener without the consent of the others.[a]

30. A single individual may alienate self-acquired property of any kind, if the alienation be made by himself. A married man, too, without male issue, may alienate self-acquired immovable property.[b]

31. Under the *Mitakshara* a co-parcener has full power of alienation over his own share, and the son cannot interfere. It has been held to be otherwise under the Mitakshara law in Bengal, Western India, and North Behar (Mithila.)[c]

32. There may be a valid sale of such a share upon an execution.[d]

33. Under the *Mitakshara,* however, a co-parcener cannot *before partition* convey away as his interest any specific portion of the joint property.[e]

34. It may be broadly stated that in Bengal at least a man may alienate as he pleases, property of any kind by gift, sale, or will; for although thoro is an undoubted

a 2 Strange's Hindu Law, 436, Colebrooke; 1 Macnaghten's Hindu Law, 2-3; 2 Digest, 32, Vrihaspati; 1 Madras Reports, 412; 7 Madras Reports, 25.

b 1 Strange's Hindu Law, (200-202) and above cases.

c 1 Madras Reports, 471; 2 Ibid., 416; 4 Ibid., 60.
3 Bengal Reports F. B., 39.
5 Sutherland's Weekly Reporter, 221.
9 Ibid., 469.
3 Bombay Reports, A. C., 66.

d 1 Madras Reports, 471.

e 8 Ibid., 6.

restriction as to the alienation of ancestral *real* property, yet the alienation when made is valid upon the principle of *factum valet,* which prevails in that school. [a]

35. An alienation made with the consent of the son cannot be questioned by the grandson. [b]

Causes of alienation.

36. To justify an alienation of ancestral property a legal necessity must be strictly proved and such necessity cannot be inferred from the habits and general character of a vendor. [c]

37. The *Shraadh* of a mother is not a legal necessity, as that of the father is, to justify a sale. [d]

38. The payment of family debts, or the existence of a decree which may at any time be executed against ancestral property is a clear necessity for an alienation. A debt under ordinary circumstances is presumed to be contracted for the benefit of the family. [e]

39. Mere knowledge will not make a member of an undivided family a party to an alienation so as to bar his right to recover in ejectment. [f]

a 1 Strange's Hindu Law, 21, 23-25; 1 Madras Reports, 54; 4 Bengal Reports O. C., 31, 159; 3 Ibid., F. B., 39; 5 Sutherland's Weekly Reporter, 221; 9 Ibid., 469; 3 Bombay Reports A. C., 66; 6 Moore's Indian Appeals, 344,

b 9 Sutherland's Weekly Reporter, 337.

c 8 Bengal Reports, Appendix, 5.

d 7 Sutherland's Weekly Reporter, 146.

e 1 Madras Reports, 398; 11 Sutherland's Weekly Reporter, 446.

f 2 Ibid., 428.

40. When the alienation is for the common benefit, or where it has been made for the liquidation of a charge, &c., payable out of the common stock, the co-heirs are concluded by it; although a case may arise in which the remedy of the alienee may be against the alienor only.[a]

Duties of purchaser.

41. When a purchaser of immovable property deals with a person having a qualified power of dealing with that property, it lies upon the purchaser to give some reasonable account of the need which actually existed was to alleged exist for the sale.[b]

42. In the case of a sale, when the dispute is with the vendee, and the money had not been advanced to discharge a prior debt, positive proof must be adduced. When it had been so advanced, it is enough to show a *primá facie* case by presumptive evidence that the charge existed, and that it was ascertained by inquiring that it was a burden on the property from which it was prudent to relieve the family, and that the advance was made in good faith for its discharge. When parceners are acting in collusion to defraud a purchaser by setting aside the alienation, the *onus* of disproving its validity would lie upon them.[c]

43. Where in the particular instance the charge is one that a prudent owner would make, the *boná fide* lender, is

a 1 Strange's Hindu Law, 200; 2 Ibid., 336—338, Colebrooke.

b 2 Madras Reports, 407.

c 6 Ibid., 371.

not affected by the precedent mismanagement of the estate. The actual pressure on the estate, the danger to be averted, or the benefit to be conferred on it in the particular instance is the thing to be regarded. If a lender, before making a loan, makes enquiries and acts honestly, the real existence of an alleged sufficient and reasonably credited necessity, is not a condition precedent to the validity of his charge, and under such circumstances he is not bound to see to the application of the money. [a]

44. Where a person alienated property in which he had merely a life-interest, it was held that the alienation was invalid as against the party entitled as reversioner. [b]

Alienation by widow.

45. The above *dicta* apply with greater force to alienations by Hindoo widows of their husbands' estates—the widows' interest being a *restricted* estate of *inheritance*, with power of *exclusive* enjoyment. [c]

46. An alienation by a widow for necessary purposes *e. g.*, for religious, or charitable, or even wordly ones, is binding upon the reversioners without their consent. [d] The *Shraadh* of her deceased husband, the marriage of his daughter, the maintenance of his grandsons, and the

a 6 Moore's Indian Appeals, 393.

b 2 Madras Reports, 378.

c 3 Ibid., 116. See case of *Kasheenath Bysack* v. *Hurooso𝑜ndery Dossee*, decided by Sir Hyde East, Chief Justice of Bengal (1819) and confirmed by the Privy Council, 2 Morley's Digest, 198 and Clarke's Reports (1834) 91.
8 Moore's Indian Appeals, 550.

d 1 Strange's Hindu Law, 246, 247 ; Colebrooke's Digest, Bk. V. Ch. 8, § 399.

payment of her husband's debts are legitimate grounds for alienation. What are necessary purposes, however, would always be a question of fact in each case.

47. The restriction placed upon a widow's power of alienation of her husband's estate extends to all the property left by him, movable and immovable, ancestral and self-acquired. Her power of disposition of both is limited to certain purposes.[a]

48. An alienation by a widow, even for other than legitimate purposes, is however good for her life, and the reversioners are not entitled to dispute it during her life, unless their own interests are endangered thereby, *e. g.* as by causing waste.[b]

49. The widow of an undivided Hindoo has no right to sell his property for payment of his debts even though it be self-acquired.[c]

50. Even if there are no reversionary heirs, the widow's power of alienation is still restricted. The Crown can then interfere to set aside the alienation.[d]

51. A widow has no right to alienate the *accumulations* of her husband's estate: they should be treated in the same way as the *corpus*. She would be allowed to dispose of the *income*.[e]

a 11 Moore's Indian Appeals, 487.
b 6 Ibid., 445.
c 1 Madras Reports, 374.
d 8 Moore's Indian Appeals, 550.
e 4 Bengal Reports, O. C., 40. See also 6 Ibid., 732, 7 Ibid., 93, and 15 Sutherland's Weekly Reporter, C. R., 63.

52. A widow cannot alienate when the reversionary heirs offer to supply her with the money she requires.[a]

Alienations by women generally.

53. The same restrictions with reference to ancestral estates are placed upon mothers and daughters during the lifetime of other heirs.

54. The restrictions placed upon alienations by women under the Bengal school are greater than under the *Mitakshara.*

55. The rules already stated with reference to the conduct of purchasers from males, having only a qualified interest in property, apply of course with greater force to purchasers from females.

Gifts.

56. By Hindu, as by English law, a man may make a gift of any of his property binding as against himself.[b]

57. The Hindu law recognizes the validity of a gift on condition. There is nothing against the principles of Hindu law in allowing a testator to give property whether by way of remainder, or by way of executory bequest, upon an event which was to happen, if at all, immediately upon the close of a life in being.[c]

58. A *voluntary transfer* of property, if made *bonâ fide,* and not with the intention of defrauding creditors, is valid as against creditors.[d]

a Sham Churn's Vyavastha Darpana, 57.

b 1 Madras Reports, 393.

c Ibid., 403; 9 Moore's Indian Appeals, 135.

d 4 Madras Reports, 84. The Hindu and the English Law on the subject is discussed in this case.

59. There are gifts of several kinds under Hindu law forming different species of property—gift by a woman's affectionate kindred would form her *Sondayaka*—~~a~~ gift from a father or grandfather would be impartible, a gift by a stranger would be partible and so forth.

60. A father~~-in-law~~ cannot by virtue of a special custom disinherit his son, and give all his property to his son-in-law. [a]

61. A donor, having made a gift upon a certain consideration, cannot set it aside afterwards on the ground that he erred as to the consideration. [b]

62. A gift of immovable property to a man by a woman living under his guardianship cannot be enforced as against her husband. [c]

63. A gift or any alienation made so as to leave the family destitute, or unable to defray necessary expenses, would be invalid in countries governed by the *Mitakshara*. Otherwise in Bengal. [d]

64. A gift by a minor is invalid. A gift by a leper is valid; and a lunatic may *take* by gift. A gift to an idol, or to a religious institution, would be valid. [e]

a. 1 Madras Reports, 51.
b Ibid., 393.
c 2 Ibid., 360.
d 1 Strange's Hindu Law, 18; 2 Ibid., 431 *et seq.* Colebrooke.
e 6 Sutherland's Weekly Reporter, 68; 7 Ibid., 5.

65. A gift or other alienation may be always set aside on the ground of physical or moral incapacity in the person making it. [a]

66. To constitute a valid gift, there must be a giving either orally, or by writing, with the intention to pass the property in the thing given, accompanied by its *actual* delivery and acceptance in the donor's lifetime. [b]

67. If these requisites be fulfilled, a gift may be made in contemplation of death. [c]

68. A gift which is to take effect after the death of the donor does not go to the heir of the donee, without express stipulation, if the latter dies before the former.[d]

69. It has been held, that the absence of *seisin* is no objection to the validity of a gift by a Hindoo. [e]

70. To make a gift of land complete under the Hindu law there must either be possession, or receipt of rent by the donee. The grant need not be in writing. [f] *Benamee* transactions, *i. e.*, gifts and purchases in the names of others are valid under Hindu law. [g]

Stridhanum. 71. Besides ancestral and self-acquired property, there is another species of property called *Stridhanum*, or, as

a 1 Strange's Hindu Law, 23.
b 6 Madras Reports, 270.
c Ibid.
d Sham Churn's Vyavastha Darpana, 601.
e 6 Sutherland's Weekly Reporter, 245.
f 5 Bombay Reports, O. C. 83 ; 6 Moore's Indian Appeals, 267.
g 6 Moore's Indian Appeals, 53.

the name imports, woman's property. It may consist of anything of value, such as land, jewels, &c.[a] The word *Stridhanum* is not a technical term.

72. Generally speaking, a woman has absolute control over her *Stridhanum.* There are occasions, however, when the husband also may make use of it, as when the family is in want, when distress prevents the performance of an indispensable, particularly of a religious duty, or in sickness, imprisonment, or even on account of the distress of a son, nor is he obliged afterwards to account for it.[b]

73. This right, however, is only personal in the husband.[c]

74. Any gross abuse of her *Stridhanum* by a woman will be controllable by her father while single, by her husband during coverture, and by her guardians after his death, such interference being itself subject to revision by the judicial power.[d]

75. Ordinarily, what a woman derives by gift, earnings, and inheritance constitutes *Stridhanum.* A stricter rule would be that *Stridhanum* consists of what a woman may dispose of independently of her husband or of others.[e]

a 1 Strange's Hindu Law, 26.

b Ibid., 27; 2 Ibid., 22, 23, Colebrooke citing *Mitakshara,* Chap. II, sect. ix, § 31 *et seq.*; W. H. Macnaghten's Hindu Law, 40; 3 Madras Reports, 360; 1 Ibid., 85, citing Sutherland.

c Ibid.

d 1 Strange's Hindu Law, 28.

e Dayabhaga, Chap. IV, Secs. 1, 18.

76. Gifts to a woman during marriage by a stranger would not be *Stridhanum*; so also some of her earnings would not be hers absolutely; and with regard to what she inherits, it will be her *Stridhanum* or not, according to the relationship of the person from whom she inherits.[a]

77. With regard to gifts, earnings, and inheritance she would of course stand on a different footing, if she were unmarried: they would, perhaps, be less under her control than if she were married.

78. The gift must be made by her husband or some one of her near relatives: if from a stranger, it is without reserve at the disposal of her husband.[b]

79. A gift by a son to his mother for maintenance forms her *Stridhanum.*[c]

80. According to the *Mitakshara* property which a woman acquires, by inheritance, purchase, partition, seizure, a finding is woman's property. The text of *Yajnyawalkya* of which this is a commentary, runs thus: "What was given to a woman by the father, the mother, the husband or a brother, or received by her, at the nuptial fire, or presented to her on her husband's marriage to another wife, *as also any other* (*separate acquisition*) is denominated a woman's property.[d]

a 3 Madras Reports, 272.
b 1 Strange's Hindu Law, 26, 27.
c 5 Sutherland's Weekly Reporter, Miscellaneous Reports, 53.
d Mitakshara, Chap. II, sect. xi, §§ 2, 3.

81. It has been held, however, in Madras upon this text, that all property inherited by a woman is not *Stridhanum.* In one case it was held that property inherited by a woman from her mother, or husband is not *Stridhanum,* and in another that property inherited by a mother from her son was not of that description. These cases were decided according to Bengal law, in opposition to the above passage in the *Mitakshara,* which was dissented from, as being ambiguous, and opposed to other authorities chiefly the *Smriti Chandrika.*[a]

82. In Bengal it has been held that according to the *Mitakshara, movable* property inherited by a woman from her husband would be her *Stridhanum,* and in Bombay that property of both kinds inherited by a married woman from members of her own family, or from her husband, or her son is *Stridhanum.*[b]

83. The Privy Council have, however, decided that all property, movable or immovable, inherited by a woman, from her husband is not *Stridhanum.*[c]

a 3 Madras Reports, 312; 2 Ibid., 402; 8 Ibid., 88. The soundness of these decisions has been questioned and apparently with reason. See West and Buhler's Digest, Vol. 1, 107, Appendix.

b 2 Bombay Reports, 10; 6 Ibid., A. C., 215; Ibid., O. C., 1.

c 11 Moore's Indian Appeals, 487. The reason for this is evident, for the widow does not take as *heir* in the strict sense of the term to her deceased husband but by *survivorship.* She had an interest in the property during his lifetime. This judgment therefore does not decide the question that property *inherited* by a woman from any one else is not *Stridhanum.*

Madras and Bengal rulings as to *Stridhanum.*

84. In Madras it is held that no property inherited by a woman, except *perhaps* what she inherits from her mother, can become her *Stridhanum.* The decisions are based almost entirely upon Bengal authorities which greatly restrict the rights of women, and upon the position that, if the *Mitakshara* be correct, then property vesting in a widow on her husband's death would become her *Stridhanum.* But, it is submitted, there is no real analogy between a widow's estate and property coming to a woman by *inheritance.* A wife is called "half the body of her husband," and therefore when she succeeds to her husband's property on his death, she succeeds as the *surviving half* and not as his *heir,* in the strict sense of the term.[a]

Bombay rulings.

85. In Bombay the definition of *Stridhanum* according to the *Mitakshara* is very general, and includes even property inherited by a woman from her husband, over which however she would have no power of alienation. *Stridhanum* there is divided into two kinds, viz., that over which a woman would have absolute control, and that over which she would not. The property, however, must be inherited from members of her own family.[b]

Madras and Bengal rulings as to property inherited by daughter from her father.

86. According to Madras decisions, under the *Mitakshara,* property inherited by a woman, married, or unmarried, from her father would not be *Stridhanum.* This is also the rule in Bengal.[c]

a 11 Moore's Indian Appeals, 487; 9 Ibid., 610; 10 Ibid., 312.

b Mitakshara, Chap. II, sec. ii, § 4. West and Buhler, Bk. 2, App.

c 2 Madras Reports, 402; 3 Ibid., 312; 6 Ibid., 310 (*Shivagungah* case); 8 Ibid., 88.

87. In Bombay, however, under the *Mitakshara* property inherited by a married, or unmarried woman from her father is her *Stridhanum;* but with reference to the unmarried this is doubtful. Her interest perhaps would be greater than a widow's.[a]

Bombay rulings.

88. The following kinds of property have been classed as *Stridhanum:*

Kinds of property forming *Stridhanum.*

(i.) Gift to a woman as to her husband in trust for her at the time of marriage, and on account of the marriage;

(ii.) Her fee, a gift to her in the bridal procession upon the final ceremony, when the marriage is about to be consummated;

(iii.) Gift to her on her arrival at her husband's house.

(iv.) Gifts subsequent by her parents or brothers. (*Sondayaka*).

(v.) Gift to her by her husband to reconcile her to the supersession when he is about to take another wife.

(vi.) Gift to a woman from the bridegroom on the marriage of her daughter.

(vii.) Gift to her by her husband by way of reward, for performing well her business in the house.

a 1 Bombay Reports, O. C.. 130; Ibid., A. C., 209; 1 Ibid., 117; 2 Ibid., 10; 8 Ibid., 244; 4 Ibid., 150. It is difficult to see on what ground the Madras Courts preferred the Bengal authorities to those of the *Mitakshara* and the Western school. See, however, as to daughter's interest, 2 Indian Appeals, 126.

(viii.) Special gifts to her at any time by any of her relations.

(ix.) The earnings of her industry.

(x.) Gift to a woman for sending or to induce her to send her husband to perform particular work.

(xi.) Property which a woman may have acquired by inheritance, purchase, finding, seizure or partition.

(xii.) The savings of her maintenance. [a]

Menu's definition of *Stridhanum*.

89. The most comprehensive description, however, of the *Stridhanum* of a married woman is from Menu: What was given before the nuptial fire, what was given at the bridal procession, what was given in token of love, and what was received from a mother, a brother, or a father, are considered as the six-fold separate property of a married woman. This enumeration according to the *Mitakshara* commenting on this passage, is intended not as a restriction of a greater number, but as a denial of a less. [b]

No difference between schools as to property forming *Stridhanum*.

90. There is not much difference, generally speaking, between the schools as to the kinds of property which constitute a woman's *Stridhanum*.

Sondayaka or gifts by affectionate kindred.

91. In that which constitutes woman's property, a distinction obtains of what has been given to the woman

a I Strange's Hindu Law, 20—32; Mitakshara, Chap. II, sect. ix, § 2; 1 Digest, Chap. IX, Sec. 1, 3rd Ed.

b Menu, Chap. IX, 194.

whether it be immovable or movable by her father, mother or brothers between the period of her betrothal and that when she is taken to her husband's house (for form sake) on the completion of the marriage—being usually five days. Over such she has exclusive control without regard to her husband or heirs. This is called her *Sondayaka* or gift by affectionate kindred. [a]

92. *Katyayana's* definition of *Sondayaka* is, that which is received by a married woman, or by a maiden in the house of her husband, or of her father, from her brother, or from her parents. So also *Vyasa*. According to the *Smiriti-Chandrika* the above passage shows that *Sondayaka* is the same as the wealth called *Yantaka*, or the like received by a woman from her own parents, or persons connected with them, in the house of either her father, or her husband, from the time of her betrothment to the completion of the ceremony to be performed on the occasion of her entering her lord's house. [b]

93. Ornaments worn by the wife during her husband's lifetime and not distinctly given to her by her husband are not considered her property as long as he lives, but become

a Strange's Manual, §§ 147, 165. *Smiriti Chandrika*, 122 123.

b *Smiriti Chandrika*, 122, 123. According to the *Smiriti Chandrika* the term *Yantaka* means property given by any one to the bride or bridegroom while seated together at a marriage or the like.

so at his death if she survives him, and are afterwards inherited as *Stridhanum*. So also ornaments worn with the husband's consent even if they have not been given to her. [a]

94. The different acquisitions included in *Stridhanum* may for all practical purposes be included in gifts, or the like, from her husband or kindred before, during, or after her marriage. Gifts to a married woman from a stranger, that is from other persons than her husband and kindred, and *not* made at the time of her marriage, belong to the husband's estate and are considered as his property, and so are all her acquisitions by the practice of any mechanical art, as spinning, weaving, or the like; but what she acquires by her own exertions in a state of widowhood belongs of course to her own property. [b]

Madras and Bengal law as to *Stridhanum* losing its character by descent.

95. In Madras it has been suggested that property *inherited* by a woman from her *mother* would *probably* be classed as *Stridhanum*, but not property inherited by her from any one else. In Bengal *Stridhanum* that has once devolved loses its character as such and is ever afterwards governed by the ordinary rules of inheritance. Thus property, given to a woman on her marriage is *Stridhanum*, and at her death passes to her daughter; upon the daughter's death it passes to the heir of the daughter like other property, and the brother of her mother would be heir in

a Elberling, 84; Chintamani, 260.

b Ibid., Mitakshara, Chap. II, sect. 2.

preference to her own daughter if she was a widow without issue. [a]

96. A wife or widow may alienate her *Stridhanum*, movable or immovable, with the exception, perhaps, of land given her by her husband. [b] This doctrine has been approved by the Privy Council.

Alienations of *Stridhanum*.

97. According to Regulation XXV of 1802, Section 8, alienations by Zemindars, Meerasidars and other landed proprietors shall be invalid, unless such alienations shall have been regularly registered at the office of the Collector, and unless the public assessment shall have been previously fixed and determined. Nor shall such alienation exempt a Zemindar for payment of any part of the public land-tax assessed on the entire Zemindary previously, but the entire Zemindary shall continue to be answerable for the total land tax in the same manner as if no such transaction had occurred.

Regulation XXV of 1802.

a 2 Madras Reports, 405; W. H. Macnaghten's Hindu Law, 41. This doctrine seems to be approved in 3 Madras Reports, 312; 2 Bengal, Reports A. C., 144. See *post*, Chap. VI for descent *Stridhanum*. The following are authorities on the subject of *Stridhanum*, *Manu* 9, 194; *Vyavahara Mayukha*, Chap. IV, sect. viii, §§ 10, 14. The *Madhaviya*, 1 Norton's Leading Cases, Appendix 8, 13; 1 Strange's Hindu Law, 26, 32, 49, 52, 137, 140, 246, 250; Strange's Manual, §§ 145, 310, 326, 343, 364, (366-368); Colebrooke's Digest, Volume II, West and Buhler, Volume II, (67-112,) Appendix. *Mitakshara*, Chapter II, sect. xi, §§ 458, 466; *Smiriti Chandrika*, Chap. IX.

b 1 Madras Reports, 85; 2 Ibid., 360; 5 Madras Reports, 111.

Old doctrines as to *status* and power of alienation of Zemindars.

98. In the earlier Reports of the Madras High Court various positions were maintained with reference to the *status* of Zemindars and their powers of alienation, but these have to some extent been abandoned. He was compared to a tenant in tail under the Statute of Westminster, II (13th Ed. I. c. 1 A. D. 1295,) and his power of alienation was considerably circumscribed. It was accordingly held that a transfer of land made by a Zemindar, or other landed proprietor, without conforming to the terms of the above Regulation, would not be binding upon his successor.[a]

Explosion of old doctrine.

99. This doctrine is exploded and it is now held that these provisions apply only to Government. The point was first mooted by Lord Kingsdown in the course of his observations in the *Yettiapuram* case in which he is reported to have said with reference to this Regulation: "That the language of the Regulation would seem to apply to questions between the Zemindar and the Government and to have been formed with a view of preventing a severance of the Zemindary without public notice to the Government. It is not very obvious upon what principle it can be held that an instrument good against the party making it, is bad against an heir if the ancestor had an absolute power of alienation." It is held in Madras that a Zemindar is in the position of a manager of family property and that no alien-

a 1 Madras Reports, 455; Ibid., 265; Ibid., 141; 2 Ibid., 128; 3 Ibid., 5; 4 Ibid., 463.

ation of his estate will be valid as against his successors except for purposes of necessity.[a]

100. Questions of title to property are now decided by English law, and the Hindu law of limitation has been supplanted by Act XV of 1877, the Indian Statute of Limitations.

Questions of title how decided.

a 8 Moore's Indian Appeals, 337.

8 Madras Reports, 157, 189. The Privy Council (9 Moore, 539) have compared a Zemindar's widow's Estate to an *Estate tail*, the power of alienation being absolute for some purposes but qualified for others. The propriety of adopting the nomenclature of English real property law to estates under Hindu Law has always been open to question: since these terms do not truly represent the *quantum* of the estate possessed by a Hindu owner. In the case under notice, if a Zemindar is in the position of a Manager, then his estate is not correctly represented as an estate tail. For the owner of the latter has an *absolute* estate, except when the estate is not in possession, but expectant upon the determination of prior estates, in which case alone a *partial* restraint upon alienation exists. There really does not seem either to be any difference between the estate possessed by a Zemindar and that possessed by a Zemindarni. In each case the Zemindary is held under Regulation XXV of 1802: and in each case an Istimrar Sannad is granted. It is submitted that it is incorrect to compare the latter estate to a life tenancy (another misapplication of terms) and to hold that a Zemindarni has an estate less absolute, so to speak, than a Zemindar's. It is submitted that this view depends not upon the question as to whether or not property inherited by a woman becomes her *Stridhanum*, but upon the alleged analogy between Zemindaries and Rajs. It might as well be contended that the Queen of England had less power than her predecessors, because she is a woman.

CHAPTER III.

MARRIAGE.

Time of marriage.

101. The time when a girl should be given in marriage (betrothment) is before puberty, even before the age of eight years.[a] This rule, however, is not observed by Sudras: among Brahmins, however, it is essential that the marriage ceremony be performed before the age of puberty.

102. Girls are, however, given in marriage at the age of two, and upwards, till they attain their maturity. A Brahmin girl attaining maturity without having contracted marriage, forfeits her caste.[b]

103. The three superior classes, viz., the Brahmins or the sacerdotal order, the Kshetryas, or the military tribe, and the Vysyas, or the mercantile body, may not contract marriage until they have completed the stage of studentship, the opening of which period is marked by performance of the *Oopanayaṅa,* or investiture with the sacred thread, and the close by a ceremony termed *Samavurthana.* For the Sudras, or servile class, who have no stage of studentship, there is no limitation as to the time for marriage.[c]

a 1 Strange's Hindu Law, p. 36.

b Strange's Manual, § 19.
Ibid., § 20.

c Ibid., § 24.

Selection of husband.

104. If a husband be not selected for a girl for three years after she has attained her eighth year, she may select one for herself.[a]

105. The right of selection vests first in the girl's father, and, at his death, in her paternal grandfather, brother, kinsman, remote relations (*saculya*), and mother in succession.[b]

106. A divided brother has not during the life-time of his brother's widow an exclusive right to betroth his deceased brother's infant daughters to whom he will without consulting the mother. In a divided family the widow is legally the guardian of her daughters and the proprietor of her husband's estate.[c]

Relation of parties before and after betrothment.

107. Previous, and up to betrothment, the affair rests legally in promise, which may be broken subject to consequences as the breach can or cannot be justified. What is termed the betrothal is really the first stage in the marriage. A suit will not lie for specific performance of *a promise of marriage*[d]

108. Wherever, from the existence of a legal impediment or the death of the girl, the marriage has been prevented from taking place, the bridal presents are returnable, the bridegroom, in the latter case, paying the

a Strange's Manual, § 24.

b 2 Strange's Hindu Law, 28, Colebrooke citing *Mitakshara.*

c 4 Madras Reports, 344.

d 2 Strange's Hindu Law, p. 28, Colebrooke citing Mitakshara.
7 Bombay Reports, O. C., 122.

expenses incurred on both sides. If the breach be on the girl's side without discovery of legal impediment, her family are to bear the expenses. [a]

109. According to Menu, a woman should not marry a man of a caste below her, though a man may marry in his own caste or in an inferior one. [b]

110. After betrothment, the girl remains under the care of her family till her maturity admits of her husband claiming her, of which it is the province of the mother to give notice. [c]

The essence and principal ceremony of marriage.

111. The essence of the rite of marriage consists in the consent of the parties, that is, of the man on the one hand, and on the other of the father or whoever else gives away the bride. [d]

112. The ceremony most essential to marriage is that of the bride and bridegroom walking seven steps (*saptha-pathi*) hand in hand during a particular recital. The contract is perfected upon their arriving at the seventh step, and may be enforced by the husband on completion of the time. [e]

a 2 Strange's Hindu Law, p. 38, Mitakshara, Chapter II, sect. xi, § 29.
Strange's Manual, § 31.

b *Mitakshara*, Chapter I, sect. viii, § 7.

c 1 Strange's Hindu Law, p. 37.

d 2 Ibid., p. 44.

e 1 Ibid., p. 37.

113. The question whether there has been a marriage ceremonially complete must be decided in each case with reference to the question what formalities are customary among the parties concerned. The omission of the usual formalities will raise a presumption that there was not a valid marriage. [a]

Death of husband before consummation entails widowhood.

114. If the husband die before consummation, the girl is in every respect considered a widow. [b]

115. When either party incurs forfeiture of caste intercourse between them ceases, and should the loss of caste be on the side of the woman, and she be sonless, she is accounted as dead, and funeral rites are performed for her. If she have a son, he is bound to maintain her, and in this way, under such circumstances, her existence is recognised notwithstanding her loss of caste. [c]

Parties to be of the same class.

116. The parties must be of the same class, but of distinct and unconnected families: this precept, however, is not binding upon Sudras. [d]

117. The general law, however, applicable to all the classes or tribes, does not seem opposed to marriage

a Cunningham's Digest, § 79.

b 2 Ibid., 32, 33, Ellis, W. H. Macnaghten's Hindu Law, 2nd ed., 58. As to re-marriage of widows, see Chap. 1, ante: also Act XV of 1856, relating to the re-marriage of widows, minors, as well as those of full age, and which also gives particulars as to what constitutes a valid re-marriage.

c Strange's Manual, § 32.

d 1 Strange's Hindu Law, 39, 40.
1 Madras Reports, 478.

between individuals of different sects or divisions of the same class or tribe, and even as regards the marriage between individuals of a different class or tribe, the law appears to be no more than directory.[a]

118. In all cases where there has been a marriage *in fact*, the Court will declare the marriage to be valid.[b]

Prohibited degrees of relationship for marriage.

119. The relations with whom it is prohibited to contract matrimony are thus enumerated by Menu: "She who is not descended from his *paternal* or *maternal* ancestors within the sixth degree, and who is not *known by her family name to be* of the same primitive stock with his *father* or *mother*, is eligible by a twice-born man for nuptials and holy union." This rule may or may not be observed by Sudras. It is to a great extent practically disregarded by Brahmins.[c]

120. Upon the principle that an adopted son identifies to all intents and purposes with a natural one, a marriage by such a son with the daughter of him by whom he has been adopted would be incompetent.[d]

121. Various texts of Menu discountenance the marriage of a younger brother or sister before the elder. This too is practically disregarded at the present day.[e]

a 1 Madras Reports, 478.

b 13 Moore's Indian Appeals, 58.

c W. H. Macnaghten's Hindu Law, 2nd ed., 61.
1 Strange's Hindu Law. 41. Strange's Manual, § 47.

d Ibid.

e Ibid.

122. By the Hindu law, a marriage is not a contract: it seems therefore that a Hindoo idiot's marriage would be valid. A lunatic's marriage has been held valid. [a]

Marriage not a contract.

123. There are eight different forms of marriage:—the *Brahma, Daiva, Arsha* (or *Rishis*), *Prajapatya* (or *Caya*), *Asura, Gandharva, Rakshasa,* and *Paisacha.* Of these, the four first, being approved ones, are proper for the Brahmin: the *Gandharva* and *Rakshasa* are permitted to the *Cshatrya* or military class, and the *Asura* to the mercantile and servile ones—the *Paisacha,* being prohibited to all, is universally reprobated. [b]

Different kinds of marriage.

124. Of these the *Brahma* and *Asura* appear to be the forms most observed in Southern India, the former being disinterested; while the characteristic of the latter is the payment of money by the bridegroom to those who give the bride away. [c]

a 1 Madras Reports, 214, Note, citing *Dabychurn Mitter* v. *Radachurn Mitter,* 2 Morley's Digest, 99. See, however, W. H. Macnaghten's Hindu Law, 2nd ed., 57, where it is said that among the Hindoos marriage is not merely a *civil contract* but a *sacrament.*

b 1 Strange's Hindu Law, 42, 43. A wife is called "Patni" which implies her capability of performing religious ceremonies in conjunction with her husband during his lifetime. See Mitakshara, Chap. II, sect. i, § 5. According to the Smiriti Chandrika, however, the term is applied only to a wife married in one of the approved forms.

c 1 Strange's Hindu Law, 42, 43.

125. The *Asura* form is peculiar to *Vysyas* and *Soodras*. Though each class has its peculiar form of marriage, there is nothing to bind it to the species appropriate to it. A Brahmin may contract an *Asura* marriage and a Soodra a Brahmin one. [a]

126. Brahmins are divided into *Gotras*, the head of each *Gotra* being some particular sage. Most of the *Cshatryas* and all the *Vysyas* follow the *Gotras* of their *Purohitas*, or family priests. The descent in these *Gotras* is in the male line exclusively, and females after marriage are transferred to the *Gotras* of their husbands. [b]

Rights and duties of husband and wife.

127. The union once effected, involves reciprocal rights and obligations of a personal nature as between husband and wife. It involves also special rights of property, and the right of supersession. [c]

128. The right of inheritance as between husband and wife is in a great degree reciprocal; the latter succeeding as heir to the property of the husband dying a divided member of a Hindoo family, and leaving no male issue. [d]

129. A Hindoo widow's title to maintenance as well as also to inheritance on her husband's death depends upon her preserving her chastity. [e]

a Strange's Manual, § 26.
b Ibid., § 44.
c 1 Strange's Hindu Law, 44.
d Ibid.
2 Madras Reports, 117, citing Mitakshara, Chap. II, sect. i, § 39. See further, Chap. VI, *post*.
e 1 Strange's Hindu Law, 45.

130. A Hindoo wife leaving her husband for a justifying cause is entitled to maintenance, otherwise if there be none. The husband's marrying a second wife is not such justifying cause. [a]

131. If a Hindoo husband marries a second wife and his first wife thereupon leaves him, the first wife has no implied authority to borrow money for her support. [b]

Wife presumed to be husband's agent for contracting debts.

132. In the case of husband and wife living together, the presumption is that the wife is the husband's agent for contracting debts for the necessities of the family. But by Hindu law, perhaps this presumption is not so strong as it is by English law. [c]

Grounds of separation between husband and wife.

133. Infidelity in the husband or the wife: confirmed barrenness in the woman and corporal imbecility in the man: and loathsome or incurable disease in either, or production of only daughters, are some of the causes which authorize a separation or a supersession but not a divorce in the English sense of the term, except in the case of infidelity in the wife, which, it is said, "puts an end to the marriage." The absence of these causes will not however, invalidate a second marriage. [d]

a 1 Madras Reports, 375.
b Ibid.
c Ibid.
d 1 Strange's Hindu Law, 47. See Reporter's Note to; 1 Madras Reports. 374; 2 Ibid., 337; Strange's Manual, § 35.

134. Infidelity in the woman except in certain of the lowest classes, occasions forfeiture of caste, and therefore puts an end to the marriage: so also does conversion to a new faith of either the man or the woman. Act XXVI of 1866 provides for the dissolution of marriage of Christian Converts.

135. The prohibition against a plurality of wives, save under certain circumstances, is merely directory and not imperative. [a]

136. A wife superseded but not divorced, must be provided for, she residing in the house of her husband. And if she live apart from him, it is her duty to seek protection from his relations; and failing them, from her own. [b]

137. The first wife's assent supplies the want of a justifiable cause for a second marriage, she being reconciled to her lot by a suitable settlement, which, according to Colebrooke, with her previous *stridhanum*, should be of a value equivalent to the expenses of the second marriage. [c]

Status of wives. 138. Where a plurality of wives exists, the one first married not having been suspended for any fault, takes precedence. She also succeeds eventually to her husband as heir, maintaining the others who inherit in their turn on

a 1 Madras Reports, 375.

b 1 Strange's Hindu Law, pp. 54, 55.

c Ibid., p. 53.

her death, or even during her life in the event of her re-marriage, &c. [a]

139. An innocent wife abandoned without justifying cause does not lose her *status,* nor any of her rights to her husband's property.

140. The right of divorce by Hindu law is not competent to the wife, unless by custom, in contradistinction to the Sastras. It is competent to both among some of the lowest castes and the women may marry again. Such marriage is called *Natra* and is common in Bombay. This custom, however, has been declared invalid by the High Court of Bombay. [b]

Right of divorce.

141. Adultery is not a sufficient cause for the wife to desert her husband, and there are not many predicaments in which such an act on her part is justifiable. Insanity, impotence, and degradation might perhaps be considered justifying causes. [c]

Adultery and its effects.

142. A woman divorced for adultery may, in some cases claim a bare subsistence or what is called a *starving maintenance;* but a woman divorced for adultery who has con-

a 1 Strange's Hindu Law, 56, 136, 137. Degradation, as a disqualification for inheritance, is removed by Act XXI of 1850.

b Ibid., p. 52 ; 2 Bombay Reports, 125, the custom set up was that the re-marriage takes place *without the consent of the husband.*

c W. H. Macnaghten's Hindu Law, 2nd ed., 61, 62.

tinued in adultery during her husband's life, and in unchastity after his death, is not entitled even to such subsistence.[a]

143. When the adultery has been condoned, a Hindoo wife or widow may recover maintenance, or may inherit if she has inherited, her estate not being forfeited by subsequent acts of unchastity.[b]

Punishment of adultery.

144. Adultery being regarded as a criminal offence by the Hindu law and punishable as such, the adulterer would not be liable to an action of damages at the instance of the husband.[c] It is said the Hindu law does not grant discretionary damages. From the authorities this seems doubtful. The adulterer of course would be liable now under the Penal Code, but there seems no reason why a suit may not be brought by a Hindoo husband for damages against the adulterer.

145. Adultery, though a criminal offence, is nevertheless expiable under Hindu law, if the parties are of the same caste. Menu gives the penances to be performed for adultery.[d]

a 2 Madras Reports, 337.
1 Ibid., 372; 8 Ibid.

b Ibid; 13 Bengal Reports, 1.

c 2 Strange's Hindu Law, 40—44, Colebrooke and Ellis.

d 9 Menu, 178, 179.

146. Though the Hindu law regards marriage with an eye of favor, it by no means discountenances illegitimacy. Independently of special usage or custom, it does not make illegitimacy an absolute disqualification for caste, so as to effect in the relations of life not only the bastard, but also his legitimate children.[a]

Status and rights of illegitimate children.

147. A Hindoo of a caste governed by the Sastras may contract a valid marriage with the daughter of a bastard, whilst the Hindu, unlike the English law, recognizes a bastard's relation to his father and family.[b]

148. Among the lower classes of *Sudras,* marriage with women who have lived in concubinage is allowed.[c]

149. By birth, and without any form of legitimation, bastards of the three twice-born classes are now recognized as members of their fathers' family and have a right to maintenance. So also the offspring of a marriage of a man of one of the above classes with a woman of an inferior class.[d]

150. In the case of Sudras, the law has been and still is that, bastards succeed their fathers by right of inheritance. And the illegitimate son of a Sudra is not an outcaste.[e]

a 1 Madras Reports, 478.
b Ibid.
c Strange's Manual, § 40.
d 1 Madras Reports, 478.
Cunningham's Digest, § 74.
e 1 Strange's Hindu Law, 69, 132; 1 Madras Reports, 478, and the authorities there cited.

151. The illegitimate son of a Sudra by a concubine, not being a female slave, is entitled to maintenance, that is, where he does not possess the inheritance. [a]

152. It has been held, however, that the illegitimate son of one of the mixed classes, between the second and third of the regenerate classes, has no title to inherit by the ordinary rules of Hindu law, and the circumstance that the father was illegitimate does not alter the law. [b]

Act XV of 1856.

153. Act XV of 1856 not only permits the re-marriage of widows, but declares their issue by such re-marriage to be legitimate. It however deprives them afterwards of all right to their deceased husband's property.

154. A suit for restitution of conjugal rights will lie to compel a Hindoo wife to return to her husband and live with him. A suit however will not lie by a husband to recover possession of the person of his wife. In a suit for restitution of right the wife may be imprisoned, or her property attached. [c]

CHAPTER IV.

GUARDIANSHIP AND MINORITY.

Limit of minority.

155. Agreeably to the Hindu law as current in the Benares school, minority is held to last until after the expir-

a 2 Madras Reports, 293.

b Ibid., 369.

c 6 Sutherland's Weekly Reporter, 105.

ation of sixteen years of age; and according to the doctrine of Bengal the end of fifteen years is the limit to minority. [a] These periods, however, have been extended by Act IX of 1875 (the Indian Majority Act) to *eighteen* years. This Act, of course, has no restrospective effect, and applies to both sexes.

156. Under Regulation V of 1804, for constituting a Court of Wards, the period of minority is extended by Act IX of 1875, to twenty-one years *in the case of those under its care*, or of those for whom or whose property a guardian has been appointed by a Court of Justice.

Regulation V of 1804, and other Regulations relating to minors.

157. Regulation V of 1804 contains various provisions relating to the appointment of guardians under the Court of Wards. Amongst others, that female guardians are to be appointed for females and male guardians for males, and that in the case of males, the female relations are not to have charge of them after they have attained the age of seven, at which time the guardians are to appoint proper persons to educate them. [b]

158. Regulation X of 1831 extends portions of Regulation V of 1804, to estates not subject to the Court of Wards, by which the District Court, on the report of the Collector, may appoint a guardian to a person to whom property descends by inheritance, and who is disqualified by minority,

a W. H. Macnaghten's Hindu Law, 2nd ed., 103, 291.
2 Strange, 76, Colebrooke.

b See Act XXI of 1855 as to the education of male words and the marriage of minors without leave of the Court.

sex, or natural infirmity for its management. Such appointment may be sanctioned or annulled by the High Court.

159 Act XXI of 1855 and Act XIV of 1858, relate to the guardianship of minors. Act IX of 1861 refers to the mode of preferring claims to the custody and guardianship of minors. Act XV of 1856 contains provisions as to the guardinship of the children of a Hindu widow on her re-marriage. [a]

Guardians of minor.

160. The natural guardians of a minor, (male or female,) are first, the father; then the mother and elder brother; in their absence, the paternal male kindred; and failing such relatives, the office devolves on the maternal kinsmen, according to their degree of proximity. [b]

161. As under the Hindu dynasties, the sovereign was the legal and supreme guardian of all minors, so also now the ruling power, acting through the Courts, may appoint a guardian in lieu of any other guardian where necessary. [c]

a The corresponding Bengal Regulations are XXVI of 1793 and XL of 1858; Act XX of 1864 is a Bombay Regulation and is similar to Act XL of 1858, (Bengal Code) which extends the provisions of the previous enactment.

b W. H. Macnaghten's Hindu Law, 2nd ed., 103, 104.
2 Strange's Hindu Law, 74, Colebrooke.

c 1 Ibid., 71.
2 Ibid., 74, 75, Colebrooke.
W. H. Macnaghten's Hindu Law, 2nd ed., 104, 105. The pre-supposition to the exercise by the state acting through the Courts of the right to appoint a guardian is that there shall he no guardian existing by the provision of the law itself. See 7 Madras Reports, 179.

162. Where a mother, which of course implies a step-mother also, is both manager and guardian of the minor and his property, she as manager is necessarily subject to the control of her husband's relations: and with respect to the minor's person likewise, there are some acts to which she is incompetent, such as the performance of the several initiatory rites, the management of which vests with the paternal kindred. [a] Mother and step-mother.

163. A step-mother is not to be preferred to a paternal grandmother as guardian of a minor step-son, since relationship subsists between the two latter, which does not with regard to the stepmother and step-son. She is preferable however to a paternal uncle, or other kinsman. [b]

164. The adoptive mother of a boy has a claim to be guardian preferable to that of the boy's natural father. [c]

Appointment of guardian by will.

165. It has been said that a testamentary appointment of a guardian is not noticed in Hindu law; but such an appointment will now be recognized by the Courts, since Hindu wills are held to be valid. Further, such an appointment has been sanctioned by special enactment. [d]

a W. H. Macnaghten's Hindu Law, 2nd ed., 103.

b 7 Sutherland's Weekly Reporter, 321.
1 Norton's Leading cases, 118.

c Cunningham's Digest, § 44, citing Regular Appeal 18 of 1876 (Madras).

d 2 Strange, 73, Colebrooke.
Madras Regulation V of 1804, sect. xix, cl. 5. A testamentary guardian however, does not come within the scope of, the Regulations and Acts prior to Act IX of 1861 and cannot apply to the District Court for permission to remove minors from the custody of their mother. See 8 Madras Reports, 94.

Liability of minor.

166. A minor, so long as his minority lasts, is not liable for the debts of him whose property he has inherited. He will only be liable on coming of age. Subject to this condition, a minor must not only pay the debts above specified, but also all necessary debts contracted on his account during his minority. While his liability for the former will depend upon his inheriting the assets of the deceased, his liability for the latter will be the same, whether he inherits the assets or not. [a]

167. Colebrooke says heirs succeed to the obligations of ancestors without any reference to the adequacy of the property, and the rights of inheritance must be relinquished when its obligation are repudiated.

Powers of minor.

168. A minor legally can have no will, though if of a competent understanding, the concurrence of a minor as to the appointment of a guardian should not be disregarded. A minor may appoint a person to perform his own *Shraaddhas,* as well as those of his ancestors. [b]

Powers of guardian.

169. The power of the manager of an infant heir to charge an estate not his own, is, under Hindu Law, a limited and qualified power. It can only be exercised rightly in a case of need, or for the benefit of the estate. It is the duty of guardians scrupulously to regard the

a W. H. Macnaghten's Hindu Law, 2nd ed., 105.
2 Strange's Hindu Law, 279, Colebrooke.

b Sutherland's Synopsis, Note viii.
1 Strange's Hindu Law, 72.

interest of minors in dealing with their estates, and the Court will, when necessary, enforce the performance of this duty.[a]

170. Minors are under the protection of the law favored in all things which are for their benefit, and not prejudiced by anything to their disadvantage. A minor, however, may be arrested in execution of a decree.[b] Minors protected by law.

171. All acts of the guardian of a Hindoo infant which are such as the infant might, if of age, reasonably and prudently do for himself, must be upheld when done for him by his guardian.[c]

172. A minor may sue through his legal guardian to establish his rights; but where the legal guardian himself invades the minor's right, any friend of the minor may sue on his behalf. The consent of the minor to the institution of a suit on his behalf is unnecessary. In the same way, a minor may defend a suit as well as sue. An idiot or lunatic, too, may sue, or be sued, through a guardian, manager, or *prochein ami*. Guardians *ad litem* should always Power of minor to sue, &c.

a 6 Moore's Indian Appeal, 393.
14 Ibid., 393.

b W. H. Macnaghten's Hindu Law, 2nd ed., 105, citing Colebrooke on Obligations and Contracts.
2 Madras Reports, 47.
17 Sutherland's Weekly Reporter, Civil Rulings, 374.

c 1 Strange's Hindu Law, 203.
2 Madras Reports, 47.

be appointed by the Court in which the litigation is pending [a]

Unmarried females.

173. An unmarried female of whatever age is under the guardianship of her father, and failing him of his kindred. [b]

Guardians of women.

174. "Day and night," says Menu, "must women be "held by their protectors in a state of dependence. Their "fathers protect them in childhood; their husbands protect "them in youth; their sons protect them in age. A "woman is never fit for independence." After her marriage, a woman is subjected to the control of her husband's family. [c]

175. The guardians of a widow are the sons of her husband, if he have left any; and, if not, guardians are to be selected from his other relations by the ruling power; if there be no relations of her husband within the degree of a *sapinda*, then the kin of her own father are the guardians of the widow. In disposing of any property she may have

a 2 Strange, 79, Colebrooke citing Vyasa and Vrihaspati. Also Act XXXV of 1858; 5 Madras Reports, Appendix 8. Guardians may sue for personal injuries done to their wards, but are not liable for torts committed by them; 9 Sutherland's Weekly Reporter, 327; 3 North West Reports, 191.

b Strange's Manual, § 136. A girl under sixteen years of age (*now eighteen*) has not such a discretion as enables her, by giving her consent to protect any one from the criminal consequences of inducing her to leave the protection of a lawful guardian: *secus*, if over eighteen. 5 Bengal Reports, 418.

c W. H. Macnaghten's Hindu Law, 2nd ed., 104. 1 Strange's Hindu Law, 244, 245.

inherited from her husband, she is subject to the control of her legal guardians and advisers, as well as of her husband's heirs. [a]

Position of female managers.

176. A female in management of a minor's property is subject to the control of those who are her guardians. Practically the Courts do not require assurance of the support of the guardian to acts by a female of mature age, and would not hold invalid such acts by reason of the concurrence of the guardian being wanting thereto. [b]

177. In some of the laboring classes, the woman who contribute to the maintenance of the family may contract obligations, if for the uses of the family and render their husbands liable for the same. [c]

Suit on behalf of minor.

178. A suit cannot be brought on behalf of a Hindu minor to secure his share in undivided family property, unless there is evidence of such malversation as will endanger the minor's interest, if his share be not separately secured. The Court may relieve the minor from the guar-

a W. H. Macnaghten's Hindu Law, 2nd. ed., 104.
1 Strange's Hindu Law, 244, (245—247).
2 Ibid., 272, 273, 310, 401, Colebrooke.
W. H. Macnaghten's Hindu Law, 2nd ed., 104.
Daya Bhaga, Chap. XI, sect. i, 64.
See, however, 3 Madras Reports, 116.

b Strange's Manual, § 138.

c Ibid., § 135.

dian's authority, (*e. g.*, brother's) and appoint another; but a case requiring relief must be made out. [a]

Act XV of 1856.

179. Under Act XV of 1856 provisions is made for the appointment of guardians to children whose mothers have re-married with the proviso that when the children have not property of their own sufficient for their support and proper education whilst minors, no such appointment shall be made otherwise than with the consent of the mother unless the proposed guardian give security for the support, and proper education of the children whilst minors.

CHAPTER V.

ADOPTION.

Grounds of adoption.

180. MARRIAGE failing in its most important object, (the birth of sons;) in order that obsequies in particular might not go unperformed, and celestial bliss be thereby forfeited, as well for ancestors as for the deceased, a son (*puttra*, a deliverer from *Put*, the place of torment,) must be adopted. [b]

181. The right to adopt attaches not only where there has been a failure of male issue, but also where there is male issue and they have become disqualified for inheriting,

a 1 Madras Reports, 105, 106.
3 Ibid., 69, 94.
See, however, 3 Madras Reports, 94, where this doctrine has been slightly modified.

b 1 Strange's Hindu Law, 74.
Dattaka Mimansa, sect. i, § 6.

the right of inheritance and that of performing funeral obsequies being correlative. [a]

182. A Hindoo's obsequies may be performed by his widow; or, in default of her, by a whole brother or other heirs; but not with the same benefit as by a son. Hence the necessity for adoption on failure of sons, or of competent issue.

183. By the expression "failure of issue," is meant son's sons and grandsons, these on being an equality as heirs. [b]

Meaning of term "issue."

184. The ancient law admitted of twelve kinds of adopted sons; of these, the one now recognized is *Dattaka*, or the son given, as distinguishable from *Aurasa*, the son by birth. The *Kritrima* form of adoption prevails in *Mithila*. In this no particular ceremonies are essential, and the adopted son does not leave the family of his natural parents. [c]

Form of adoption now practised.

185. There is but little difference if any, between the schools as to the law of adoption, except, perhaps, in Mithila.

a 1 Strange's Hindu Law, 77.
Sutherland's Synopsis, Head First.
W. H. Macnaghten's Hindu Law, 2nd ed., 66, 67, Note.

b 1 Strange's Hindu Law, 76.
Ibid., 78.
W. H. Macnaghten's Hindu Law, 2nd ed., 66.

c 1 Strange's Hindu Law, 74.
2 Ibid., 194—217.
W. H. Macnaghten's Hindu Law, 2nd ed., 65.

Power of wife or widow to adopt.

186. The right of adoption, where it exists, is, as between husband and wife, absolute in the husband. The father may give in adoption without the mother's consent. [a]

Age of adoptee.

187. In making an adoption, preference is always given to the tenderest age. It may, however, be stated generally, that adoption may take place among the three superior classes any time before the performance of the *Oopanayana;* and among Sudras, any time before marriage. There is a great difference between the two leading authorities, the *Dattaka Mimansa* and the *Dattaka Chandrika,* as to the time when adoption should take place among the superior classes. The former maintaining that, after the performance of the initiatory rite of *tonsure* in the natural family, the son cannot be adopted. The latter that the performance of the *Oopanayana* in the natural family is the only bar to the adoption. The rule laid down by the latter (which is the great Bengal authority) is the one generally followed. [b]

Time for performance of Oopanayana among the superior classes.

188. The time for the performance of the *Oopanayana* varies among the three superior classes. Among Brahmins

a 1 Strange's Hindu Law, 78. As a general rule, the wife, however, should consent to the gift of a son, though she need not be privy to the acceptance of one. See 2 Strange, 131, Colebrooke citing Mitakshara.

b 1 Strange's Hindu Law, 88—91.
W. H. Macnaghten's Hindu Law, 2nd ed., 72.
Morley's Digest, Old Series, 22, note 9.
3 Madras Reports, 28.

it is generally performed at the eighth year, and among the Cshatryas and Vaisyas at the eleventh and twelfth respectively.[a]

Procedure at adoption.

189. Adoption is not required to be in writing any more than an authority to the widow to adopt. The ceremony of adoption, however, should be as public and solemn as possible, where this is not the case there will be ground for suspicion.[b]

190. The procedure is thus described by Vasishtha as cited in the *Dattaka Mimansa* :—" A man being about to adopt a son should take an unremote kinsman, having convened his kindred and announced his intention to the king, and having offered a burnt offering *(Datta-homam)* with recitation of the holy words in the middle of his dwelling."[c]

The sacrifice of Datta-homam.

191. The sacrifice of *Datta-homam* is important only in a *spiritual* point of view, and only so with regard to Brahmins. And even with regard *to them*, it does not appear

a W. H. Macnaghten's Hindu Law, 2nd ed., 72, 73.

b 1 Strange's Hindu Law, 93, 94.

c Dattaka Mimansa, sect. iv, § 51 ; and sect. v, § 31.

As to the form of adoption, see Dattaka Mimansa and Dattaka Chandrika, *passim ;* also as to the ritual of the *Datta-homam,* see 2 Strange, 218, *et seq.*

"Ceremonial adoption" is, generally speaking, practised only by Brahmins. Among Sudras generally there is no such ceremonial ; " But public avowal or general notoriety of the fact is sufficient with them to establish its validity."—2 Strange, 39, Ellis.

that its absence will invalidate an adoption performed correctly in other respects. [a]

192. The other classes, and particularly the Sudras, perform an imitation of the *Datta-homam* with texts from the *Puranas.* [b]

Effect of an agreement to adopt on subsequent adoption.

193. A mere intention to adopt may be abandoned; and even an agreement for the purpose resting there would not invalidate a subsequent adoption. [c]

Assent necessary to adoption.

194. To render an adoption valid and complete, it is necessary that the person adopted should assent, or, being a minor, be given by a competent party. [d]

The essentials of adoption.

195. The validity of an adoption for *civil* purposes consists generally in the consent of the necessary parties, the adopter having at the time no male issue, and the child

a 1 Strange's Hindu Law, 95—97.
2 Ibid., 126, Colebrooke, and 226, Ellis.
Ibid., 130, 131.
4 Madras Reports, 165.
The *datta-homam* is considered necessary when the adopted son does not belong to the same *Gotra* as his adoptive father. Generally however the adopted son is selected from his adoptive father's *Gotra.* So that this ceremony is seldom actually necessary.

b See, however, note previous page.

c 1 Strange's Hindu Law, 95.
2 Ibid., 113—115, Colebrooke.

d 1 Strange's Hindu Law, 88.
Sutherland's Synopsis, Head Second.

to be received being within the legal age, and not being one considered ineligible for adoption. [a]

196. In Bengal it has been held that something more than a mere *constructive* giving and taking of the boy in adoption is necessary. There must be an *actual* transfer of the proprietary interest in him. In Madras too it has been held that there must be a valid giving as well as receiving, and that where both parents are dead, and there is no one to give the child, it cannot be received. No amount of ratification can supply the essentials of such a transaction. [b]

Dwyamushyayana.

197. The *Dwyamushyayana* (son of two fathers) form of adoption is still recognized in the present age. This form of adoption may be the result of agreement between the parties. Practically, however, this form of adoption no longer exists, except perhaps in the case of the only son of a brother. [c]

a 1 Strange's Hindu Law, 96, 97.
1 Madras Reports, 363. An adoption invalid on account of there being a son does not become valid by death of that son.
1 Norton's Leading Cases, 78.

b 2 Bengal Reports, A. C., 279.
4 Madras Reports, 165.
This case over-rules *Veerapermal Pillay* v. *Narrain Pillay*, 1 Strange's Notes of Cases, 78.

c Sutherland's Synopsis, Head Fifth.
W. H. Macnaghten's Hindu Law, 2nd ed., 101.
1 Madras Reports, 54: also Reporter's Note.

Rights and duties of adoptee.

198. Adoption being a substitution for a son begotten, its effect is, by transferring the adopted from his own family, to constitute him son to the adopted with a consequent exchange of rights and duties. [a]

199. Of these, the principal are the right of succession to the adopter on the one hand, with the correlative duty of performing for him his last obsequies on the other. In the *Dwyamushyayana* form of adoption, however, the adopted performs the funeral rites of his natural father as well. The right of succession attaches to the entire property of the adopter, real and personal, and operates *lineally* and *collaterally*. [b]

Relation of adoptee to his natural family.

200. The severance of an adopted son from his natural family is so complete that no mutual rights as to succession to property can arise between them. [c]

Share of adoptee in the inheritance when legitimate son subsequently born.

201. The right of inheriting also, in general, is subject to the existence of a legitimate son born subsequent to the adoption, in which case the share of the adopted son is

a 1 Strange's Hindu Law, 97.
Sutherland's Synopsis, Head Fourth.
1 Madras Reports, 420.

b 1 Strange's Hindu Law, 97, 98; 2 Ibid., 116, 117.
W. H. Macnaghten's Hindu Law, 2nd ed., 70, 79.
Sutherland's Synopsis, cited above.

c 2 Strange's Hindu Law, 124, 125, 129, Colebrooke.
Sutherland's Synopsis, cited above.
1 Madras Reports, 180.

one-fourth of the share of the son so begotten. In Bengal it is one-third. [a]

202. By virtue of adoption, an adopted son belongs to the "*gotra*" (family) of his adoptive father, while he disowns that of his natural parent. Adoption is generally made, however, from the same *gotra*. His relation, too, as *sapinda* in the family of his adoptive father, commences from the date of his adoption. According to Bengal law his relationship with his natural family is not severed. [b] Adoptee's gotra and sapindaship.

203. It is by the performance of the *Datta-homam* that the adopted son is converted from the gotra of his natural to that of his adoptive father. [c]

204. The adopted son, who is son of two fathers, (*Dwyamushyayana,*) inherits the estate and performs the obsequies of both fathers; but the relation of his issue obtains exclusively to the family of the adoptive father. [d] The rights of the Dwyamushyayana.

a 1 Strange's Hindu Law, 98, 99.
W. H. Macnaghten's Hindu Law, 2nd ed., 70.
Sutherland's Synopsis, Head Fifth.
Mitakshara, Chap. I, sect. xi, § 24, as explained in the Saraswati Vilasa.
1 Madras Reports, 45, and Reporter's Note, where all the authorities are cited.
Dayabhaga, Chap. X, sect. 7.

b Sutherland's Synopsis, Heads Third and Fourth, and Note xx.
The *Dwyamushyayana,* however, will be sapinda in both families. See Dattaka Chandrika, sect. iii, § 25. Shamchurn's Vyavastha Darpana, 889.

c 2 Strange, 89; 220, Ellis. In Bengal *Datta-homam* is essential.

d Sutherland's Synopsis, Head Fifth.

205. In the case of the above form of adoption, where a legitimate son is born to the adopter subsequent to the adoption, it would appear from the *Dattaka-Chandrika*, that such son *(Dwyamushyayana)* would only take half the share to which the son absolutely adopted would be entitled in participating with a legitimate son subsequently born. [a]

206. On the same principle, this author appears to provide that where legitimate issue is subsequently born to the natural father, the *Dwyamushyayana* only takes in the estate of such father, the half of the share of a legitimate son. [b]

207. An adopted son is incapable of contracting marriage in the family from which he was taken. Nor can the son of two fathers marry into the general family of either. [c]

Rights of person where adoption invalid.

208. The natural rights of a person adopted remain unaffected when the adoption is invalid. [d]

When second adoption can and cannot be made.

209. A second adoption may be made where the first has failed, whether effected by the man himself, or by his widow or widows after his death duly authorized. [e]

210. A double adoption is invalid. This was decided in the well known case of *Rungammah* v. *Atchumma* in

a Sutherland's Synopsis, Head Fifth.

b Ibid.

c 1 Madras Reports, 420. That is, of course, within the prohibited degrees. See Sutherland's Synopsis, Head Fourth.

d 1 Madras Reports, 363.

e 1 Strange's Hindu Law, 78.

the Madras Presidency, in which the late Sudder adopting the opinions of the Pundits held that a second adoption, while the first adopted son was living, was valid. This, however, was over-ruled by the Privy Council, and the law on the subject is now settled. [a]

211. Nor can more than one son be adopted at a time. [b]

212. In a selection for the purpose of adoption, consideration is to be had of the *class* to which the child to be adopted belongs; of his *relation* as well to the adopted as to his own family; of his *age*; and, lastly, with regard to Brahmins, to what extent his *initiatory ceremonies* have or have not been already performed. [c] Qualification of adoptee.

213. As in marriage, so in adoption, the parties must be of the same class. [d]

214. The necessity of adoption applies whether a man be single, married, or a widower. [e] Adoption necessary to all.

215. An impotent man may adopt, and so may a minor. At least there is no provision in Hindu law against adoption by a minor. A minor widow also may adopt. The

a 2 Strange's Hindu Law, 85, Sutherland.
4 Moore's Indian Appeals, 89.

b 2 Indian Jurist, New Series, 24. Bourke's Reports, O. C., 189.

c 1 Strange's Hindu Law, 82.

d Ibid.

e Ibid., 77.
W. H. Macnaghten's Hindu Law, 2nd ed., 66, Note.
2 Madras Reports, 367. 4 Ibid., 270.

consent of the guardian will be sufficient, unless the minor has attained to years of discretion. [a]

216. One who has been adopted can himself adopt. A family may thus be kept up by a succession of adoptions. [b]

Adoption not to be made during pregnancy.

217. An adoption should not be made during the wife's pregnancy, for there is the possibility of the birth of a son: such an adoption is invalid even though a daughter should be born. [c]

Power of widow to adopt.

218. A wife, or widow, cannot adopt without the assent of her husband. She may, if the distress be urgent, but the adoption is on his account, not hers. If the husband be dead, physically, or civilly, or have permanently emigrated, she may then adopt without his consent. [d]

Dravidian law.

219. According to the law of the *Dravida* School in an undivided family, a widow not having her husband's permission, may adopt with the consent of her husband's kinsmen. If the father of the husband be alive, his sole assent would be sufficient, as the head of the family, and the

a Dattaka Chandrika, sect. 6.
Dattaka Mimansa, sect. 1, § 4.
Ibid., sect. 5, § 3.

b Strange's Manual, § 64. See case of *Rawutpore Raj*, 5 Moore's I.A., 169.

c Ibid., § 56.

d 1 Strange's Hindu Law, 79.
2 Ibid., 84, Sutherland.
1 Strange's Hindu Law, 82.
W. H. Macnaghten's Hindu Law, 2nd ed., 66, citing Dattaka Mimansa.

natural guardian of the widow. If there be no father; then the consent of all the brothers would probably be required. [a]

220. In a divided family the difficulty to lay down a rule is greater. In such a case the consent of the father-in-law as the natural guardian and "venerable protector" of the widow would be sufficient. Where there was no father-in-law, there should be such evidence of the assent of kinsmen as would suffice to show that the act is done by the widow in the proper and *bonâ fide* performance of a religious duty, and neither capriciously, nor from a corrupt motive. [b]

221. The power to adopt cannot be inferred, when a prohibition by the husband either has been directly expressed by him, or can be reasonably deduced from his disposition of his property, or the existence of a direct line competent to the full performance of religious duties, or from other circumstances of his family, which afford no plea for a supersession of heirs, on the ground of religious obligation to adopt a son, in order to complete or fulfil defective religious rites. [c]

222. The authority to adopt need not be in writing, nor is any particular form required. [d]

a 12 Moore's Indian Appeals, 397.

b Ibid.

c Ibid., The *above dicta* as to adoption by a widow over-rule the doctrine propounded by the Madras High Court in 2 Madras Reports, 206 and 7 Ibid., 301, as to the assent of one sapinda being sufficient for such adoption.

d 1 Strange's Hindu Law, 80.

223. When a particular child is adopted under the authority, the power of adoption ceases, and cannot be revived to effect another adoption. If the child dies or becomes disqualified before adoption, the widow may select another under the authority. [a]

224. Where a widow exercises a power of adoption after her husband's property has vested in another, the son adopted cannot succeed to her husband's property. He is only entitled to maintenance. (Theoretically) the only object gained by adoption is the performance of obsequies. [b] Practically, however, the object appears to be to perpetuate the family name.

225. A widow cannot modify or alter an illegal authority to adopt. [c]

226. There cannot be a conditional adoption, but there may be a conditional power of adoption, so as to provide for successive adoptions.

227. A widow's refusing, or omitting to adopt under the authority given to her, does not thereby affect her own heritable right. [d]

228. A widow who has become unchaste, is living in concubinage, and is in a state of pregnancy, is incompetent to receive a son in adoption. [e]

a 1 Norton's Leading Cases, 94.
b 10 Moore's Indian Appeals, 304.
7 Sutherland's Weekly Reporter, 392.
c 5 Sudder Dewanny Reports, (Bengal) 461.
d 7 Moore's Indian Appeals, 169.
e 5 Bengal Reports, 362.

229. A widow's right to adopt is not affected by the fact that she takes as heir of a deceased son, and not immediately from the husband.[a]

230. Where there are two widows they may, if so authorised, adopt in succession.[b]

231. A mother, however, cannot adopt to her son, nor can permission be given her to adopt. Power of mother to adopt.

232. In Bengal the authority of the husband is essential, and cannot be dispensed with under any circumstances. Bengal law.

233. In Bombay, however, it has been held that in the *Maharashtra* country, a widow may adopt *without* the consent of her husband, or of his kindred, if done by her *bonâ fide*, as a religious duty.[c] Bombay law.

234. In Mithila the *Kritrima* form prevailing, the widow may adopt with or without her husband's consent, but it has been held that such son would only succeed to her property, and not to her husband's. He does not cease to be a member of his own family, and he inherits also in it. If adopted by the husband, he would inherit his property.[d] Mithila law.

235. A dancing-girl may make adoption of a daughter, if authorised by the Pagoda to which she is attached. She Dancing girl may adopt.

a Cunningham's Digest, § 282, citing *Rajah Vellanki Venkata Kistna Row* v. *Rajah V. V. Lakshmi Narrayan*, Privy Council, 3rd November 1876.

b 1 Norton's Leading Cases, 81.

c 5 Bombay Reports, A. C., 181.

d 7 Sutherland's Weekly Reporter, 500 ; 8 Ibid., 155.

cannot do so of a son. To adopt, the dancing girl must be daughterless. It is immaterial whether she have a son or not. It is questionable however whether an adoption by a dancing-girl is legal. It has been held that the ordinary Hindu law of adoption and division is totally inapplicable to dancing-girls. It has been held, too, that such adoptions are not necessary for the devolution of their property, for sons may inherit as well as daughters.[a]

Who may not adopt.

236. A leper, or person with incurable disease, cannot adopt, except he performs the prescribed penance, but he may authorise his wife or widow to adopt without performing any expiation.[b]

237. Nor for the same reason can a lunatic, or an idiot, or an outcaste adopt, but their wives or widows may.

238. A person under pollution in consequence of the death of a relative, or other cause, cannot adopt.[c]

239. A minor under the Court of Wards cannot give his widow authority to adopt, without the permission of the Court.[d]

a Strange's Manual, § 98.
Ibid., § 99; 2 Madras Reports, 56; Ibid., 196; Cunningham's Digest, § 257, citing Special Appeal, 579 of 1876, (Madras).
b Shamchurn's Vyvastha Darpana, 757.
c 9 Moore's Indian Appeals, 506.
Strange's Manual, § 63.
d 9 Moore's Indian Appeals, 295.

240. Adoptive parents cannot give their son in adoption, for it would be against the agreement on which they received the boy in adoption.

Who cannot give in adoption.

241. One brother cannot give another away in adoption, even when both parents are dead, their rights being co-ordinate. For the same reason, an uncle cannot give a nephew away. [a]

242. As to relationship, the general principle is that one with whose mother the adopter could not legally have married must not be adopted. [b]

Degree of relationship prohibited for adoption.

243. Under these circumstances, brother's, paternal and maternal uncles; daughters' and sisters' sons cannot be adopted. In Bombay it has been held that an adoption of a sister's son among the *Vysyas* is valid. These two latter, however, are eligible to adoption among Sudras. [c]

244. Subject to the above general principle, the nearest male relation of the adopter is the proper object of adoption. This is a whole brother's son, whose right to be adopted in preference to any other person, where no legal impediment exists, may be regarded as a received rule of

Who may be adopted.

a Strange's Manual, §§ 97, 80.

b 1 Strange's Hindu Law, 83. Sutherland's Synopsis, Head Second. 2 Madras Reports, 462.

c 1 Strange's Hindu Law, 83, 84.
W. H. Macnaghten's Hindu Law, 2nd ed., 67.
1 Madras Reports, 424 ; 7 Ibid., 250 ; 4 Bombay Reports A. C., 130.

law. On failure of *sapindas,* one must be sought from more distant kindred.[a]

Bengal law. Who cannot be adopted.

245. In Bengal, a Brahmin's widow cannot adopt her uncle's son, nor can a sister's son be adopted there. And nowhere can an adopted son adopt his own natural brother, nor can a widow adopt the natural brother of her deceased husband.[b]

246. The adoption of an eldest or an only son (except as a *Dwyamushyayana*) though considered improper, is, when made, valid according to Hindu law. This ruling has been adopted by the Bombay High Court. In Bengal it has been held otherwise, the principle of *factum valet* was said not to apply to such a case. The adoption of a wife's brother, too, is considered valid, it being customary.[c]

247. According to Hindu law, an orphan cannot be adopted, nor an illegitimate son.[d]

a 1 Strange, 84; 2 Ibid., 102, 103, Colebrooke.
Sutherland's Synopsis, Head Second.
W. H. Macnaghten's Hindu Law, 2nd ed., 68.
Mitakshara, Chap. I, sect. xi, § 36, citing Menu, 9, 182.

b 1 Madras Reports, 420, and Reporter's Note.
2 Madras Reports, 399.

c 1 Strange's Hindu Law, 87.
Strange's Manual, § 91.
1 Madras Reports, 54.
W. H. Macnaghten's Hindu Law, 2nd ed., 67, note.
4 Bombay Reports, A. C., 191.
1 Bengal Reports, A. C., 221.

d 2 Madras Reports, 129.

248. The adopted son of one, whose alleged adoption has been held invalid, can make no claim through his adoptive father to be maintained by the alleged adopter.[a]

Right to maintenance and inheritance of certain adoptees.

249. A person excluded from inheritance may nevertheless adopt; but the person adopted will be subject to the same disqualification, and cannot inherit, where the claim to inheritance can only be made through the adopter. He will be entitled to maintenance only.[b]

250. A member of a Hindu family cannot, as such, inherit the property of one taken out of that family by adoption.[c]

251. A son, whether adopted or begotten, can claim maintenance of his father until put into possession of his share of the ancestral estate.[d]

252. When an adopted son dies issueless, the property he has inherited from his adoptive father goes to the father's heirs.[e]

253. It has been held in Bengal that an adopted son cannot succeed to the property of his adoptive maternal *bandhus*, nor do they succeed him.[f]

a 2 Madras Reports, 129, citing Sutherland and over-ruling decision on this point in 1 Madras Reports, 45.

b 1 Strange's Hindu Law, 98.
See, however, Sutherland's Synopsis, Note iv, citing Dattaka Chandrika and Mitakshara.

c 2 Strange, 124, 225, Colebrooke, citing Menu and Mitakshara.
1 Madras Reports, 180.

d 1 Madras Reports, 45.

e Madras Sudder Decisions 1859, 265.

f Sutherland's Full Bench Rulings, 121.

254. A son adopted to one wife does not become an heir to a co-wife, and *vice versâ*, the co-wife is not his heir. He may, however, inherit the latter's *Stridhanum.* [a]

Effect of adoption on widow's inheritance.

255. Where a widow adopts, her husband's estate descending to her on his death, adoption subsequent divests her succession, like the case of a posthumous child. While, on the other hand, where the adopted, surviving his adopted father, dies unmarried and issueless, the widow of the latter, if living, succeeds as legal mother to the adopted. [b]

256. An adopted son is liable for debts contracted by his natural father, whether contracted by the father in person, or by the adopted as his father's agent. [c]

Roman Law.

257. There is a similarity between the Hindu and the Roman law as to adoption. Under Roman law there were two kinds of adoption—*adoptio* properly so-called and *adrogatio.* The first was the ceremony by which a child or grandchild, *under the power of its parents,* was transferred to another. When the person *was not in the power of his parent,* the ceremony was called *adrogatio.* The peculiarity of this latter adoption was that, if a man had sons, and was adopted by another, he became the son, and his sons the grandsons of the adopted. [d]

a Weekly Reporter for 1864, 71; 3 Ibid., 49.

b 1 Strange's Hindu Law, 101.
2 Ibid., 129, Colebrooke.
W. H. Macnaghten's Hindu Law, 70, 71, 2nd ed.

c 2 Strange, 124, 225, Colebrooke, citing Menu and Mitakshara.

d Institutes of Justinian, 1, 11.

258. The capacity to contract marriage was the only qualification necessary to enable a man to adopt. [a]

259. Women at one time under Roman law were not permitted to adopt, but subsequently they were allowed to do so to console them for the loss of children. [b]

260. A person older than the adopter could not be adopted, for a son should not be older than his father. The adopter therefore was obliged to be eighteen years older than the person adopted, that is, the adopted had to be older by the full age of puberty. [c]

261. A person without a son could adopt a grandson, if he had a son, he could not adopt a grandson without the son's consent.

262. According to the ancient Roman law an adopted child, as in Hindu law, became one of the adopter's family, and lost all connection with his natural family. This was found to create inconvenience, and in some instance injustice, and a distinction therefore was drawn between an adoption by *a stranger,* and one by a relative, an ascendant, *e.g.,* grandfather. In the former case, the tie with the natural family subsisted, in the latter it did not, for the existence of the relationship, it was supposed, would prevent injustice. [d]

a Institutes of Justinian, 1, 11, 10.
b Ibid.
c Ibid., 1, 11, 4.
d Ibid., 1, 11, 2.

263. A son used to be named sometimes by will. Under the ancient law, a son could not object to be adopted, but under the new legislation, he had a right to object.

264. Adoption is permitted under the Civil Code in France, but it is not legalized either in England or Scotland.

CHAPTER VI.

INHERITANCE.

Co-parcenery the normal condition of a Hindu family.

265. THE normal condition of a Hindoo family is that of co-parcenery with the right of survivorship resembling joint tenancy under English law: the estate being under the control of a managing member, generally the eldest of the family whose acts to be of validity must be for the general good. The exception to this rule of co-parcenery is the case of the succession to a Raj or Zemindary or other impartible estate in which the descent is to a *single* heir.[a]

Parcener's undivided rights represented by his sons in case of death.

Inheritance in an undivided family.

266. Where a man dies undivided leaving sons, grandsons, or great-grandsons, as the case may be, they represent his undivided rights, while the females of his family continue to depend on the aggregate fund till a partition takes place. In the absence of male issue, the property will vest equally in his surviving undivided brothers. On the deaths of any of these, their male issue, if any, will succeed

a See further post, 1 Strange's Hindu Law, 120, 198, 199, 200.

in like manner, after whom the property will descend to the widow of the last surviving. It afterwards goes to divided relations in their order. [a]

267. The sons in an undivided Hindoo family although they have a proprietary right in the paternal and ancestral estate have not independent dominion.

268. Where, however, the co-parcener possesses self-acquired immovable property, he may, at his death, dispose of it as he pleases, provided he has no male issue. Self-acquired movable property, however, may be disposed of under any circumstances. Self-acquisition not disposed of, descends, of course, to the heirs. [b]

Power of parcener over self-acquisition.

269. The self-acquired immovable property of an undivided co-parcener also will not, at his death, without issue, be subject to the right of survivorship, but will descend to the widow. If he have issue, it will descend to them and his widow will be entitled only to maintenance. In default of issue or widow, it will go to the collaterals. [c]

Descent of self-acquired immovable property of parcener.

270. An undivided co-parcener is entitled, during his life-time, to the separate enjoyment of his self-acquired property, movable and immovable. [d]

Right of parcener to enjoy self-acquisition.

a 1 Strange's Hindu Law, 120, 198, 199.
W. H. Macnaghten's Hindu Law, 17, 18, 2nd ed.

b 1 Strange's Hindu Law, 20, 21.
1 Madras Reports, 412.

c *Katama Nachyar* v. *Rajah of Shivagengah*, 9 Moore's Indian Appeals, 604.
1 Madras Reports, 374.

d Ibid., 412.

Bengal law.

271. In Bengal, where an undivided co-parcener dies leaving a childless widow, his share does not vest in the surviving parceners, but descends to his widow as his heir; whereas the *Mitakshara* restricts her right of inheriting to the case of her husband so dying separated; allowing her, where he dies undivided, a maintenance only. The widow, however, will inherit where there are no undivided heirs. [a]

Course of descent of divided and undivided property of parceners.

272. Where a residue is left undivided upon partition, what is divided goes as separate property; what is undivided follows the family property—the law of succession follows the nature of the property and of the interest in it. [b]

Two principles upon which succession depends.

273. There are two principles on which the rule of succession, according to the Hindu law, appears to depend: the first is that which determines the right to offer the funeral oblation, and the degree in which the person making the offering is supposed to minister to the spiritual benefit of the deceased; the other is, an assumed right of survivorship. [c]

a 1 Strange's Hindu Law, 121; 2 Ibid., 231—233.
W. H. Macnaghten's Hindu Law, 19, 2nd ed.
Mitakshara, Chap. II, sect. i, § 39.
1 Madras Reports, 412.
2 Ibid., 117.
Ibid., 325.
Under Madras Law, widow will take property vesting in the husband, although actual possession of the husband is postponed. 2 Madras Reports, 462.

b 9 Moore's Indian Appeals, 539. The mere performance of funeral rites, however, gives no right of inheritance; 2 Madras Reports, 325.

c Ibid.

274. The principal ground on which the leading rule of inheritance is based in all the Schools is the *spiritual benefit* to be derived by the deceased from the performance of funeral obsequies.

275. This is the latest development of Hindu law of which the *Dayabhaga,* the chief authority in Bengal is the principal exponent. According to the *Mitakshara,* however, preference is given to the principle of survivorship, which is supposed to have been the rule of succession prevailing amongst Hindoos in the earliest stages of society, when partition was unknown. As the succession under the Bengal school devolves entirely according to the principle of *spiritual benefit,* and not by *survivorship,* it is easy to see why in Bengal females are so generally postponed to males, and the interest that is allowed them in property is so very limited.

276. The principle of *survivorship* applies on the failure of male issue, and it conflicts with the rights of the widow.

277. In Madras it has been held that the right of survivorship depends upon the *status* of the deceased co-parcener only, and not upon the nature of the estate he has left. This is opposed to the *Mitakshara* generally and to the decision of the Privy Council in the *Shivagunga* case, which decided that the rule of survivorship did not apply when the property was self-acquired [a]

[a] 1 Madras Reports, 412; 9 Moore's Indian Appeals, 539.

278. It is not necessary that the heir should be born when the inheritance falls in. It is sufficient that he should have been begotten, and afterwards born with vitality. [a]

When right of inheritance attaches in a divided family.

279. The right of inheritance attaches, not only upon the father's demise, but upon his renunciation of worldly concerns, or after long absence from his family. [b]

Sons.

280. In the series of a Hindu's heirs, the first in order is his male issue, legitimately born; or, in default, its substitute and equivalent, a legally adopted son. [c]

281. The heirs of a man include not only his sons, but his grandsons and his great-grandsons. All these constitute but one heir, possessing co-ordinate rights and stepping into each other's places in case of death. [d]

282. The right of lineal representation stops at the *fourth* degree, except in the case of absence in a distant country, when it extends as far as the *seventh* degree. The inheritance is kept open to the remotest *sapinda* on the

a Elberling, 40.

b 1 Strange's Hindu Law, 122, 131, 132, 184, 185.

According to Colebrooke, a man may be considered dead after 20 years' absence if he be in the first period of life; after 15 years, if of the middle age; and after 12 years, if in the latter period of life. See 2 Strange, 238.

See also 1 Indian Law Reports (Allahabad), 53.

c 1 Strange's Hindu Law, 123.

d Ibid., 123, 124, 198.

presumption that an intermediate descendant may have survived to transmit it to him. [a]

283. When, however, the great-grandson survives his ancestor and dies, the property inherited by him would devolve upon his son in consequence of its having vested in the father. Lineal succession is *per stirpes* and not *per capita*. [b]

a 1 Strange's Hindu Law, 124, 125. Strange's Manual, § 324.

It has been held in Madras that the right of representation does not exist under Hindu Law, and that the law of inheritance is "*the law of inheritance of the offerings to the dead.*" But it is submitted that the doctrine of representation does prevail in Hindu law : otherwise why such expressions as "the widow being half the body of her husband," or, "the son and daughter being said to proceed from the limbs of the father." Besides it must not be forgotten that the use of the son is as much to keep up the lineage of the ancestor, as to offer funeral obsequies. With regard to the latter being the only criterion of heirship, Mr. Maine in his Village Communities, p. 53, observes that, no trace of this theory is found in the ancient unwritten customs of the Hindoos, and that the idea is purely one of modern growth. It must also be remembered that it is this right of representation which has broken up the joint system of inheritance with its rights of survivorship which anciently prevailed, and has helped to form the system of separate and lineal succession which is now in vogue. See also 1 Strange's Hindu Law, 124, and 2 Bombay Reports, 10, in which Arnould, C. J. held that, the doctrine of representation prevails among daughters, as well as sons, and that a daughter's son succeeds as his mother's representative. The theory of tracing the heir by the funeral cake is entirely a Bengal one, and is the leading idea of the *Dayabhaga*. The *Mitakshara*, which is more in accordance with the ancient law, does not give prominence to this idea, but rather traces the heir by relationship. See also 1 Indian Law Reports, (Allahabad), 105.

b 1 Strange's Hindu Law, 123.

284. The son's preferable right of inheritance rests on his presenting the greatest number of beneficial offerings, while the same degree is attributable, in default of their respective fathers, to the grandson, or great-grandson, but not to any ulterior representative.[a]

285. Upon this principle also, if a man leave a son, and the son of another son and the son's son of a third son, they take equal shares of his estate, *because* they confer the benefit equally.[b]

286. In deciding the question of right of inheritance, however, payment of the deceased's debts, as well as nearness of kin, or proximity by birth, should enter as conjoint considerations.[c]

287. The mere performance of exequial rites, however, gives no title to inheritance; but, on the other hand, the heir being the nearest of kin, the most competent, is bound to the due performance for the deceased, to whose property he has succeeded.[d]

Grandsons and great-grandsons.

288. Grandsons and great-grandsons inherit *per stirpes* and not *per capita*, that is, the sons, however numerous, of

a 1 Strange's Hindu Law, 128. The relation of foster son is not recognized by Hindu Law. 1 Madras Reports, 326.

b 1 Strange's Hindu Law, 128, 129.

c Ibid.

d 1 Ibid., 129, 130.
2 Ibid., 242, Colebrooke.
W. H. Macnaghten, 36, 2nd ed.

one son and grandson respectively, take no more than the sons, however few, of another son and grandson respectively—their shares being the same as those to which their respective fathers would have been entitled, had they survived. [a]

289. The share of a son demising before the inheritance falls in, is not kept alive for his widow. [b]

Apratibandha and sapratibandha.

290. The heritable pretension of a son being immediate, is termed *apratibandha*, "heritage not liable to obstruction;" while that of remoter heirs is termed *sapratibandha*, "liable to obstruction," by the intervening birth of nearer ones, the title in the one case being *apparent*, in the other *presumptive*. [c]

291. Illegitimate children are a charge upon the inheritance, but do not inherit by the Hindu, any more than by the English law, excepting in the Sudra class. So also do the sons of illegitimate sons. [d]

Illegitimate sons.

292. Amongst Sudras, illegitimate participate with legitimate sons, if there be any, to the extent of a half share;

a 1 Strange's Hindu Law, 18.
2 Ibid., 242, Colebrooke.
W. H. Macnaghten, 66, 2nd ed.,

b 2 1 Strange's Hindu Law, 231, 232, Colebrooke.

c Ibid., 131.

d Ibid., 132.
1 Madras Reports, 478.
Mitakshara, Chap. I, sect. xii, §§ 1, 2, 3.
12 Moore's Indian Appeals, 203.

and if there be none, nor daughters nor daughter's sons, they are then not distinguishable in point of inheritance from legitimate ones. [a]

293. In Bengal it has been held that the right belongs only to the illegitimate sons of a Sudra by a female slave, or a female slave of his slave. [b]

294. The sons of a Brahmin woman living in concubinage with a foreigner (*Meleecha*) are Hindoos (Sudras), or a class still lower, and their rights are to be determined by the rights of the class to which they belong. In the absence of preferable heirs, too, they inherit the property of their mother and of one another. [c]

Rights of sons by different wives.

295. Where a man has more wives than one of the same caste, all his sons are upon an equality, though they are the offspring of several wives, and though the number of sons by each differs. They severally take *per capita*, and their rights in the distribution of property are not affected in any way by the order of their mothers' marriages. [d]

a 1 Strange's Hindu Law, 132.
W. H. Macnaghten's Hindu Law, 18, 2nd ed.
See also Mitakshara above cited.

b 1 Indian Law Reports, (Calcutta), 1.
Ibid., (Bombay), 97.
See also 4 Madras Reports, 204. This case decides that the intercourse must have been continuous and the woman unmarried, if the intercourse is adulterous, the issue will not inherit.
8 Ibid., 142.

c 2 Madras Reports, 196.

d 1 Strange's Hindu Law, 205.
3 Madras Reports, 75.

296. A man cannot disinherit his heir in favor of another. And even where this has prevailed as a custom, it has not the force of law. The law of inheritance extends to all persons and classes alike. [a] An heir cannot be disinherited.

297. A Hindu widow, whether childless or not, stands next in the order of succession on failure of male issue. [b] Widows.

298. Where a man left two wives, and one pre-deceased him leaving three daughters while the other survived him and was childless, it was held that the childless widow succeeded to the husband's property in preference to the three daughters. [c] So also, where two married undivided brothers died in succession without male issue leaving widows, the widow of the one who died last would succeed, while the other would be only entitled to maintenance

299. A widow's right to succeed her husband, however, is subject to the single condition of her having been faithful to him during coverture, an unchaste wife being excluded from the inheritance. But nothing short of actual infidelity in this respect disqualifies; the presumption of guilt, however, suffices for her disinherison. [d]

a 1 Strange's Hindu Law, 159, Note.
1 Madras Reports, 51.
b Ibid., 223.
c Ibid.
d 1 Strange's Hindu Law, 136.
2 Ibid., 270, 272, Colebrooke and Ellis.
Mitakshara, Chap. II, sect. i, §§ 2, 37.

300. In Bengal the reason of the widow's succession is her celebration of acts after her husband's death spiritually beneficial to him only in a degree less than those performed by a son. She succeeds in Madras on the principle of *survivorship,* she being the *surviving* half of her husband's body, as well as on the ground of her competence to perform funeral rites. The doctrine that a woman can only inherit, through having male issue, is untenable. [a]

301. A widow, being the mother of daughters, takes her husband's property, both movable and immovable, where the family is divided; but a childless widow takes only the movable property. Where there are two widows, one the mother of daughters and the other childless, the former alone takes the immovable estate, and the movable property is equally divided between them. This is not Madras law. [b]

302. A Hindoo widow has an absolute right to the fullest beneficial interest in her husband's property inherited by her for her life. She takes, as heir, a proprietary estate in the land, absolute for some purposes, although, in some respects, subject to special qualifications, and her disposition of the property is good for her life. The proposition that a widow has no estate in her husband's immovable pro-

a 1 Strange's Hindu Law, 135, 136.
2 Ibid., 239, Sutherland.
Mitakshara, Chap. II, sect. i, § 15, et seq.

b W. H. Macnaghten's Hindu Law, 21, 2nd ed., citing Smriti Chandrika.

perty, but only the personal enjoyment of the usufruct, is untenable.[a]

303. The application of such terms as *life-estate* and *life-tenancy* to the inheritance of a widow is improper. It seems doubtful, upon the Hindu authorities, whether a widow really takes the limited interest which she is supposed to do in her *divided* husband's estate. The opinion seems to be founded upon passages like the following from *Katyayana :* Let the sonless widow preserving unsullied the bed of her lord and abiding with her venerable protector (Guroo) enjoy *with moderation* the property until her death. After her let the heirs take it. The author of the *Smriti Chandrika,* however, explains that this passage applies to the case of a widow belonging to an *undivided* family. The decisions of the Courts have, however, authoritatively decided the question.

304. Where, of course, a widow does not inherit, she is entitled to maintenance. And in allowing her this, regard must be had to her separate property, so that her allot- Widow to be maintained when she does not inherit.

a 3 Madras Reports, 116, citing *Collector of Masulipatam* v. *Kavaly Vencata Narrayanappa*, 8 Moore's Indian Appeal Cases, 350, and the *Shivagunga Zamindari* case, 9 Moore's Indian Appeal Cases, 604.

* 2 Madras Reports, 393. See also, as to functions of widow over property, 2 Madras Reports, 409 ; 1 Ibid., 374 ; Ibid., 384 ; 2 Ibid., 462. Also 2 Madras Reports, 402, which places a mother inheriting from her son in the same position as a widow inheriting from her husband. It also decides that all property inherited by a woman is not stridhana. See Chap. II on Property.

ment, including her separate property, must be made equal to a full share. In an undivided family, the widow does not inherit, but is only entitled to maintenance. [a]

305. An unchaste widow forfeits her right to maintenance. [b]

Daughters. 306. In default of sons and widow, the daughters succeed, on the ground of their conferring proportionate benefits on the deceased. They take, in common, not indiscriminately, but in order as they are single, married, or widows. The *Mitakshara*, however, citing *Vrihaspati* bases her right upon *relationship*. *Vrihaspati* says, :—"As a son, so does the daughter of a man proceed from his several limbs. How then should any other person take her father's wealth?" The daughter therefore takes as *heir*, and not like the widow, as the *surviving half*. She obtains ownership, like the son, by birth. [c]

a 1 Strange's Hindu Law, 134, 171.
2 Ibid., 290, 295—297, Colebrooke.

b 1 Ibid., 172; 1 Madras Reports, 372. See however, 1 Indian Law Reports (Allahabad), 46.

c 1 Strange's Hindu Law, 138.
Smriti Chandrika, 51, 127.
As to daughter's estate, see Madras Sudder Reports for 1854, 153; 6 Madras Reports, 310; 3 Perry's Oriental Cases, 5.
2 Sevestre's Reports, 1; Weekly Reporter for 1864, 197; 12 Ibid., C. R., 453.
2 Agra Reports A. C., 166. *Devcoorerbai's* Case, 1 Bombay Reports, 130.
2 Indian Appeals, 126. This last decision however seems to limit her interest.

307. The single, though there should be but one of that description, takes the whole of the inheritance first, to the exclusion of the rest of her sisters during her life. The single having enjoyed it, it vests next in the married ones, and, finally, in such as are widows. They hold the estate jointly and they take by survivorship. [a]

308. No preference is given to a daughter, who has, or is likely to have male issue, over a daughter who is barren or a childless widow. The unendowed, however, succeed before the endowed. This is also the law of Bombay. [b]

309. According to Bengal law, married daughters who have, or who are likely to have male issue, are together entitled to succession, while under no circumstances can the daughters, who are either barren, or widows destitute of male issue, or the mothers of daughters only, inherit the property. [c] Bengal law.

a 1 Strange's Hindu Law, 138.
W. H. Macnaghten's Hindu Law, 22, 2nd ed.
2 Digest, 542, 3rd ed.
Mitakshara, Chap. II, sect. ii.

b Ibid.
2 Bombay Reports, 5.
6 Ibid., A. C., 183.
2 Strange, 242, Colebrooke.
It has been thought by some that, according to the Benares school, daughters could only inherit through their sons, and this doctrine appears to be upheld by the Smriti Chandrika, but the Mitakshara, the paramount authority in Southern India, entirely controverts the notion.

c W. H. Macnaghten's Hindu Law, 21, 2nd ed.
2 Digest, 543, 3rd ed.

310. The above rule of succession applies in Bengal to every possible case, but, according to the Benares school, only where the family is divided. [a]

311. In Bengal the daughter takes a more limited estate than the widow, but, under the *Mitakshara* she seems to take a larger estate. Representation obtains among them, and they take as *heirs*. There is no authority in the Hindu Law books for the proposition that a daughter, inheriting from her father, takes a mere life-estate. [b]

312. Where there are daughters by more wives than one, the estate vests in them equally, without regard to the mothers. [c]

Daughters' sons.

313. According to the law of Bengal and that of Benares, the daughters' sons inherit, in default of the qualified daughters. If there be sons of more than one daughter, according to the law of *Benares* they take *per stirpes*. In Bengal, they take *per capita*. [d]

Daughters' daughters cannot inherit.

314. Daughters' sons succeed, because, in regard to the obsequies of ancestors, they are considered as sons' sons. Daughters' daughters do not inherit. [e]

a W. H. Macnaghten's Hindu Law, 22, 2nd ed.

b See however 2 Indian Appeals, 126.

c 6 Madras Reports, 310.

d 1 Strange's Hindu Law, 124.

e 1 Ibid., 138, 139.
Mitakshara, Chap. II, sect. iii, § 6, citing Menu.
1 Morley's Digest, 258, 319, 325, 326.

315. If a maiden daughter should succeed to her father's estate in preference to her married sisters, and she should then marry, her son succeeds to the property in preference to her married sisters and their sons, these sisters having been married at the date of their father's death. [a]

316. In Bengal, whether the inheritance descends from the daughter to her son or not, depends on the fact of the daughter inheriting before or after marriage. If the former, it goes to her sons; if the latter, to her sisters, if any; and if there are none, the property will be equally shared by her sons and her sister's sons. [b]

Inheritance stops with daughter's son.

317. The succession stops with the son. If there be no son, the inheritance, on the death of the daughter, goes to those who would have succeeded, if it had never vested in the daughter. It does not class as *stridhana* and vest in the husband, at least it is so held in Madras and Bengal. [c]

Parents.

318. In default of the daughter's son, the inheritance ascends, and the mother succeeds as the nearest *sapinda*, and, after her, the father. This is the generally received law of the Benares school, though in Bengal the father inherits first, under the *shraadh* theory, because he offers

a 6 Sutherland's Weekly Reporter, 147. Sham Churn's Vyavastha Dapana, 23, 147; Dayabhaga, Chap. II, § 30. These were precisely the facts in the recent *Shivagungah* case.

b W. H. Macnaghten's Hindu Law, 24, 2nd ed.

c 1 Strange's Hindu Law, 139.
2 Madras Reports, 402.
14 Bengal Reports, 235.

more oblations than the mother. According to the *Mitakshara*, the mother succeeds first, because, as being the nearest of the two parents, it is most fit she should take the estate. [a]

319. Step-mothers are excluded from the inheritance. [b]

320. The interest of the mother in the property is not absolute, that is, it is of a nature similar to that of the widow. [c]

Brothers. 321. On failure of parents, the estate passes to the brother, or brothers of the deceased, those of the whole being preferred to those of the half blood; those of the half succeeding only on failure, or in default of those of the whole. [d]

322. Generally, the brothers succeed on the ground of the benefits they confer by the offer of oblations, while the whole brother is preferred to the half, on account of his

a W. H. Macnaghten's Hindu Law, 25, 2nd ed.
Mitakshara, Chap. II, sect. iii, §§ 3, 5.
Menu, 9, 187.

b 1 Strange's Hindu Law, 144.
Mitakshara, Chap. II, sect. iii, §§ 3, 5.
Menu, 9, 185.

c W. A. Macnaghten's Hindu Law, 25, 26, 2nd ed.
See also, 2 Madras Reports, 402, and 3 Ibid., 116.
8 Ibid., 91; 8 Moore's Indian Appeals, 500.

d 1 Strange's Hindu Law, 144.
Mitakshara, Chap. II, sect. iv, §§ 1, 5, 6.
1 Indian Law Reports, (Calcutta), 27.

being the nearer *sapinda,* he of the half blood being remoter, as the son of a different mother. [a]

323. If the deceased lived in renewed co-parcenery with a brother, then, in case of all being of the whole blood, the associated whole brother is heir in the first instance; but on failure of him, the unassociated whole brother. So, in case of all being of the half blood, the associated half brother inherits in the first place, and on failure of him, the unassociated half brother. But if there be an associated half brother and an unassociated whole brother, then both are equal heirs. [b]

324. Sisters are not enumerated in the order of heirs. This is Bengal law (a sister however may succeed a sister in Bengal); but it is not so under the *Mitakshara.* She may succeed in the absence of heirs. She may succeed her brother as a *bandhu,* but not as a *sapinda.* She may also object to alienations by her deceased mother in favour of a stranger. In Bengal however, she does not succeed a brother. In Bombay she does, and, according to the *Vyvahara Mayukha,* she is placed next in order after the paternal grandmother. In Bombay it has been held that after the death of a widow, her husband's sister succeeds

Sisters do not inherit.

a 1 Strange's Hindu Law, 144, 145.
Mitakshara, Chap. II, sect. iv, § 5.

b 2 Strange's Hindu Law, 254.

as next heir before the sister's son, and sisters and daughters both take absolutely. [a]

Brothers' sons.

325. In default of brothers, their sons inherit in the same order, that is, those of the whole before those of the half blood, and the undivided before the divided. [b]

326. There is this peculiarity in the succession of brothers' sons, viz., that a brother's sons, whose father died previously to the devolution of the property, claim by right of representation; they take *per stirpes* with their uncle, being, in that case, grandsons inheriting with a son; but where the succession devolves on the brothers' sons alone as nephews, they take *per capita.* [c]

Brothers' sons and grandsons.

327. In default of brothers' sons, their grandsons, and, after them, sisters' sons inherit. Brothers' daughters have no claim to the inheritance. In Bengal however, it has

a 2 Strange's Hindu Law, 243, 244, 246, Colebrooke, Ellis, and Sutherland.
1 Morley's Digest, 325, 326.
8 Madras Reports, 88.
7 Sutherland's Weekly Reporter, 227.
5 Ibid., 215.
9 Moore's Indian Appeals, 516.
6 Bombay Reports, O. C., 1.

b 2 Strange's Hindu Law, 254.
W. H. Macnaghten's Hindu Law, 27, 2nd ed.
Mitakshara, Chap. II, sect. iv, § 7.
3 Sutherland's Weekly Reporter, 43.

c W. H. Macnaghten's Hindu Law, 27, 2nd ed ; 9 Sutherland's Weekly Reporter, 464. According to Sir T. Strange the right of representation does not subsist in the case of brother's sons. 1 Strange's Hindu Law, 145. But see 1 Indian Law Reports, (Allahabad) 105. See also § 282, *ante*.

been held that under the *Mitakshara* all descendants in the male line who can offer funeral oblations may succeed.[a]

Heirs on failure of brothers' sons and grandsons.

328. On failure of brothers and brothers' sons, that is, of the father's descendants, the heirs are successively the paternal grandmother, the paternal grandfather, the uncles, and their sons and the father's sister's son. On failure of the paternal grandfather's line, the paternal great-grandmother, the great-grandfather, his sons, and their issue, inherit. These belong to the same general family, and are connected by funeral oblations. In Bengal, according to *Srikrishna Terkalankara,* the grandfather and grandmother are placed at the bottom of the list of heirs.[b]

329. In Bengal on failure of the father's descendants in the male line down to the brother's grandson, the father's daughter's son succeeds, and after her, the father's son's daughter's son, and the father's grandson's daughter's son.

330. Generally speaking, the Hindu law is against the heritable pretensions of women. There are however, four exceptions, viz., the widow, the daughter, the mother and the paternal grandmother, which are sanctioned by express texts.

a W. H. Macnaghten's Hindu Law, 28, 2nd ed.
6 Madras Reports, 280.
6 Sutherland's Weekly Reporter, 158.
12 Moore's Indian Appeals, 448.

b 1 Strange's Hindu Law, 147, 148, citing Srikrishna Terkalankara.
W. H. Macnaghten's Hindu Law, 33, 2nd ed.
Mitakshara, Chap. II, sect. v.

331. If there be none such, the succession devolves on remoter kindred, belonging to the same general family, and connected by libations of water. [a]

Gotraja.

332. Those of the lineal kindred who succeed next after the brothers' sons are called "*gotraja*" *(gentiles)*, indicating that they belong to the same general family. And they comprise the *sapindas* and the *samonadakas*, or *saculyas*. The cognate kindred are called *bandhus*. [b]

333. Where there are no lineal kindred, cognate kindred succeed, that is, those who are sprung from a different family, and who, as such, offer no funeral oblations. They are connected through females. [c]

Sapindas and samonadakas.

334. The relation of *sapindas*, or those connected by the funeral cake, extends to the seventh person, or sixth degree of ascent, or descent; and that of *samonadakas*, or those connected by a common libation of water, extends to the fourteenth degree; or, as some affirm, it reaches as far as the memory of birth and name extends. This is signified by *gotra*, or the relation of family name. [d]

a 1 Morley's Digest, 328.
Mitakshara, Chap. II, sect. v, § 6.
b W. H. Macnaghten's Hindu Law, 33, 2nd ed.
Mitakshara, Chap. II, sect. v, §§ 1, 3; and sect. vi.
c W. H. Macnaghten's Hindu Law, 33, 2nd ed.
Mitakshara, Chap. II, sect. vi.
d W. H. Macnaghten's Hindu Law, 33, 2nd ed.
2 Digest, 568, 3rd ed.
Mitakshara, Chap. II, sect. v, § 6.

335 The *sapindas* are in two classes, the nearer, and the remote. The former are the three in direct descent from the person to be traced from, and the three in ascent above him, and their descendants to the second degree. The rest are the remoter *sapindas.* The wife, daughters, daughters' sons, mother and paternal grandmother are included among the nearer *sapindas.* [a]

336. The *bandhus* are of three descriptions: the personal, paternal, and maternal cognate kindred of the deceased. The personal kindred are the sons of his own father's sister, the sons of his own mother's sister, and the sons of his own maternal uncle. The paternal kindred are the sons of his father's paternal aunt, the sons of his father's maternal aunt, and the sons of his father's maternal uncle. His maternal kindred are the sons of his mother's paternal aunt, the sons of his mother's maternal aunt, and the sons of his mother's maternal uncle. [b] Bandhus.

337. In default of natural kin, the series of heirs, in all the classes, terminates with the preceptor of the deceased, his pupil, or his fellow-student, each in his order. [c] Heirs on failure of kin.

a Strange's Manual, § 310.

b W. H. Macnaghten's Hindu Law, 33, 34, 2nd ed.
Mitakshara, Chap. II, sect. vi.

c 1 Strange's Hindu Law, 148.
W. H. Macnaghten's Hindu Law, 34, 2nd ed.
2 Digest, 569, 3rd ed.
Collector of Masulipatam v. *Kavaly Vencata Narrainappa,* 8 Moore's Indian Appeal Cases, 500, 523.
Mitakshara, Chap. II, sect. vii.

Heirs of hermit, &c.

338. In the case of the hermit *(vansprastha)*, the ascetic *(yati or sanyasi)*, and the professed student of theology *(brahmachari)*, who, in abdicating all worldly ties, lose their title as heirs to those to whom they are by nature related, their property descends among themselves, and not according to the general law of inheritance. [a]

339. Under the ancient Hindu law, primogeniture existed. Originally, the eldest son had preferential claims to the younger sons. Menu says, the eldest brother may take entire possession of the patrimony, and the others may live under him, as they lived under their father. And even at partition, a double portion was given to the eldest son, the best chattel was given to him, and the best room in the house, because, through him, the father discharges his debt to his ancestors. [b]

340. This is now abolished, and primogeniture exists only in connection with the inheritance of Rajs or Principalities, large Zemindaries, and other impartible estates in the nature of Principalities. Primogeniture is, therefore, at the present day, an exceptional rule of inheritance. [c]

a 1 Strange's Hindu Law, 150, 151.
2 Digest, 577, 578, 3rd ed.
Mitakshara, Chap. II, sect. viii.

b 1 Strange's Hindu Law, 193.

c 6 Madras Reports, 105.
7 Moore's Indian Appeals, 476.
9 Ibid., 539.

341. Primogeniture, however, where it exists, *must be proved to exist as a long and well established custom.* It will not be *assumed* to exist in connection with every impartible estate, as was done in the case of the *Shivagungah* Zemindary. [a]

342. In connection with the succession to a Zemindary, in which the rule of primogeniture prevailed, it has been decided that, as regards the rights of sons by different wives to inherit, except, perhaps, the son of the *first* wife, the priority in point of time of their mothers' marriages has never been regarded, when the wives were equal in caste and rank, and that the rule of primogeniture was and is the same in the case of sons by several wives of equal caste and rank, as in the case of sons by one wife. [b]

343. The succession to impartible estates may also be regulated by a special family custom, other than that of primogeniture, *e.g.*, that of the *Tipperah Raj* in which it is the family custom *(Kulachar)* for the Rajah to name a *Jobraj* and a *Burrah Thakore,* of whom the former succeeds him and the latter becomes *Jobraj.* [c]

344. Where a custom is proved to exist, it supersedes the general law, which, however, still regulates all beyond

a 1 Bombay Reports, App., 42.
5 Ibid., Appeal Cases, 161. See Steele on Caste, *passim.*

b 3 Madras Reports, 75.
14 Moore's Indian Appeals, 570. This was the decision in the *Oordkad* Zemindary from the *Tinnevelly* District.

c 12 Moore's Indiau Appeals, 523.

the custom. And a claimant who fails to establish a title by family custom, must fall back on the general principles of law. [a]

345. By *Kulachar* or family custom also, an estate may remain impartible, and its descent regulated by the rule of primogeniture. [b]

Three kinds of impartible estates.

346. There appear to be three classes of impartible estates :-

First, the true ancient Raj, or Principality proper, whose characteristics are indivisibility, descent to a sole heir, and whose mode of descent is *almost universally* (though not necessarily, as in the case of the *Tipperah Raj* above noticed) according to primogeniture : examples of this kind are the *Tirhoot Raj* (12 Moore), the *Tanjore Raj* (7 Moore) and others.

Secondly, estates *in the nature* of a true Raj, or Principality, whose characteristics are indivisibility, descent to a sole heir, and whose mode of descent may be according to primogeniture, or by any *Kulachar,* or special family custom, or by the general Hindu law, male or female holding it, according as he or she may be the heir under the general Hindu law, the estate at the same time retaining its *impartible* character : examples of this kind are the *Naragunty* Polliem (9 Moore), and the *Shivagungah* Zemindary (Ibid).

a 12 Moore's Indian Appeals, 523.

b 2 Indian Appeals, 263.

Thirdly, estates which are impartible by *Kulachar,* or family custom, and whose characteristics may be as above. Such an estate, however, would be partible, if the members thought fit to divide it: [a] example, the Taluq of *Gungore,* (2 Indian Appeals).

347. *Primogeniture* under *Hindu* law means a descent to the eldest *male* heir, lineal or collateral, and where this rule of descent prevails, no *female* can enter. It does not simply mean *seniority in age,* as is sometimes understood, it implies that the heir must be a *male* as well. [b]

Rule of descent by primogeniture.

348. When this rule of descent prevails, the estate descends to the eldest son, and at his death to his eldest son, if he have left male issue, the descent in each case being to the eldest son, and on the failure of the male issue of such son, to the next son and his male issue; and on the failure of all the sons and the male issue of such sons, to the next male collateral and his male issue; and on the failure of collateral males, the estate will escheat to the Crown, as it did in the case of the *Tanjore Raj,* (7 Moore), but this may be avoided by the adoption of a son, as was frequently done in the *Rawutpore Raj* (5 Moore). The descent in the case

a *Raj Kishen Singh* v. *Ramjoy Surma Mazoomdar,* (Privy Council), cited in above case.

b 9 Bengal Law Reports, 274.
5 Moore's Indian Appeals, 100, 169.
6 Ibid., 164.
7 Ibid., 476.
12 Ibid., 1.
Maine's Ancient Law, Chap. VII, 4th ed.

of the latter Raj is a very good example of descent by primogeniture [a]

349. The descent to a sole heir by primogeniture does not interfere with the general rules of succession further than to vest the possession and enjoyment of the *corpus* of the whole estate in a single member of the family, subject to the legal incidents attached to it, as the heritage of an undivided family, (where the estate belongs to an undivided family), that being all that the purpose of the usage, viz., the preservation of the estate as an impartible Raj renders necessary. The unity of the family right to the heritage is not dissevered any more than by the succession of co-parceners to partible property; but the mode of its beneficial enjoyment is different. Instead of several members holding the property in common, one takes it in its entirety, and the common law rights of the others, who would be co-parceners of partible property, are reduced to rights of survivorship to the possession of the whole, dependent upon the same contingency as the rights of survivorship of co-parceners *inter se* to the undivided share of each; and to a provision for maintenance in lieu of co-parcenary shares. [b]

350. Descent by primogeniture is not a necessary incident to an impartible estate; but where primogeniture holds as a rule of descent, the estate must necessarily be impartible.

a 9 Moore's Indian Appeals, 446.
b 6 Madras Reports, 105.
9 Moore's Indian Appeals, 539.

351. Where an impartible estate is the self-acquisition of the last holder, it will descend to his direct heirs first, in preference to the collaterals, as was decided in the *Shivagungah* case. [a]

Descent of self-acquired Zemindary.

352. Some portion of the family estate may be impartible, and the rest governed by the ordinary law of inheritance. The private property of a Zemindary, consisting of movables and land not appurtenant to the Raj, would come under the latter description and would be liable to partition when demanded. [b]

Impartible and partible estates may co-exist in same family.

353. In a recent case (the *Shivagungah* Zemindary), it was held that where an impartible estate descends to daughters as a class, it will on the death of the last daughter pass to the *eldest* son of a daughter alive at the time *under the rule of primogeniture,* in preference to the son of the last holder. [c]

Descent of Zemindary to daughters as a class.

354. The existence of proprietary estate in Polliems, or other lands not permanently assessed, and the tenure by which it is held, are matters to be judicially determined on the evidence in each case. [d]

Evidence as to estates of inheritance in Polliems, &c.

355. Proof of possession, or receipt of rents by a person who pays the land revenue immediately to Government, is

a 9 Moore's Indian Appeals, 539.
b 5 Madras Reports, 31.
7 Moore's Indian Appeals, 46.
c 6 Madras Reports, 310.
d 6 Ibid., 227; 1 Indian Appeals, 282; 8 Madras Reports, 114; 1 Indian Appeals, 268.

primâ facie evidence of an estate of inheritance in the case of an ordinary Zemindary. The evidence is still stronger if it be proved that the estate has passed, on one or more occasions, from ancestor to heir. [a]

Escheat. 356. Where a man of whatever caste dies without heirs, and without having alienated his property, it passes to the Crown by escheat. [b]

357. Where property has escheated to the Crown, it has the right to impeach an unauthorised alienation by a widow, in the same way as reversionary heirs might. [c]

358. A lawful charge upon escheated property, or trust, will bind the Crown. [d]

Heirs to a woman's stridhanum. 359. The above relates to inheritance among males. As to *stridhanum,* or woman's separate property, it is not governed by the ordinary rules of inheritance. It is peculiar and distinct, and the succession to it depends upon the *form of marriage,* the *source* from which it has been derived, or the *time* when it was *acquired.* [e]

a 6 Madras Reports, 227; 1 Indian Appeals, 282; 8 Madras Reports, 114; 1 Indian Appeals, 268.

b 8 Moore's Indian Appeals, 500.
11 Ibid., 619.

c 8 Ibid., 529.

d 11 Ibid., 619.
The superintendence of escheats vests in Board of Revenue under Regulation 7 of 1817.

e 1 Strange's Hindu Law, 249, 250.
W. H. Macnaghten's Hindu Law, 37, 2nd ed.

360. Where it belongs to an unmarried female, with exception of a nuptial present, (which, where it exists, reverts on her death to the bridegroom), her *stridhanum* goes first to her uterine brothers, whom failing, to her parents in succession, the mother taking before the father.[a]

361. Where it belongs to a married woman, whether she die living her husband, or a widow, the immediate heirs to it, including personalty inherited from her husband, are her lineal descendants in the female line, whether daughters or granddaughters, the granddaughters taking *per stirpes*; the unmarried and unendowed of the one, or the other, taking first.[b]

362. Where there are both daughters and granddaughters, it vests in the daughters exclusively, subject to such a provision for granddaughters as usage may warrant. In Bengal the granddaughters get no share. Daughters take equally, subject to the above distinction of married and unmarried. Failing female issue, daughters' sons' sons and grandsons succeed. These also take *per stirpes*.[c]

363. In default of all issue, the succession varies according to circumstances. The marriage having been in an

Descent according to form of marriage.

a 1 Strange's Hindu Law, 249.
W. H. Macnaghten's Hindu Law, 38, 2nd ed.
2 Digest, 618, 619, 3rd ed.

b 1 Strange's Hindu Law, 51, 249.
W. H. Macnaghten's Hindu Law, 38, 39, 2nd ed.
Mitakshara, Chap. II, sect. xi, §§ 9, 12, 13, 18, 19.

c See authorities last cited.

approved form, *(Brahma, Daiva, Arsha, Prajapatya)*, the husband (surviving) and his kin successively, are heirs; if in any of the less approved ones, *(Asura, Gandharva, Rakshasa, Paisacha)*, the parents of the woman succeed. On failure of them, their next of kin take the succession. [a]

Wife's fee.

364. The wife's *fee* or *perquisite*, given to her in the bridal procession, descends, by way of exception, to her brothers of the whole blood. [b]

Descent of property given at nuptials and property not so given.

365. Some distinction has been drawn as to the course of inheritance with reference to what was given by a woman's father, but not at the time of the nuptials, and what was so given. But this distinction does not appear to be generally observed. [c]

Descent of a woman's ornaments.

366. Ornaments, &c., given to a woman by her husband, or some of her relations on, before, or connected with her marriage, are her *stridhanum*, and descend to her heirs. But those not so given, and worn by her occasionally, are her husband's property, and are descendible to his heirs; although, if they were habitually worn by her, they would

a 1 Strange's Hindu Law, 250.
2 Digest, 614, 615, 616, 624, 625, 3rd ed.
Mitakshara, Chap. II, sect. xi, §§ 10, 11.

b 1 Strange's Hindu Law, 51.
2 Digest, 619, 3rd ed.
Mitakshara, Chap. II, sect. xi, § 14.

c W. H. Macnaghten's Hindu Law, 39, 40, 2nd ed.
See Table of Succession, *post*.

be considered her property, habitual wear, says Jagannatha, being considered as a mode of acquisition. This property corresponds to a lady's *paraphernalia* under English law.[a]

367. In the line of heirs, the daughter's husband is preferred to the sister; but would be postponed, if the latter had a son, the sister's son being first heir, after the husband, in the case of a woman's separate property.[b] Daughter's husband preferred to sister.

368. Maintenance allowed to a widow does not pass at her death to the heirs of her *stridhanum*, but to her husband's heirs. Gift of money however by a son to his mother has been held to be *stridhanum*[c] A widow's maintenance not stridhana.

369. There is no material difference between the Benares and the Bengal schools, as to the order of heirs to a woman's *stridhanum.* The distinctions that do exist are somewhat nice, and therefore unimportant.[d]

370. Unchastity in a woman does not incapacitate her from inheriting *stridhanum:* nor does it preclude her from keeping possession by right of inheritance of *stridhanum.*[e]

a 1 Strange's Hindu Law, 50, 211.
2 Ibid., 55, Colebrooke.
Menu, IX, v. 200.
2 Digest, 592, 3rd ed.
Mitakshara, Chap. I, sect. iv, § 19.

b 2 Strange, 403, Colebrooke citing Smriti Chandrika and Madhavya.

c 2 Strange, 404—406, Colebrooke, Ellis, and Sutherland; 5 Sutherland's Weekly Reporter, Miscellaneous, 53.

d W. H. Macnaghten's Hindu Law, 40, 41, Note, 2nd ed. See Table.

e 1 Indian Law Reports, (Allahabad), 46.

Descent of property amongst prostitutes.

371. The trade of prostitution being recognized and legalized by Hindu law, the law of inheritance amongst professional prostitutes, as indeed among prostitutes generally, is the same as that amongst other Hindoo females, that is, their offspring, natural or adopted, succeed, the female being preferred to the male.[a]

372. Prostitute daughters, living with their prostitute mothers, succeed to their mother's property, in preference to a married daughter, living with her husband.[b]

373. It has been held that the undegraded relatives, whether offspring or other of a prostitute, cannot inherit her property. This, however, seems doubtful even according to Hindu law. Further, a prostitute's right of inheritance is secured to her by specific legislation (Act XXI of 1850), and there seems no reason, therefore, why her undegraded relatives cannot inherit to her, if she can inherit to them.[c]

a 2 Madras Reports, 56.
Ibid., 196.

b Ibid., 56.
Morley's Digest N. S., 186.

c Ibid. 2 Madras Reports, 56. See, however, 3 Madras Reports, 50, citing the Vyavahara Mayukha, the Daya-bhaga, and the Mitakshara.

Order of succession to ancestral property in a divided family (Madras).

Son (natural or adopted).
Grandson.
Great-grandson.
Widow.
Daughter. Unmarried first, then married, and among these, the unendowed before the endowed.
Daughter's son.
Mother, but not step-mother.
Father.
Brother, whole blood first, then half.
Brother's sons do.
Brother's grandsons do.
Paternal grandmother.
Do. grandfather.
Do. grandfather's sons (uncles), whole first, then half.
Do. grandfather's grandsons (cousins) do.
Do. great-grandmother.
Do. great-grandfather.
Do. great-grandfather's son, and grandson successively.
Do. great-grandfather's mother.
Do. do. father.
Do. brother, whole first, then half.
Do. brother's son do.

Then the remoter *sapindas* in the same order, to the seventh degree. In default of sapindas, the *samanodacas* succeed. These include the above enumerated heirs in the same order, as far as the fourteenth degree. In default of these, the *bundhoos* or cognates succeed. [a]

[a] 1 W. H. Macnaghten's Hindu Law, 34.

There is some difference in the order of succession between the Madras, and other schools, chiefly Bengal. This may be accounted for from the fact that, a greater number of females are admitted as heirs under the Mitakshara, in which the doctrine of *consanguinity* over-rides that of *spiritual benefit,* which prevails in the other schools, chiefly in that of Bengal. The leading rule of inheritance under the *Mitakshara* is the text of Menu: To the nearest sapinda the inheritance belongs.

Order of succession to Stridhanum according to all the schools.

Of unmarried woman:

Brother whole first, then half.

Mother.

Father.

Her paternal kinsmen in due order.

Of married woman given at time of nuptials.

Daughters including granddaughters, unmarried, then married, and among these unendowed before endowed, —unendowed are such as are destitute of wealth, or without issue. The barren and widows failing the two first succeed as co-heirs.

Son.

Daughters' sons.

Sons' sons.

Sons' grandsons.

Son of rival wife.

Son's son of do.

Son's grandsons of do.

If marriage of approved form:

Husband.

Brother whole first, then half.

Mother.

Father.

If marriage of a disapproved form:

Mother.

Father.

Brother whole first, then half.

Husband.

In default of these the order is as follows:—

Husband's younger brother.

His younger brother's son.

His elder brother's son.

Sister's son.

Hnsband's sister's son.

Brother's sons.

Son-in-law.

Father-in-law.

Elder brother-in-law.

Sapindas.

Samanodacas.

If the property be given to her by her father, but not at the time of her nuptials, the heirs are:

A maiden daughter.

A son.

A daughter who has, or is likely to have, male issue.

Daughter's son.

Son's son.

Son's grandson.

The great-grandson.

Son of rival wife.
Her grandson.
Her great-grandson.

In default of these the barren and the widowed daughters succeed as co-heirs, and then the succession goes on as in the approved forms of marriage.

If property is not given by her father, and not given at the time of marriage, the heirs are as above except that the son and unmarried daughter inherit together and not successively, and that the son's son is preferred to the daughter's son. [a]

CHAPTER VII.

DISABILITIES TO INHERIT.

Grounds of exclusion.

374. EXCLUSION from inheritance rests in general upon the same principle with succession to it, that is, it is connected with the obsequies of the deceased; from their incapacity to perform which the excluded are incompetent as heirs. [b]

a W. H. Macnaghten's Hindu Law, 39, 40, *et seq.* Macnaghten says with reference to the above order of succession to *stridhanum* that it does not vary materially in the different schools; except that (as in the case of succession to ordinary property) a distinction is made by the law of Benares and other schools between reality and indigent daughters.

b 1 Strange, 152.

375. The causes of it are sufficiently numerous; defects both of body and mind, and devotion to any of the religious orders. [a]

376. Hence idiots and madmen; the deaf, the dumb, and the blind, that is, those deprived of any one of the faculties of hearing, speaking, seeing; the lame, that is, those who cannot walk on either foot, or who have lost both hands and the impotent; those suffering from obstinate or incurable disease, as well as devotees, are excluded from the inheritance. [b]

377. Disqualified heirs are entitled to maintenance. [c]

378. The sons however, or the grandsons and great-grandsons of the disqualified person succeed to the inheritance in default of each other.

379. In Bengal it was held that a deaf and dumb father could not inherit to the grandfather, and that the grandson, born after the grandfather's death, could not succeed to the grandfather's estate. This ruling does not apply to the

a 1 Strange, Chap. VII.
Mitakshara, Chap. II, sect. x.
The orders are—1, the professed student; 2, the hermit; 3, the ascetic.

b 1 Strange, Chap. VII.
2 Digest, 435, *et seq.* 3rd ed.
Mitakshara, Chap. II, sect. x, § 2, and Note. In cases of disease, the stricted proof will be required. 2 Sutherland's Weekly Reporter, 125.

c 1 Strange's Hindu Law, 174.

case of the son of an excluded person, if having been begotten and being in the womb at the time of the ancestor's death, he is afterwards born capable of inheriting.[a]

Vice not a ground of exclusion.

380. Under Hindu law, generally speaking, vice, constructive as well as actual, is considered a disqualifying cause, since in some instances it even excluded from caste. Act XXI of 1850, however, removes the disability, arising from exclusion from caste. Under Hindu law, as administered at the present day, vice is no disqualification. When vice becomes developed into crime, it is punishable by the Indian criminal law, and the provisions of the Hindu civil law on this point are therefore ignored.[b]

Bengal law.

381. In Bengal, however, it is held that under Hindu law unchastity alone was not a ground of exclusion: but that degradation from caste was. Peacock, C. J. observed that the estate taken by a Hindoo widow by inheritance is not an estate only so long as she continues chaste, or an estate liable to be forfeited by an act of unchastity. If this were so, he held that a widow would be in a worse position than a wife, since a wife may inherit if her offence is expiated before the death of her husband; but if a widow's estate cease, expiation would not restore it.[c]

a 2 Bengal Reports, (Full Bench Rulings), 103.
See also 1 Ibid., A. C., 117.

b Mitakshara, Chap. II, sect. x.

c 4 Bombay Reports, A. C., 25.
5 Bengal Reports, 466.

382. In Bombay it is held that under Hindu law incontinence excludes a widow from succession. If, however, the estate be once vested in her, it is not liable to be divested, unless she loses her caste from subsequent incontinence. Act XXI of 1850 removes the disability. Bombay law.

383. Under Act XV of 1856, a widow may re-marry, but she loses her right to inherit, or to be maintained out of her husband's property. Under Act XXI of 1850 she may lead the most immoral life, be degraded from caste in consequence, and yet secure all the benefits of inheritance. Effect of Acts XV of 1856 and XXI of 1850.

384. It has been held in Bengal that under Act XV of 1856, a widow on her re-marriage loses only *vested* rights of inheritance, and not those which have not accrued. She might succeed to the estate of her son who died after his mother's re-marriage, and who had succeeded to her first husband's estate. [a]

385. A dumb widow cannot inherit from her husband when the dumbness is congenital, but she must be maintained, and is capable of possessing *stridhanum*. [b]

386. According to the Mitakshara, an idiot is a person deprived of the internal faculty, meaning one incapable of discriminating right from wrong. [c] Definition of term idiot.

a 2 Bengal Reports, A. C., 199.
b 4 Bombay Reports, A. C., 135.
c Mitakshara, Chap. II, sect. x, § 2.

387. It has been held, however, that the mental incapacity which disqualifies a Hindoo from inheriting, on the ground of idiotcy, is not necessarily utter mental darkness. [a]

388. A person of unsound mind, who has been so from his birth, is, in point of law, an idiot; such unsoundness is to be determined not upon wire-drawn speculations, but upon tangible and unmistakable facts. [b]

389. The reason for disqualifying a Hindoo idiot is his unfitness for the ordinary intercourse of life. [c]

Defects should be co-eval with birth.

390. The other defects of body and mind enumerated must be co-eval with birth, with the exception, perhaps, of madness and impotence. For in practice, the succession of one who becomes deaf, blind, &c., in the course of his life, occurs even though such defect be incurable. [d]

Maladies how regarded.

391. Maladies, if extreme, are regarded as an expression of the divine displeasure at vice and crime indulged and perpetrated in a prior form, which it remains for the actual sufferer to expiate, forfeiting in the meantime his succession. [e]

392. With regard to leprosy the late Sudder Court at Madras held that, it is a fact well known in medical

a 1 Madras Reports, 214.
b Ibid.
c 1 Strange's Hindu Law, 152.
See also above decision.
d 1 Strange's Hindu Law, 153.
2 Digest, 435, *et seq.* 3rd ed.
14 Bengal Reports, 273.
e 1 Strange's Hindu Law, 155.

science that the disease of leprosy assumes in some cases a mild and curable form, while in others it appears in a virulent and aggravated type. The Sudder Court find, on consulting the best authorities on the subject, that it is in the latter case only that the disease is regarded in Hindu law as a disqualification entailing forfeiture of inheritance. This doctrine was approved by the High Court of Bombay. [a]

Where defect is removed.

393. If the disqualifying cause be removed by medicaments, or other means, the right to inherit takes effect. If this happens after division, the person succeeds by analogy to the case of the son born after partition. [b]

Heir must be in same predicament as delinquent to bar inheritance.

394. In every case of exclusion, the son or other heir must be in the same predicament as the delinquent himself, in order to bar his inheritance. [c]

Law of disqualification applies to all.

395. In general, the law of disqualification applies alike to both sexes. [d]

396. An adopted son may be disinherited for like reasons as the legitimate son, but he cannot forfeit the relation of son. [e]

a Madras Sudder Reports, 1860, 238.
5 Bombay Reports, A. C., 145.

b 1 Strange's Hindu Law, 164.
Mitakshara, Chap. II, sect. x, § 7.
2 Bengal Reports, (Full Bench Rulings), 103.

c 1 Strange's Hindu Law, 163.

d Ibid., 164.
2 Bombay Reports, 5.

e 2 Strange's Hindu Law, 126, Colebrooke.
As to exclusion of unchaste wives and illegitimate sons, see Chap. on Inheritance.

Non-application of rule in certain cases.

397. The doctrine of Hindu law, that out-castes are incapable of inheritance, has no bearing upon the case of the members of new families, which have sprung from persons so degraded. [a]

Estate once divested will not revert.

398. If the estate has once vested in a remoter heir in consequence of the disqualification of the nearer heir, it will not divest on the removal of the disqualification, or in consequence of the subsequent birth or conception of a son of the disqualified heir. [b]

399. As to the exclusion of illegitimate sons, such are only excluded when they are the issue of adulterous or incestuous intercourse. [c]

In competent marriage another cause of exclusion.

400. Another cause of exclusion stated in the books is an *incompetent marriage,* that is, where the husband and wife are descended from the same *stock.* Such a marriage being incongruous, the issue of it cannot inherit excepting among Sudras. And the consequence is the same where the marriage has not been according to the order of *class.* [d] But cases of this sort do not appear to have arisen in any of the courts; nor indeed does it seem to be taken as a ground of objection in the present day.

a 3 Madras Reports, 50.

b 2 Bengal Reports, (Full Bench Rulings), 103.

c 2 Madras Reports, 293.
3 Ibid., 134.

d 1 Strange's Hindu Law, 165.

CHAPTER VIII.

CHARGES ON THE INHERITANCE.

Charges on the inheritance.

401. The charges to which the inheritance is liable, are of three kinds. *First,* debts and other obligations in the nature of legacies. *Secondly,* certain specific duties to be provided for out of it, where it has descended to a single heir, and out of the common fund, where it has vested by survivorship in undivided parceners, such as the providing for the initiatory and marriage ceremonies of the members of the family. *Thirdly,* maintenance of all requiring and entitled to it.[a]

Rule as to discharge of debts.

402. The rule as to the discharge of debts is, that they follow the assets into whosesoever hands they come, the obligation to pay attaching, not upon the death only of the ancestor, but on his becoming an anchorite, or having been so long absent from home as to let in a presumption of death. Where there are no assets, there is no liability.[b]

403. A man's private debts (in opposition to family debts) must be paid by him who inherits, either his separate, or self-acquired property.[c]

a 1 Strange's Hindu Law, 166.

b Ibid.
See further Chap. on Guardianship.
See also 3 Madras Reports, 161.
11 Bombay Reports, 76.

c Ibid.

404. This obligation is inculcated upon the heir as of importance to the peace of the deceased, equally with the performance of his funeral ceremonies, the two together constituting the true consideration for inheritance. [a]

When a debt is binding on the heirs.

405. To be binding, a debt must have been incurred on a good consideration. This excludes such as have arisen from gaming, and such as have been recklessly incurred, *and not for the benefit of the family.* [b]

Qualification of the rule.

406. It does not follow that because the ancestral estate has been encumbered, that the sum borrowed has been a wasteful expenditure. It may well be that the managing member has obtained by it something much more valuable than the original estate. [c]

407. All that is necessary is that the speculations of a managing member should be entered into with the *bonâ fide* hope and reasonable expectation of increasing his property for those who are to come after him, and then his co-parceners will be also liable for the losses he may sustain. [d]

Power of manager.

408. In cases of trade, the manager has the power to pledge the property and credit of the family, and minors and other members of the family will be bound by all acts of the manager, which are incident to the carrying on of the trade. Unless the manager had this power, the family trade

a 1 Strange's Hindu Law, 166.

b Ibid., 166, 167.

c 3 Madras Reports, 177.

d Ibid.

could not be carried on, for the acts of the manager might be set aside by the minor.[a]

409. Where self-acquired property has descended burdened with any debts, the estate is in the hands of the heirs liable for those debts, nor will it be discharged on the ground that, tho managing member ought to have paid the debts.[b]

Self-acquisition liable for debts.

410. The passage in the *Mitakshara* as to the right of sons to prohibit excessive expenditure by no means involves the logical consequence that, if that right of prohibition has not been, or, from the non-age of the sons, could not have been exercised, there would be after the lapse of any period, how long soever, a right of restitution. It may be that the case of a minor requires a different consideration; the law counter-balances his disabilities with many privileges, and it may well be that he might be entitled to restitution, although a son of full age would not be. But it may also be that, the absence of the power of interposition would be a loss attendant upon his disability, from which no law could relieve him.[c]

Meaning of passage in the Mitakshara.

411. The course for the payment of debts on partition may be either by disposing of a sufficient part of the property for the purpose, and thus paying them off at once, or by apportioning them among the parceners, according to

How payment of debts provided for.

a 1 Bombay Reports Appendix, 61.
Ibid., A. C., 27.

b 3 Madras Reports, 177.

c Ibid.

their respective shares, an arrangement which, to be binding upon creditors, would require their assent.[a]

Gifts. 412. Gifts made by a man during his life-time to take effect after his death are a charge upon the inheritance: and, according to *Devala,* that which a husband has promised to his wife for separate property must be made good by his sons even as a debt.[b]

Shraaddhas. 413. The exequial rites *(shraaddhas)* of a deceased individual, namely, his monthly, six-monthly, and annual ceremonies, are to be paid for out of the estate.[c]

Initiation and marriage. 414. Not less obligatory upon the heirs is the charge for the *initiation* of the unitiated, and the *marriage* of the unmarried members of the family.[d]

What constitutes initiation. 415. Initiation involves a succession of religious rites attended with more or less of expense; commencing with purification and terminating in marriage. They are ten in number; of which marriage is the only one competent to females and Sudras; the rest being confined to males of the three superior classes.[e]

a 1 Strange's Hindu Law, 168.
2 Ibid., 283, 284, Colebrooke.
See further Chap. on Partition, post.

b Strange's Hindu Law, 169.
Vyavahara Mayukha, Chap. IV, sect. x, § 4, citing Devala.

c 1 Strange's Hindu Law, 170.

d Ibid.

e 1 Strange's Hindu Law, 170.

416. The duty of initiating attaches to those who have themselves been initiated; and the provision for it is to be made before partition out of the common stock. [a]

Duty of initiation to whom attaches.

417. Charges of this nature to be available against the inheritance must be reasonable; though this is seldom attended to. They regard brothers and sisters only, not extending to collaterals. [b]

Charges of initiation, &c., to be reasonable.

418. Of course, when the family is undivided, sons, grandsons and great-grandsons must be maintained out of the estate as well as the other members; and the same duty attaches to each partner after division with reference to the members of his own family, his own family then being in a state of undivision. Where there is no ancestral estate, they are not entitled to maintenance after they have attained majority. This applies also to adopted sons. [c]

Charges in undivided family.

419. As already observed, the widow, where she does not inherit, must be maintained by the heir. It is a charge upon the whole estate, and therefore upon any part thereof. It may be supplied by an assignment of land, or an allowance of money; in either case proportioned to her support, and that of those dependant upon her, including the performance of charities and the discharge of religious obligations; and this always with a reference to the amount of property,

Widow to be maintained where she does not inherit.

a 1 Strange's Hindu Law, 170.

b Ibid., 170, 171.

c 1 Madras Reports, 45; 4 Bengal Reports Appendix, 23. 12 Sutherland's Weekly Reporter, 494.

so as at the utmost not to exceed a son's or other parcener's share. This is also the law in Bengal [a]

420. In Bombay it has been held that a destitute widow must be maintained by her husband's relations, although she may have shared her husband's estate and supported herself for a long time by trading. [b]

421. It has been held that the heir cannot turn out the widow and others entitled to maintenance from the family dwelling-house, and that these may remain in the dwelling-house and claim maintenance from the estate, even though they have passed into other hands. [c]

422. A brother's widow must be maintained by her husband's brother on his succeeding to the estate. [d]

423. A woman forfeits her right to maintenance if she leaves the protection of her legal guardian without sufficient cause. [e]

a 1 Strange's Hindu Law, 171.
2 Ibid., 305, 307, 383, Colebrooke.
4 Bombay Reports, 273.
Ibid., A. C., 73.

b 1 Bombay Reports, 13.
9 Sutherland's Weekly Reporter, 475.

c 4 Bengal Reports, O. C., 81.
15 Sutherland's Weekly Reporter, C. R., 263.
17 Ibid., 433.
1 Agra Reports, 42.

d 10 Sutherland's Weekly Reporter, 359.

e 1 Madras Reports, 372.
4 Sudder Dewanny Decisions (Bengal), 491.
6 Sutherland's Weekly Reporter, 116.
9 Ibid., 413.
Ibid., 152; But see 5 Madras Reports, 150; and 2 North-West Reports, 170.

424. A widow's right to maintenance is *personal.* It cannot be alienated nor can she alienate lands charged with her maintenance. [a]

Liabilities of widow succeeding.

425. Where the widow succeeds as heir, she takes subject among other things to defray the education and nuptials of an unmarried daughter;—as also to maintain those whom the deceased was bound to support. [b]

Claim of adulterous wife, &c.

426. A wife leaving her husband's house without sufficient cause, and an adulterous wife, are not entitled to maintenance, but may claim, under certain circumstances, a bare subsistence. [c]

427. A wife however does not permanently forfeit her right to maintenance by leaving her husband's house, or for any ordinary fault. If she returns to her husband after leaving him, he is bound to maintain her. [d]

Grandmother and stepmother to be maintained.

428. The grandmother forming a part of the family, is alike entitled to maintenance; as are also the step-mothers: the daughter too, but not to a separate subsistence. A step-mother should be supported by her step-sons. [e]

a 5 Sutherland's Weekly Reporter, 111.
3 North-West Reports, 324.
b 2 Strange's Hindu Law, 404, Colebrooke.
c 1 Ibid., 372; 2 Madras Reports, 327.
3 Ibid., 144.
d 9 Sutherland's Weekly Reporter, 475.
e 1 Strange's Hindu Law, 172.
1 Madras Reports, 372.
6 Sutherland's Weekly Reporter, 116.
This is Bengal law, but see 5 Madras Reports, 377.

Unmarried and widowed sisters also.

429. Married sisters are considered as provided for. Unmarried ones maintainable out of the family property till marriage are, upon partition, a charge upon it to the extent, as is commonly said, of a quarter of a share; an allotment explained by various authorities, including the *Chandrika* and *Madhaviya*, as meaning a sufficiency only for the expenses of the marriage; and widowed ones not otherwise provided for are entitled to be maintained. [a]

Sister's allotment.

430. The allotment of a quarter share to a sister is not a fourth to each sister to be deducted from the share of each brother, but a participation out of the whole equivalent to the fourth of a brother's share without regard to the number of brothers. [b]

Widowed daughter-in-law.

431. The daughter-in-law (widow) has no right to maintenance from her father-in-law when he has no ancestral property, but she has when he possesses it. [c]

Maintenance of illegitimate issue.

432. In all the classes, it is the duty of the parent to maintain illegitimate issue; an obligation that attaches to the survivors and is to be provided for upon partition. [d]

Mothers of such.

433. The mothers of such children have the like claim. [e]

a 1 Strange's Hindu Law, 173.
b Ibid.
2 Ibid., 404, Colebrooke.
c 2 Bengal Reports, A. C., 17.
5 Madras Reports, 150.
d 1 Strange's Hindu Law, 174.
Ibid., 187.
e Ibid., 174.

434. All those who, on account of natural defects or disease, are excluded from the inheritance, are likewise a charge upon the estate. [a] Those excluded from inheritance.

435. Under Act XXI of 1850, outcastes are entitled to maintenance. Under Hindu law they are entitled to food and raiment only. [b] Maintenance and rights of out-castes, &c.

436. Of persons disqualified to inherit, their childless wives, continuing chaste, are to be provided for; as are also the maintenance and nuptials of their unmarried daughters. [c]

437. A successor to a Raj or Zemindary would be bound by the debts of his predecessor contracted for necessary purposes, *e.g.*, the payment of Government revenue, or for reproductive works upon the estate. Charges on Zemindaries.

438. The illegitimate son of a Zemindar of the Sudra caste is entitled to maintenance, and the maintenance is a charge on the Zemindary. [d]

439. A Hindoo whose adoption is invalid is entitled to maintenance in his adopter's family. [e] Maintenance of adoptee.

a 1 Strange's Hindu Law, 174.

b Ibid.; 3 Madras Reports, 50. Mitakshara, Chap. II, sect. *x*, § 5, and note by Balambhatta.

c Ibid., 175.

d 5 Madras Reports, 405. As to claims of illegitimate sons generally, see Chapter on Inheritance, *ante*.

e 1 Ibid., 45.

Arrears of maintenance when recoverable.

440. No rule of Hindu law prohibits the recovery of arrears of maintenance. The Limitation Act specially provides for such a suit. Arrears of maintenance due to a widow at her death do not necessarily revert to the estate from which they were derived, on the ground that they were not separated from the *corpus* during her life. [a]

CHAPTER IX.

PARTITION.

Partition defined.

441. PARTITION, in its most general sense, comprehending as well the division of the paternal property during the life of the father, as that which usually takes place at some period or other among co-heirs, is the adjusting by distribution the possession of different parties to a pre-existing right: as the divesting of exclusive rights in specific portions of property, and revesting a common one over the whole, is implied in re-union. [b]

442. It is an inchoate right, founded on a claim of succession, originating in birth. [c]

Who can claim partition.

443. In the Madras school, sons as well as grandsons, irrespective of all circumstances, may maintain a suit against their father and grandfather respectively for compulsory division of ancestral family property. [d]

a 2 Madras Reports, 36; 16 Sutherland's Weekly Reporter, C. R., 76.

b 1 Strange's Hindu Law, 176, 177.

c Ibid.

d 1 Madras Reports, 77, citing Mitakshara.

444. This differs from the law in Bengal. There, the father's consent is requisite to partition, and, while he lives, the sons have not the power to exact it, excepting under such circumstances as would altogether divest him of his proprietary right, such as his adoption of a religious life. The father of course may divide with his sons when he pleases.[a] Bengal law.

445. In Bengal, sons have not a right of ownership in the wealth of the living parents, but in the estates of both when deceased. They have, however, a proprietary right in their shares, though not in the whole estate. And this title is always considered distinct, though the family is undivided.[b]

446. In the Madras school, the father may enforce partition as against his sons, there being no distinction between a father and other co-parceners. In Bombay it has been held that partition cannot be enforced by sons against their father as regards movable property.[c] Bombay.

447. A father, in making a partition with his sons, must make an equal distribution of the ancestral property. Not so in Bengal. Of ancestral property the father may retain Partition must be equal, otherwise in Bengal.

a W. H. Macnaghten's Hindu Law, 43, 2nd ed.

b Daya Bhaga, Chap. I, sects. 8, 9 & 30.

c 2 Madras Reports, 416.
10 Sutherland's Weekly Reporter, 273.
1 Bombay Reports, Appendix, 76.

a double share, or divide it as he pleases.[a] According to the Mitakshara, wives may claim a share equal to a son's, where they have no *stridhanum*, and where they have, half a share.[b]

Partition according to Bengal and Madras law.

448. In Bengal, *partition* is a separation of property into particular shares corresponding to the previously distinct title of each owner. In Madras, where each member has no separate title before division, but the title is joint, partition of title, without partition of estate, is sufficient to constitute a division, regard being had to the intention of the parties.[c]

Share and rights of son subsequently born.

449. Where pregnancy is apparent in the mother, at the time of partition, either the partition should wait, or a share be set apart to abide the event: but if it were then neither manifest nor apprehended, in such case, should a son who was at the time in the womb, be born after, he

a 1 Strange's Hindu Law, 194, 195, 223.
W. H. Macnaghten's Hindu Law, 44, 2nd ed.
As to father's right of partition in Bengal, see further, Ibid., 43.
Mitakshara, Chap. I, sect. ii, § 14 ; also sect. vii, § 2.
Dayabhaga, Chap. II, sect..xx, as to the Bengal law; see, however, 2 Strange, 325, citing Sutherland.

b Mitakshara, Chap. I, sect. ii, § 9.

c 3 Bengal Reports, Full Bench Rulings, 39.
6 Sutherland's Weekly Reporter, 139.
7 Ibid., 488.
9 Ibid., 61.
11 Moore's Indian Appeals, 75.

should obtain his share from his brothers by contribution. He must however be conceived before partition. [a]

450. After the death of the father, an equal partition must be made both of self-acquired and ancestral property. The widow and mother also will come in for shares equal to that of a son. The shares of the sons will be according to the number of sons, and not according to the number of mothers, *i.e.*, where there has been a plurality of wives. [b]

Partition subsequent to father's death.

451. The heirs of parallel grade who are in natural co-parcenary are a father and his sons, son's sons and son's grandsons: brothers and their sons, son's sons and son's grandsons: male cousins of male descent: widows of the same husband: daughters; daughter's sons; and daughter's daughters inheriting in the female line. [c]

Heirs of parallel grade and their mode of succession.

452. Of these the sons, brothers, widows, and daughters, when taking from the father, inherit equally or *per capita*; and the son's sons and son's grandsons, the brother's sons, son's sons and son's grandsons, the cousins, daughters' sons, daughters taking from the mothers and granddaugh-

a 1 Strange's Hindu Law, 182.
Mitakshara, Chap. I, sect. vi, § 12.
4 Madras Reports, 307.

b *Dayabhaga*, Chap. III, sect. ii, § 29; *Mitakshara*, Chap. I, sect. ii, § 9.
3 Madras Reports, 289.
12 Bengal Reports, A. C., 373, 388.

c Strange's Manual, § 234.

ters according to the share of the person through whom they derive the inheritance or *per stirpes.* [a]

453. The male issue of a man that is his sons, son's sons, and son's grandsons must have been exhausted before a lapsed share falls to those of parallel grade to himself, that is, to his brothers. In like manner daughters' sons must have been exhausted before the lapsed share of the daughter falls to other daughters. [b] In the remaining classes of co-heirs, the right of one co-heir vests in the survivors of the same grade before passing on to the next in the line of descent.

Effects of partition in some cases.

454. Partition among brothers will alter the line of succession; but not so among daughters. For on failure of male issue of a brother who has divided, the right of the widow on the daughters accrues. Partition among daughters has no such effect, since upon the death of one if married, her share vests in her own line; if unmarried, in her brothers. [c]

Rights of subsequently begotten sons.

455. A subsequently begotten son shall have recourse only to the remaining property of the father, succeeding to the whole exclusively, or dividing with it with such of the

a Strange's Manual, § 235; citing Mitakshara and Smriti Chandrika.

b Ibid., 237. This seems to be contrary to the general opinion. It is however a moot point. For the prevailing notion, see 6 Madras Reports, 310, and 1 Indian Appeals, 124. Indeed, the whole doctrine of survivorship appears to be opposed to the spirit of Hindu law. See Burnell's Varadaraja's *Vyavaharanirnaya* (Preface).

c *Mitakshara*, Chap. II, sect. xi, §§ 12, 30.

brothers as may have become re-united to the common parent.[a]

456. Where there is an adopted son and there are other sons by birth after the adoption, the adopted son gets one-fourth of what forms the share of each of the after-born sons.[b]

457. Any acquisition by a re-united father through means of his individual wealth, or personal exertions, belongs exclusively to the son born after partition, *and not to him in common with another re-united.* This latter *dictum* is doubtful and is opposed to Menu.[c]

458. Where there is no after-born issue, the sons who had received their shares take by inheritance what their parents leave.[d]

459. Where illegitimate issue would inherit in case of the death of their putative father, they are also entitled to share on partition in his life; and they are under other circumstances entitled to be provided for to the extent of maintenance. He gets among Sudras half the share that falls to a son, daughter, or daughter's son. Failing these

Shares of illegitimate sons.

a 1 Strange's Hindu Law, 182.
W. H. Macnaghten's Hindu Law, 47, 2nd ed.
3 Bengal Reports, A. C., 7.

b Elberling, 71.

c 1 Strange's Hindu Law, 182, 183.

d Ibid.

he comes in for a full share, but his obtaining a share in his father's life-time depends upon his pleasure.[a]

Share of minor.

460. A minor's share should be secured for him by the sharers. It has been held that a minor cannot enforce partition at his option, unless his interests will be endangered, if his share be left with the co-parceners. His guardian however may consent to partition on his behalf.[b]

Sons and great-grandson's share *per stirpem.*

461. As in inheritance, sons as far as great-grandsons share on partition *jure representationis,* the aggregate grandsons of each deceased grandfather being entitled *per stirpem,* not to an equality individually with their uncles and cousins.[c]

Share of absent son.

462. If one of the sons, absent at the time of partition in a foreign country, die leaving issue, their right survives to them as far as the seventh generation; and on their appearing, the brothers who remained at home and divided, or their representatives, must, to that extent, answer a claim out of their several shares: so also is one who has returned after residing in a foreign country entitled on his return to receive a share of the property, whether it has been divided or not.[d]

a 1 Strange's Hindu Law, 187.
Mitakshara, Chap. I, sect. xii, § 2.

b 1 Strange's Hindu Law, 188.
2 Ibid., 362, Colebrooke.
2 Ibid., 182; 3 Madras Reports, 94.

c 1 Strange's Hindu Law, 187, 188, 207.
Mitakshara, Chap. I, sect. v, § 2.

d 1 Strange's Hindu Law, 188, 206.

463. A partition may be made openly in the presence of arbitrators, privately by adjustment, and lastly by casting of lots.[a] How partition is made.

464. Previous to partition, debts and other charges such as maintenance and initiation, &c., must be provided for by such means as may be agreed at the time; since taking place in the life of the father, it must be looked upon as an anticipated descent of his property. For a distribution of the debts of any of the co-parceners, the consent of the creditors must be obtained.[b] Provision to be made for debts previous to partition.

465. If widows and daughters have before partition received property from the deceased equal to or more than a son's share, they will get nothing more on partition, if less, then they will receive what will equal a son's share.[c]

466. Where there are outstanding debts both of father and grandfather with assets of each, they may be distributed, analogous to the English practice of marshalling the assets.[d]

a Strange's Hindu Law, 190, 222.

b Ibid., 191, 223. See further previous Chap.

c 12 Bengal Reports, A. C., 385.

d 1 Strange's Hindu Law, 191. The marshalling of assets is such an arrangement of the different funds of the common debtor of two or more creditors as may satisfy every claim, so far as, without injustice, such assets can be applied in satisfaction thereof, notwithstanding the claims of particular individuals to prior satisfaction out of some one or more of those funds. Story's Equity, §§ 558, 560, 561.

467. But for a debt incurred by a disunited father an after born son is exclusively liable, unless it was contracted not on his own account alone, but for the benefit of the family subsequently to re-union; in which case it is eventually a charge, as well upon the re-united parceners, as upon sons born after partition.[a]

Impropriety of Court to settle a certain rate of expenditure as being just or otherwise.

468. In a suit for partition by a son, it is improper for the Court, in deciding what debts are just or otherwise, to settle a certain rate of expenditure, as being that which should have been expended by the father, and to debit the estate with all the excess.[b]

469. There is no such legal obligation to frugality, as can be enforced by rendering the father liable for all sums which a Court may think to have been unreasonably expended from the date of his coming into possession, until the date of the suit for partition.[c]

470. If the father could show that the property to be divided is equal in value to that which descended to him, he would be absolutely exempt from any duty to account at all to his son. And if for the purpose of his present acquisitions he has encumbered the ancestral estate, then the plaintiff must take his share of it *cum onere*.[d]

Waiver of share by son.

471. Where a share is not desired by a son, it may be effectually waived by his acceptance of a trifle in satisfac-

a 1 Strange's Hindu Law, 191.
b 3 Madras Reports, 177.
c Ibid.
d 3 Madras Reports, 177.

tion, his heirs being bound by his consent. But the son must be himself able to earn wealth. Without renunciation it may still be claimed.[a]

Partition need not be general.

472. Nor is it necessary, where the partition is general, *that* it should attach upon the whole of the property; a part only may be distributed, keeping what remains for future division, or to descend in a course of inheritance.[b]

Two-fold application of word partition.

473. There is a two-fold application of the word *partition.* There may be a partition of *right,* and there may be a partition of *property.* A partition of the one need not necessarily be followed by a partition of the other. That is, there must be a division of the title and the income, but not necessarily of the estate itself.[c]

474. When the members of an undivided family agree among themselves with regard to particular property that it shall thenceforth be the subject of ownership in certain defined shares, the undivided family becomes a divided family with reference to the property that is the subject of that agreement, and that is a separation in interest and in right, although not immediately followed by a *de facto*

a 1 Strange's Hindu Law, 195.
Menu, IX, 207.
Mitakshara, Chap. I, sect. ii, §§ 11, 12.
3 Madras Reports, 33.
5 Ibid., 449.

b 1 Strange's Hindu Law, 195.
2 Madras Reports, 325.

c 11 Moore's Indian Appeals, 75.
2 Madras Reports, 325. See also, 3 Madras Reports, 40.

actual division of the subject-matter. This may at any time be claimed by virtue of the separate right.[a]

Bengal law as to partition of self-acquisition.

475. In Bengal a father is entitled to a share in his son's self-acquisition. If it is acquired with the aid of family funds, the father is entitled to half, the acquirer two shares, and the others to one share each. If not so acquired, the father gets two shares, the son who acquired it two, and the rest none.[b]

When partition is valid.

476. Where there has been no fraud or undue advantage taken of a sharer's minority, and in the absence of proof of gross inequality in the distribution of the property, a division will be held valid.[c]

477. A clear intention to hold property separately, and to abandon all claim to the shares of the other partners amounts to a partition.[d]

Widow or daughter cannot call for partition.

478. Since a wife cannot claim partition as against her husband, nor a daughter a share upon its taking place in the life of the father, so neither can the one nor the other call for it after his death. This can be done by those alone who are considered as heirs; in contradistinction to those

a Above Privy Council decision.

b 2 Bengal Reports, A. C., 287.
Dayabhaga, Chap. II, sect. lxv, *et seq.*
Vyavastha Darpana, 385.

c 2 Madras Reports, 182.

d 3 Madras Reports, 40.
3 Sutherland's Weekly Reporter, 41.
10 Ibid., 273. This is a still stronger case as one of the partners was a minor.

who have a claim only to be maintained—of which latter description are the widow or widows of the deceased, the principle being that the right is co-ordinate with the gift of funeral cakes. [a] Otherwise in Bengal. They are entitled to share, however, when a partition is made. So are also the mother and grandmother. [b]

479. Where a widow sued to recover from the brothers of her deceased husband a share of her property which remained undivided at his death, it was held that she had no right to recover property which was actually undivided at the death of her husband. It must have been otherwise if the husband's share had been ascertained though he was not yet in possession. [c]

Patni-bhaga not recognized.

480. The mode of division called *Patni-bhaga*, or division by wives, in contradistinction to *Puttra-bhaga*, a division by sons, does not prevail. [d]

Impartible property.

481. Impartible property [e] —

a 1 Strange's Hindu Law, 203, 204.
2 Madras Reports, 325.
12 Bengal Reports, 373, 385.
Mitakshara, Chap. I, sect. ii, § 9.
2 Strange's Hindu Law, 307, 383, 404, Colebrooke. A widow however is capable of offering oblations.

b W. H. Macnaghten's Hindu Law, 47, 48, 49, 2nd ed., citing Digest.

c 1 Strange's Hindu Law, 234.
2 Madras Reports, 325.

d 2 Strange, 355, Colebrooke. 2 Select Reports (Bengal), 147.

e 1 Strange's Hindu Law, 208—221. Gifts not made in return for something else, and friendly gifts, which, never vesting in the donee, in consequence of his death during the life of the donor, descend to his heir, are held impartible. Ibid., 169, 170. For examples of impartible estates, see Chap. on Inheritance, *ante*.

i. (*a*) Regalities or Ancient Rajs: that is, the *ruling power* is not subject to partition, but descends to the eldest son.

(*b*) Zemindaries, Polliems and estates in the nature of a Raj.

(*c*) Estates that are impartible by agreement.

ii. Lands endowed for religious purposes not being inheritable, are impartible.

iii. Clothes and jewels habitually worn by members of the family, male or female.

iv. Separate acquisitions, where they have been made without the aid of the family funds. [a]

v. Nuptial gifts which a man receives with his wife.

vi. Wealth acquired by science, valour, or the like, where the joint property has not been employed in the acquisition.

vii. The gains of prostitution being the profits of a trade recognised and legalised by Hindu law. [b]

viii. Places of religious worship and lands appropriated for that purpose. [c]

Partible property.

Partible property relating to the above:

a As to separate acquisition being impartible, see 6 Bombay Reports, A. C., 54.

b 2 Madras Reports, 56.
6 Bombay Reports, A. C., 1.

c 8 Sutherland's Weekly Reporter, 193.

✓i. The private property and effects of a Sovereign or Zemindar.

ii. Village and religious dues: and an annuity when made to one of an undivided family and his heirs.

iii. Srotryums and Jaghires. [a]

iv. An annuity to a member of a joint family and his heirs.

v. The management of lands endowed for religious purposes.

vi. Clothes and jewels belonging to males or females, but not habitually worn.

vii. Self-acquisitions, including those obtained by science and valour, where the family property has been employed. [b]

482. Where the common stock has been augmented or improved, the benefit on partition, as well as during the period of joint occupancy, accrues to all alike, without regard to the degree in which each may have contributed to its enhancement. It is like accretion under the civil law. If there is a distinct acquisition by means of the common

Augmentation of common stock like accretion under civil law.

a 1 Strange's Hindu Law, 208—221.
On the subject of an Inam village being partible or otherwise, see 2 Madras Reports, 470. As to srotryums, see 1 Madras Reports, 465, and note.

b As to separate acquisition being partible, see 6 Sutherland's Weekly Reporter, 256.

stock, the acquirer is entitled to a double share in the acquisition, and this right is kept open for his male issue.[a]

Agreement may be made by one parcener with the others as to re-payment of self-acquired property expended upon the common stock.

483. There is no rule of law, however, which precludes one member of an undivided family, though living together, from entering into an agreement with his co-parceners in respect of the expenditure upon the family property and re-payment of self-acquired funds; and such an agreement is rendered more reasonable and probable, where portions of the family property are occupied and enjoyed by each of the members living separately.[b]

Share of parcener who has obtained self-acquisition with aid of family property.

484. If separate acquisitions have been made to which the patrimony was instrumental, the acquirer is rewarded with a double share. So says also *Jimuta Vahana.*[c]

Share of recoverer of family property.

485. When landed property has been recovered, the special claim of the recoverer is to a fourth only, instead of a double share; the merit of recovering what has only been withheld not being considered equal to that of making a new acquisition. The property however must have been taken by others or lost, it must have been recovered from

a 1 Strange's Hindu Law, 213, 223.
1 Madras Reports, 309.
1 Strange's Hindu Law, 220.
Strange's Manual, § 276.

b 1 Madras Reports, 309.

c 1 Strange's Hindu Law, 219, 220, 223, 224.
2 Ibid., 373, Colebrooke.
Mitakshara, Chap. I, sect. iv, § 29.
Dayabhaga, Chap. VI, sect. i, § 128.

strangers, and not from members of the family, as in the case of disputed inheritance.[a]

Widow of party suing for division.

486. A party suing for division and dying while the suit is pending is still undivided. His widow is not entitled to demand his share.[b]

487. A decree declaring a party entitled to a share in family property not having been carried into effect before the death of the party, he is considered as dying undivided.[c]

How partition is made when the enjoyment of the common stock has been unequal.

488. Where the enjoyment of what is in common may have been unequal, that of some having been greater than that of others, the shares upon a division are still to be the same, the law taking no account of greater or less expenditure, unless the difference be such as to exclude all idea of proportion, the object entirely selfish, or the circumstances of a kind to impute fraud.[d]

489. If the family of one brother, being more numerous than those of the rest have, in the maintaining of it, incurred a greater expense, so it has been proportionate, and not excessive, the difference is not to be regarded when they come to divide; and the same principle applies as to what may have been laid out on the nuptials of a daughter,

a 1 Strange's Hindu Law, 220.
9 Sutherland's Weekly Reporter, 70.
8 Ibid., 13.

b Strange's Manual, § 289.

c Ibid., 290.

d 1 Strange's Hindu Law, 224.
2 Ibid., 394. Colebrooke.

or the initiation of a son, occurrences, in Hindu families, which constitute a charge on the joint property where they are undivided.[a]

How partition made when a parcener has used common fund for his own purposes.

490. But if one giving a loose to pleasures in which the rest have not participated have thereby broken in upon the common fund to an extent not to be justified, he will, upon partition, receive his portion, diminished by what he has dissipated; though it is said, that if more than the amount of his share have been so expended, the law does not direct that the excess shall be considered as a debt.[b]

491. It is the same of a loan or gift even for a good (as for a religious) purpose, if made by a parcener on his sole account; or of a sale, a purchase, or an hypothecation; the principle being, that the patrimony or family property is not to be arbitrarily aliened; otherwise, where the purpose and end have been the support, the interest, or the spiritual benefit of the whole.[c]

According to Bengal law, an unproductive parcener may be shared out of acquired property.

492. In the Bengal Provinces, but not in Southern India, an unproductive parcener may be shared out of the property acquired; but must receive his portion of the original stock descended.[d]

Deed of partition not indispensable.

493. In whichever way partition is effected, the law prescribes an instrument in writing, called by Vrihaspati

a 1 Strange's Hindu Law, 224.

b Ibid., 167, 224.

c Ibid., 18, 225.
2 Ibid., 338, 339, Colebrooke.

d 1 Ibid., 197, 224, 225.

"the written memorial of distribution," but it has not rendered it indispensable. [a]

Requisites of deed where it exists.

494. Where, however, an instrument exists, it should, generally speaking, be attested by kinsmen; the want of whom, and the consequent substitution of more distant relations, or even of neighbours, is always open to be explained. Such, in fact, is the order in which witnesses for this purpose are classed; *kinsmen* being described as persons allied by community of funeral oblations, or as sprung from the same race; *relations*, as maternal uncles and other collateral and distant relations of the family. [b]

Proof of disputed partition.

495. With respect to the proof of a *disputed partition*, though the law favors separation by which religious ceremonies are multiplied, it presumes joint tenancy as the primary state of every Hindoo family; and this especially among brothers, it being most natural for such to dwell together in unity. [c]

496. Important as the question may be to strangers, appearances as to the fact are not always to be relied upon. The legal idea of *undivided*, regarding,—as it does *property*, a family may be separated as to residence, meals, and ceremonies, so as to seem, even to their neighbours as well as

a 1 Strange's Hindu Law, 222.

b Ibid., 223.

c Ibid., 225.
2 Ibid., 347, Ellis.

to others, to be divided, without being so; remaining, in truth, united in interest. [a]

497. On the other hand, having parted property, they may have become legally divided by a severance in their worldly concerns; and yet, continuing to live and eat together, performing also in common their solemn and accustomed rites, they will appear to be still united, though, in reality, and to legal purposes, they are no longer so. [b]

498. The obscurity in which this matter is sometimes involved, productive as it is not only of eventual litigation, but of occasional fraud and injustice, may be attributed to the law, allowing partition without the presence of witnesses or intervention of any deed; thus leaving a transaction of such important consequence to others as well as to the family to be performed in secret, resting in the breasts and in the consciousness alone of, the parties. [c]

499. This difficulty too, has been enhanced since it has been decided that an actual partition by metes and bounds is not necessary to a division, provided, of course, there has been a partition of title. [d]

a 1 Strange's Hindu Law, 225.
2 Ibid., 347, Ellis.
4 Madras Reports, 5.
11 Moore's Indian Appeals, 488.
b 1 Strange's Hindu Law, 225, 226.
c Ibid., 226.
d 11 Moore's Indian Appeals, 75.
2 Madras Reports, 325.
3 Ibid., 40.

500. The presumption raised by the law from the natural state of families in favor of union may be destroyed by evidence of separate acts inferring a contrary one, and amounting to proof of partition having taken place. [a]

501. Such are for this purpose religious ones, the religious duty of co-parceners being single; dressing food; transactions inconsistent with the idea of their continuing united, as making mutual loans, sales, purchases, and other contracts; separate suits by the partners; separate entries in Revenue Puttahs; or becoming sureties, or witnesses for one another on subjects of property. To which, as indicating the understanding of neighbours, may be added delivering to them, severally, of provisions and other dues by the village peasants. [b]

502. The religious ceremonies above alluded to are the five great sacraments in favor of "the divine sages, the manes, the gods, the spirits and guests" enumerated, described, and enforced by Menu, it being of such of which it is said that of undivided brethren, the religious duty is single, *i.e.*, performed by an act in which all join, severing in them and performing them separately in their respective houses *after* partition. [c]

a 1 Strange's Hindu Law, 226, 227.
2 Ibid., 387, 395.
b 1 Ibid., 277.
2 Ibid., 391, 393, 397, Colebrooke and Ellis.
Mitakshara, Chap. II, sect. 12.
See however, 8 Madras Reports, 25.
c 1 Strange's Hindu Law, 228.

503. Of the instances specified, the one the most to be relied upon is the taking food separately prepared, since, in general, a distinct preparation of food, after an agreement to separate, proves partition, and the previous agreement may in some cases be inferred from that sole evidence; but more satisfactorily in proportion as a greater number of the indicated circumstances concur. [a]

504. The fact that some of the partners separately possess some of the family lands is not *conclusive* proof of partition. [b]

505. With respect to these circumstances, they are but evidence; though concurrence of all to constitute proof is not requisite. The presumption is that a family separate in residence and food is also separate in estate. [c]

When a re-partition may take place.

506. Generally speaking, a partition once made cannot be opened. Yet, if effects that were not forthcoming at the time be afterwards *recovered* in a way to warrant a claim to participation, and much more if *concealment* had taken place, a discovery leads to a second division. [d]

a 1 Strange's Hindu Law, 228, 229.

b 1 Indian Appeals, 21.

c 1 Strange's Hindu Law, 228.
See summary of these circumstances by Jimuta Vahana, cited at 230, Ibid.

d 1 Strange's Hindu Law, 230, 231.

507. When a co-heir fraudulently appropriates any of the joint property on discovery, distribution will take place, and he will be deprived of his share.[a]

508. Wherever, from any cause not understood at the time, the division proves to have been *unequal* or in any respect *defective*, it may be set to rights notwithstanding the maxim that "once is partition of inheritance made;" a position that supposes it to have been fair and made according to law.[b]

When a new partition may take place.

509. Not only may an original partition be re-formed by means of a supplemental one, but there may be an entirely new one upon a *re-union* of any of the separated parceners competent to the purpose; and this as well after partition by a father as among co-heirs. According to the Mitakshara and other authorities the re-union must be between a father, brother or a paternal uncle. It must be between the separated partners only, for re-union between any one would not be a re-union in the sense of the law. And when this re-union is effected, the descendants of those re-united however remote, will again form an undivided family. There cannot be a re-union of the

a 1 Strange's Hindu Law, 231, 232.
Mitakshara, Chap. I, sect. ix, §§ 4, 5, 12.
Menu, IX, 213.

b 1 Strange's Hindu Law, 232.

descendants of those who have separated. Cases of re-union rarely occur. [a]

Claims of re-united parceners when of the whole and half-blood respectively.

510. Other claims being disposed of, if the surviving re-united parceners be partly of the whole and partly of the half-blood, those of the whole take in exclusion of those of the half: while consisting of half-blood only, any *dis*-united co-heirs of the whole divide with them,—union in blood being for this purpose equivalent to re-union in co-parcenery. [b]

Parceners of the half-blood share in the real estate only.

511. The participation of the half-blood at all in this case regards the real estate only; for, as to movable effects they at all events descend exclusively to the whole blood, re-united or not. [c]

Bengal law.

512. In Bengal the whole brothers and whole sisters equally divide their mother's property. [d]

Share of one disqualified on re-partition.

513. The share of one who has entered into the fourth order, or become otherwise disqualified, on re-partition, vests in his representatives; and in general, the rules pre-

a 1 Strange's Hindu Law, 233.
Mitakshara, Chap. II, sect. ix, § 3.
2 Madras Reports, 235.
3 Bombay Reports, A. C., 69.
5 Sutherland's Weekly Reporter, 249.

b 1 Strange's Hindu Law, 234.
Mitakshara, Chap. II, sect. ix, §§ 6, 9.

c 1 Strange's Hindu Law, 234, 235.

d Dayabhaga, Chap. IV, sect. ii, § 1.

scribed for an original partition are applicable to the one in question.[a]

514. Where a division has taken place amongst the members of a Hindoo family, one of whom is a minor, the circumstance that the father and minor continue to live together, and their share become mixed, does not conclusively constitute a state of re-union between the father and the minor, but is evidentiary only to prove the re-union.[b]

The fact of a father and a minor living together is only evidentiary of re-union.

515. Where the widows of a man divide the estate, the title remains joint, and the surviving takes the whole, and neither of the widows has a separate power of alienation. In a case where this was done, the Privy Council said that the partition between the widows did not operate to enlarge either widow's estate, so as to give her a greater power of disposition over it, than she would have otherwise had. The estate of two widows who take their husbands' property by inheritance is one estate. The right of survivorship is so strong that, the survivor takes the whole property even to the exclusion of daughters of the deceased widow. They are therefore in the strictest sense co-parceners, and one widow cannot alienate any portion of the estate without the consent of the other.[c]

Division among widows.

516. *Stridhanum* is divided, after the mother's death, and before the death of the father, among the daughters,

Division of *stridhanum* when.

a 1 Strange's Hindu Law, 235.
Mitakshara, Chap. II, sect. ix, § 13.

b 2 Madras Reports, 285.

c 11 Moore's Indian Appeals, 487.

the unmarried first, then the married, the unendowed first, or their issue. If there be no daughters, their sons succeed.

How sons take. 517. On partition, sons take *per capita:* other than sons take *per stirpes:*

The subjoined are cases of partition:

Examples of partition.

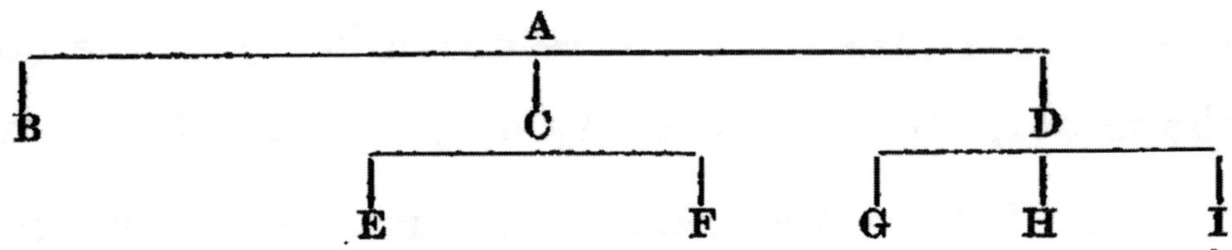

A has three sons B, C and D: C dies leaving two sons E and F; and D dies leaving three sons G, H and I. A division takes place. The property is divided into four shares, of which A and B each receive one; one is received by E and F, that is, each gets one-eighth; and E, H and I receive one, that is, each gets one-twelfth.

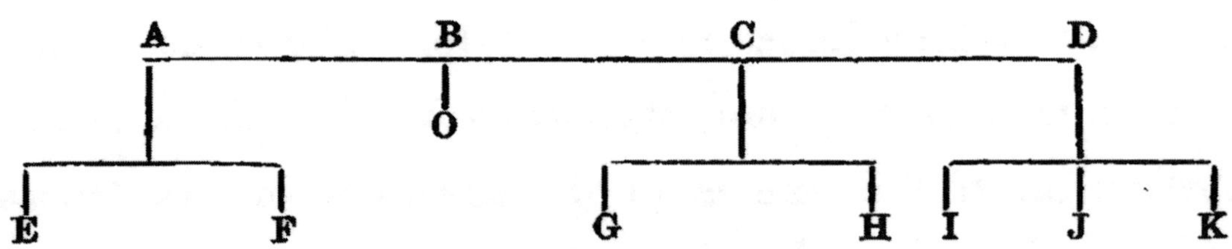

A, B, C and D are four brothers: A has two sons E and F: B has none: and C and D have each two and three sons respectively, G and H, and I, J and K.

A and B seek a division, and C and D remain united. The property is divided thus: C and D keep half between them, and A and B each gets one-fourth. B dies unmarried, and his share is divided equally between A, C and D, that is, A gets one-twelfth, and C and D one-sixth between them. A's property is now one-third of the whole, and the joint property of C and D equals two-thirds of it. A now divides with his sons, and each gets one-ninth of the whole. C and D next divide, each taking one-third. C and D and their respective sons now divide: C and his sons each gets one-ninth, and D and his sons each gets one-twelfth of the whole property originally possessed by the four brothers. On the deaths of A, C and D respectively, the shares of their sons will each be one-sixth of the whole to each of the sons of A and C respectively, and each of the sons of D, one-ninth of the whole respectively.

CHAPTER X.

WILLS.

Sir Thomas Strange's opinion as to Hindu wills.

518. ACCORDING to Sir Thomas Strange, a will is an instrument unknown to Hindu law; and citing Ellis, he maintains that if a Hindoo will is contrary to the *Dharma Sastra*, it is invalid; and if in conformity with it, it is unnecessary. [a]

Doubtful whether Hindu will of foreign origin.

519. There is some doubt as to the Hindoo will being of foreign origin, as pointed out by a writer on the subject. They appear to have been in use before the arrival of the

a 1 Strange's Hindu Law, Chap. XI. This chapter contains Sir Thomas Strange's views generally on the subject of Hindu wills.

English. Wills at any rate seem to have been adjudicated upon at the very outset of English administration in India, and there seems nothing really antagonistic to them in the Shasters. They relate merely to the posthumous devolution of a man's property, and such devolution is treated of in the Hindoo system throughout India, before the establishment of English Courts. [a]

√520. The power of a Hindoo to make a will is not of modern introduction, nor is it of local origin. Wills seem to be known to and in use amongst Hindoos, not in the Presidency towns only, but from one end of the peninsula to the other. The right to make a will is part of the Hindu law itself. The extent and nature of the disposition which a Hindoo testator is capable of making, is not a question of public expediency, or of custom, or usage, but must be regulated by rules to be found in or directly deduced from Hindu law. [b]

Advantage arising from the introduction of wills.

521. Whatever may have been the origin of wills amongst Hindoos, either in this Presidency, or elsewhere, they are now recognized by the Courts of Justice, and not without advantage, inasmuch as they stimulate the circu-

a Montriou's Hindu Will.
2 Strange's Hindu Law, 417, *et seq.*
4 Bengal Reports, O. C., 217, 289.
6 Moore's Indian Appeals, 344, (Madras Case).
12 Ibid., 1.

b 4 Bengal Reports, O. C., 103, Per Norman, J.

lation of property, and quicken the stagnation of Hindu society.[a]

The whole of the English law of wills does not apply to Hindu wills.

522. It does not follow (assuming that wills have been introduced into Hindu law from the law of a foreign country,) that as a necessary consequence, the whole of the foreign law relating to the subject-matter must be imported with it. Where such introductions take place, so far as it can be done, the foreign matter must be moulded according to analogies derivable from the indigenous law. The rules of Hindu law must be applied to the construction.[b]

523. It was accordingly held that as there is no transaction of Hindu law which absolutely requires a writing, a Hindoo might make a nuncupative will of property, whether immovable or movable. The Court saying that contracts of every description involving both temporal and spiritual consequences may be made orally; and it would be singular if it were to attempt to rule that, all other expressions of a will are valid when delivered by word of mouth, but that

a 1 Madras Reports, 326, the Leading Case.
Regulation 5 of 1829 shows their statutory effect. So far back as 1823 the Madras Sudder Reports, established the validity of wills, and in 1838 the Privy Council confirmed a decision of the Madras Sudder establishing the will of a Hindoo.
A *donatis mortis causa* however has not the same signification here as it has in England. Per *Phear*, J., in 3 Bengal Reports, O. C., 113.

b 2 Madras Reports, 37.
3 Ibid., 50.
4 Bengal Reports, O. C., 169.
7 Knapp, 247.

the expression by a man of his will, as to the disposition of his property after his decease, shall be wholly invalid, unless reduced to writing. [a]

A Hindu will need not be attested nor signed.

524. So also a Hindoo's will need not be attested: it need not even be signed. [b]

Construction of Hindoo wills.

525. The rule as to construction, too, of Hindoo wills, is not the same as that of English wills. The construction of an English will depends upon the peculiarities of the English law of property, and upon distinctions between real and personal property, which are altogether unknown to Hindu law. [c]

526. Accordingly, under a bequest by a Hindoo of ten Rupees per month followed by a direction to the following effect—"In this manner continue to pay in the legatee's name, so long as he shall be alive: after his death, continue to pay the same to his descendants from generation to generation," it was held, *first*, that the legatee took only a life-interest, and not absolutely under the bequest: *Secondly*, that the words "from generation to generation" were not technical words, and did not impart more than the words "absolutely" and "for ever:" *thirdly*, that the testator's intention was that the "descendants" at the

a 2 Madras Reports, 37.
Under English law, soldiers and sailors may make nuncupative wills. 1 Vic. c., 26, sect. xi.

b 1 Madras Reports, 328, Reporter's Note and Addenda, xi.
1 Bombay Reports, 77.

c 1 Madras Reports, 400.
2 Ibid., 37.

time of the death of the tenant-for-life should take absolutely as a class: *fourthly,* that such descendants were entitled in equal shares to an amount sufficient to produce the monthly sum of ten Rupees. [a]

527. Again, the "descendants" of A in a Hindoo will would include children and grandchildren living at his decease, but does not include A's brother or widow. The term "male issue" also is not confined to sons alone. [b]

528. The principal rule of construction is that the Court ought to gather the intention of the testator from that which the will expressly, or by implication declares. This rule is just as applicable to the wills of Hindoos as to those of persons of other religions. [c]

a 1 Madras Reports, 400 ; 8 Moore's Indian Appeals, 66.

b 1 Madras Reports, 400 ; 8 Bengal Reports, 400.

c 4 Ibid., O. C., 176.

The Privy Council say :—"The Hindu law, no less than the English law, points to the intention, as the element by which we are to be guided in determining the effect of a testamentary disposition ; nor is there any difference between the one law and the other as to the materials from which the intention is to be collected. Primarily the words of the will are to be considered. They convey the expression of the testator's wishes, but the meaning to be attached to them may be affected by surrounding circumstances, and when this is the case, these circumstances must no doubt be regarded. Amongst the circumstances thus to be regarded is, the law of the country under which the will is made, and its dispositions are to be carried out. If that law has attached to particular words a particular meaning, or to a particular disposition a particular effect, it must be assumed that the testator in the dispositions which he has made, had regard to that meaning, or that effect, unless the language of the will, or surrounding circumstances displaces that assumption. 9 Moore's Indian Appeals, 123.

Power of bequest by will.

529. A Hindoo may by will create particular estates to enure to the benefit of particular individuals. He is not bound to dispose of the *whole* of his estate. [a]

Perpetuities.

530. There is no rule of Hindu law, however, imposing any restriction in point of time on the operation of a bequest, creating a series of successive life-interests in each generation of a legatee's descendants. But the grounds of the rule against perpetuities are applicable to the property of Hindoos, and the Court will be very reluctant to construe a Hindoo will, so as to tie up property for an indefinite period. [b]

531. Trusts created under a will may and have been frequently enforced against Hindoos, and will always be enforced when they are valid. [c]

532. With reference however to the rule against perpetuities, it has been held by the Privy Council that, it would be to apply a very false and mischievous principle if it were held that the nature and extent of testamentary disposition by Hindoos could be governed by any analogy to

a 4 Moore's Indian Appeals, 137.

b 1 Madras Reports, 400. The English rule against perpetuities, as applicable to Hindoos, has been controverted and commented on in 4 Bengal Reports, O. C., 107, the great Tagore Will Case.
2 Bengal Reports, O. C., 11.

c 4 Moore's Indian Appeals, 452.
6 Ibid., 53, 531.
8 Ibid., 66.
9 Ibid., 55.
2 Bengal Reports, O. C., 103.
4 Ibid., 107.

the law of England. The law of England is concerned with a system of the most artificial character, founded in a great degree on feudal rules, regulated by Acts of Parliament and adjusted by a early course of judicial determination to the wants of a state of society, differing as far as possible from that which prevails among Hindoos. Perpetuities however, are not permitted under Hindu law. [a]

533. The English doctrine of *cypres* is not applicable to Hindoo wills. [b] *Cypres.*

534. Where plaintiff sued as the widow of an adopted son (a daughter's son, and, therefore, ineligible for adoption) for the property of the adoptive father, and also on the ground that the adopted son was the devisee of the adoptive father, it was held that as the language of the testator sufficiently indicated the person who was to be the object of his bounty, the person so indicated was entitled to take, although the testator conceived him to possess a character which, in point of law, cannot be sustained. The Court remarking that the authorities for persons taking as "*personœ designatœ,*" even in opposition to an established rule of construction of the words used are very numerous. It is unnecessary, it said, to enlarge upon this subordinate rule, which is only a particular example of the more general rule that the construction of all written instruments is to be such, as will effectuate the expressed intent of the author of the instrument. [c]

Where a will indicated the person who is to be the object of the testator's bounty, he is entitled to take although testator conceived him to possess a character which in point of law cannot be sustained.

a 10 Moore's Indian Appeals, 308.
8 Ibid., 66.
b 4 Bengal Reports, O. C., 169.
c 2 Madras Reports, 462.

Law of wills in Madras.

535. The Hindu law in Madras admits of the testamentary disposition of property, both ancestral and self-acquired. [a]

Bengal law.

536. In Bengal, the power to devise property is under fewer restrictions than in Madras. There, too, the principle prevails that how objectionable soever an act may be in a moral point of view, in point of law it will be valid and irreversible. [b]

Extent of the power of devise generally among Hindoos.

537. The legal right to make a will being settled, there seems nothing in principle or reason opposed *to the exercise of this power being allowed co-extensively with the independent right of gift, or other disposal by act inter vivos*, which by law, or established usage, or custom having the force of law, a Hindoo now possesses in Madras. To this extent, the power of disposition can reasonably be considered to be in conformity with the respective proprietary rights of the possessor of property, and of heirs and co-parceners as provided and secured by the provisions of the Hindu law. [c]

a 1 Madras Reports, 326.

b 1 Strange's Hindu Law, 260.
1 Madras Reports, 326.

c 1 Strange's Hindu Law, 258, 259.
1 Madras Reports, 326, citing *Mubana Luchmia* v. *C. Venkata Rama Jagganadha Row*, 2 Moore's Indian Appeal Cases, 54; *Nagalutchmee Ummal* v. *Goopoo Nadaraja Chetty* and others, 6 Moore's Indian Appeal Cases, 309 and *Sonatum Bysack* v. *Sreemutty Juggutsoondree Dossee*, 8 Moore's Indian Appeal Cases, 66.
2 Madras Reports, 37, following above decision.
Ibid., 369.
See, however, 3 Madras Reports 50, questioning the power of a Hindoo to devise whatever he may give.

538. Though large innovations have been made upon Hindu law in the matter of wills, yet it has never been contended that a man having male issue can by will disinherit.[a] Nor can he deprive the rest of a sufficiency for their maintenance. And where there is no land, they must all be provided for to that extent out of his personalty.[b]

A man having male issue cannot disinherit them.

539. It is by no means clear upon the authorities that he can even by gift *inter vivos* deprive them of their right to share even in his *self-acquired real* property, and it is perfectly clear that such male issue would be absolutely entitled to it at his death.[c]

540. A Hindoo's will, however, would not be invalidated merely by its omitting to provide for his widow.[d]

A will not invalid though omitting to provide for widow.

541. The Privy Council in the case above cited lay down that ancestral property may be disposed of by will, unless by reason of some inherent peculiarity, it be withdrawn from the testamentary power: that he cannot do so when he has a son, because the son immediately on his birth becomes co-parcener with his father: that the objection to bequeathing ancestral property is founded on the Hindu

Extent of power of bequest over ancestral and self-acquired property.

a 1 Strange's Hindu Law, 261.
3 Madras Reports, 50.

b 1 Strange's Hindu Law, 18—21, 261.

c 3 Madras Reports, 50. See also 2 Strange's Hindu Law, 2 Sutherland; and W. H. Macnaghten's Hindu Law, 44, Note, 2nd ed.

d 1 Madras Reports, 326.
2 Ibid., 462, citing *Nagalutchmee Ummal* v. *Goopoo Nadaraja Chetty*, 6 Moore's Indian Appeal Cases, 109.

notion of an undivided family, and that when there are no males in the family, the liberty of bequeathing is unlimited. And with regard to self-acquired property, they said that, though the law of Madras differed from that of Bengal with regard to wills, yet even in Madras it is settled that a will of property, *not ancestral*, may be good: a decision to this effect has been recognised and acted upon by the Council, and indeed the rule of law as to that is not disputed.

542. A co-parcener cannot alienate by will his undivided interest in joint property; [a] and, generally, a will opposed to the principles of Hindu law is invalid. [b]

Effect of certain words of limitation in will.

543. A gift to a man and his sons and grandsons, or to a man and his sons and son's sons, would, in the absence of anything showing a contrary intention, pass a general estate of inheritance according to Hindu law. [c]

544. A gift by will of an estate to a man under the Hindu law, even without any words of limitation, would convey a general estate of inheritance in the absence of words showing a contrary intention. But if a will should be made by gift, or conveyance to a man, or to a man and his sons and son's sons, and words should be added that the

a 8 Madras Reports, 6.
b 9 Bengal Reports, 402.
8 Moore's Indian Appeals, 18.
c 4 Bengal Reports, O. C., 182.

elder heir should always be preferred to the younger, and that every elder son of each heir in succession by descent, and his issue, as heirs male by descent, should be preferred to every younger son, or his issue, as heirs male by descent, to the exclusion of females and their descendants, and that in default of sons or son's sons the estate should go over to a third person and his heirs, such a gift could not, without doing violence to language, be construed as expressing an intention to vest in the donee a general and absolute estate of inheritance, alienable at pleasure and descendible to all heirs according to Hindu law, lineal or collateral. male or female, as the case might be.[a]

545. A gift over, upon an event which might be indefinitely postponed, is void. Or, as was ruled in the Tagore Will case, a gift by a Hindoo to a person not ascertained, or capable of being ascertained at the time of the death of the testator, cannot take effect: therefore a gift to the unborn male issue of the sons and grandsons of the testator must fail. Where there is a gift to a class, and some persons constituting such class cannot take in consequence of the remoteness of the gift, or otherwise, the whole bequest must fail.[b]

546. A Hindoo cannot make a gift by will, under any circumstances to an unborn person or persons.[c]

a 4 Bengal Reports, O. C., 183.
b Ibid., 103.
8 Ibid., 400.
c Ibid.

Entails not recognised in Hindu law.

547. Entails cannot be created under a Hindoo will, as estates tail are wholly opposed to the general principles of Hindu law. In the Tagore Will case, devises of estates tail were rejected as void, and the Court refused to convert them into larger estates than the testator intended. The words of the devise, the Court said, cannot be construed to pass a general and absolute estate. As the devisee had no sons born in the life time of the testator, the devise to the use of the first and other sons successively of the eldest son of the devisee lapsed. By Hindu law, a gift cannot operate upon property, unless the donee is in existence, so that as soon as the property is relinquished and passes out of the donor, it vests in the donee. That, in the case of a will, would be at the time of the death of the testator, from which moment the will operates as a relinquishment, except in the case of a posthumous child of the testator, or a son adopted by the widow of a testator. Therefore the devises to the sons of the devisee, to be born, or adopted after the death of the testator, are not valid, according to Hindu law. The gift to trustees does not cause the invalidity, for the law will not permit that to the donee indirectly, which cannot lawfully be done directly. [a]

When remote kinsman postponed to devisee.

548. The title of a remote kinsman, though heir of a Hindoo testator, who died without leaving issue, or any near relative surviving him, and with whom that remote kinsman had not been united in food, worship, or estate, cannot

[a] 4 Bengal Reports, O. C., 103.

prevail against the title of a devisee of that testator, whether such property was by the testator self-acquired, or held in severalty, either by virtue of a partition, or of the non-existence, or if any did ever exist, the extinction of co-parceners. [a]

549. A woman may make a will alienating her *stridhanum*, unless it is immovable property given her by her husband. [b] Woman may make will.

550. The will of a Hindoo (not executed under the Wills Act) need not be signed. No formalities are necessary. The will, however, must be complete, and express the unbiassed intentions of the testator. [c]

551. Wills made on or after the first day of September 1870, within the local limits of the ordinary Original Civil Jurisdiction of the High Court, or which relate to immovable property, situate within the said limits, so far as relates to such property, are subject to the provisions of the Hindu Wills Act of 1870. Under this Act wills must be *in writing*. Wills under Presidency Towns' Wills Act.

552. The Hindu Wills Act (1870) lays down rules for the construction of Hindoo wills. It makes a considerable part of the Indian Succession Act relating to wills and codicils, their proper execution and construction, their probate, &c., applicable to the wills of Hindoos under the Act. Rules under above Act.

a 3 Bombay Reports, A. C., 6.

b 3 Sutherland's Weekly Reporter, 49.

c 1 Bombay Reports, O. C., 77.
6 Ibid., A. C., 224.

Of course this enactment refers only to wills made within the Presidency towns, or relating to property situate therein, but the rules of construction are such as will be of use for all wills of Hindoos. See Act appended to this Chapter.

553. The following provisos, too, are embodied in it:

i. Marriage shall not revoke any will or codicil.

ii. A testator shall not acquire authority by the Act to bequeath property which he could not have alienated *inter vivos,* nor deprive any persons of any right to maintenance which he could not but for the Act have deprived them of.

iii. No property shall vest in an executor or administrator with will annexed, which the testator could not have alienated *inter vivos.*

iv. The law of adoption and of intestate succession shall remain unaffected by the Act.

v. No Hindoo shall acquire authority to create in property any interest which he could not have created before 1st September 1870.

Changes effected by the Act.

554. Great changes have been effected by the Hindu Wills Act in the matter of Hindoo wills executed in the Presidency Towns: nuncupative wills are abolished: and particulars are given as to the due *execution,* attestation, so that the law on these matters is, to some extent, assimilated to that of the English Wills Act (1 Vic. c. 26).

555. With regard to probate and administration, before the Hindu Wills Act, it had been decided that, though the Court had power to grant probate of a Hindu will if applied for, it had always been held that, a Hindu executor could not be compelled to bring in a will, and prove it in solemn form. It was not incumbent upon the representative of a Hindoo to take out administration, or probate, except in the case provided for in Act 27 of 1860, Section 2; and even then, he need not procure the certificate, probate, or letters of administration, when the Court was of opinion that, payment of a debt due to the estate was withheld from fraudulent or vexatious motives, and not from a reasonable doubt, as to the party entitled. It was optional with the Hindu executor, whether he would prove the will or not. The Court had no jurisdiction to compel him to do so. If he set up the will in a suit, its validity would be tried, just as is the case in England, when a will relating only to realty, and therefore not requiring probate, is set up, by some one claiming under it. It is a totally different matter, when the executor had actually applied for probate, and thus submitted himself to the ecclesiastical jurisdiction. The next of kin had a right then to compel him to proceed and prove the will. [a]

Position of Hindu executors and administrators.

556. A Hindu executor, not under the Wills Act, derives his title entirely from the will of the deceased, and not, as an executor under an English will, from the grant of probate by the Court. [b]

a 1 Madras Reports, 59. These observations will still apply in the Mofussil.

b 1 Bengal Reports, O. C., 24.

557. An executor to a Hindu will, not under the Wills Act, simply occupies the place of a manager of property. He takes no estate as executor. He is only a trustee for those who take under the will. He has not the same power over the movable and immovable property of the testator, as an executor under an English will would have over personalty. A Hindu executor must only exercise his powers for the benefit of the estate. A Hindu administrator stands in the same position.[a]

Duty of alienee of executor.

558. An alienee of an executor must, like a purchaser of ancestral property, satisfy himself that the executor is acting within his powers, otherwise he will be liable to refund what he may have obtained.[b]

559. The position of an executor, or administrator, is considerably altered by the Wills Act. His rights, duties and powers are specifically defined therein; but it is conceived that the general principles of Hindu law will still apply to him, as also to the testator, with regard to dealings with property under the Act.[c]

560. Under the Hindu Wills Act, though probate is, letters of administration to the property of an intestate are not compulsory. An executor or administrator under the Act is the representative of the testator: all his property vests in him under the Act, and not under the will.

a Bourke's Reports, O. C., 48; 2 Bengal Reports, O. C., 1; 6 Moore's Indian Appeals, 393.

b Ibid.

c See Section 3, Hindu Wills Act.

561. Certificates of succession under Act XXVII of 1860 can only be granted to persons claiming to be representatives of deceased persons to enable them to recover debts and receive interest or dividends; but such certificate concludes only the debtors of the estate, and the procedure given by the Act was not intended to apply to the decision of any right to succeed to the estate of a deceased person. [a]

Certificates of succession.

562. There may be a parol revocation of a will by a Hindoo, but not under the Hindu Wills Act. [b]

Parol revocation of a will valid.

563. Wills may be registered under the Indian Registration Act (Act III of 1877.)

Registration of Will.

CHAPTER XI.

TRUSTS.—PRIVATE, PUBLIC AND RELIGIOUS.

564. As to Private Trusts, see Chapter on Wills.

Private Trusts.

565. As to Public Trusts, see Regulation VII of 1817. This Regulation relates to the due appropriation of the rents and produce of lands granted for the support of Hindu Temples and Colleges, or other public purposes: for the maintenance of Chuttrums, &c., and for the custody and disposal of Escheats.

Public Trusts.

a 2 Madras Reports, 164.

b 4 Indian Appeals, 228.

As to rules for the execution, construction, &c., of Wills, see Appendix B.

566. The Regulation is intended to be supplementary of existing remedies, and the Court had unquestionable jurisdiction in such cases prior to its enactment. The expression in Section 14 is not intended to limit the jurisdiction of the Courts to the cases contemplated in it, but rather to provide against the finality of erroneous orders that may be passed by the Board of Revenue under the Regulation.

567. The Revenue Board has the superintendence of all escheats under Regulation VII of 1817. Where an endowment has been abandoned it becomes an escheat.

Religious Trusts and the provisions of the *Devastanum* Act.

568. As to Religious Trusts—Act XX of 1863, commonly called the *Devastanum* Act, regulates the administration of trusts in connection with Temples, repealing that portion of Regulation VII of 1817, on that subject. The remainder of the Regulation refers to Public Trusts.

569. With regard to the maintenance of national idol-worship, endowments have been made at different times to the various Temples in the country by the Princes of India, and by the wealthy members of communities. The management of the funds belonging to these Temples was at one time vested by Regulation VII of 1817, in the Revenue Board, but under Act XX of 1863, this has been removed, and the management is now vested in Committees appointed under the Act, who are under the supervision of the District Courts of the several Districts in which the Temples

are situated, and who are liable, civilly and criminally, for mismanagement of Temple funds and property.[a]

570. The management of a Temple may be hereditary and at the time of its endowment this stipulation may be made by the grantor. The management may vest in the family of the grantor, as it most frequently does, or it may be vested in the line of some other person and it may vest in a whole family jointly, or in a single individual.[b]

571. Under sections *three* and *four* of the Devastanum Act, two kinds of Managers of Temples are referred to. The former refers to the Manager, who under Regulation VII of 1817, was appointed by Government, or whose appointment was sanctioned or confirmed by Government, or their agent, acting on their behalf. The latter refers to the Manager who was never so appointed, but whose succession was probably hereditary. Over the former only, the Committee under the Act have control, but not over the latter; but of course both kinds are amenable to the jurisdiction of the District Court.[c]

a Under the Act no Member of a Committee can act as Trustee, Manager or Superintendent of a Temple, &c.

b 4 Sutherland's Weekly Reporter, 79.

c 7 Madras Reports, 77.

5 Ibid., 4, 8, 53.

Section 3 says:—In the case of every Mosque, Temple or other religious establishment to which the provisions of either of the Regulations specified in Section 1 are applicable and the nomination of the Trustee, Manager, or Superintendent thereof at the time of the passing of this Act is vested in, or may be exercised by, the Government, or any public officer; or in which the nomination of such Trustee, Manager, or Superintendent shall be sub-

572. Under the Devastanum Act, the Committee have power to dismiss the Trustees or Superintendents of Temples described in section *three* of the Act, without recourse to a civil suit, but such power can only be exercised on good and sufficient grounds.[a]

573. Nor do they require the sanction of the Court to institute a suit, in order to establish their authority under section *three* of the Act, or to establish it as against the Temple officials. The suits which require the sanction of the Court are only suits which refer to the malversation of Temple property by the Temple officials, and not suits with reference to other matters in connection with these Institutions, as for instance, a suit to establish a right to share in the manage-

ject to the confirmation of the Government, or any public officer, the Local Government shall, as soon as possible after the passing of this Act, make special provision as hereinafter provided.

Section 4, in the case of every such Mosque, Temple or other religious establishment which at the time of the passing of this Act shall be under the management of any Trustee, Manager, or Superintendent, whose nomination shall not vest in, nor be exercised by, nor be subject to the confirmation of the Government or any public officer, the Local Government shall, as soon as possible after the passing of this Act, transfer to such Trustee, Manager or Superintendent all the landed or other property which at the time of the passing of this Act shall be under the superintendence or in the possession of the Board of Revenue, or any local agent, and belonging to such Mosque, Temple or other religious establishment, except such property as is hereinafter provided, and the powers and responsibilities of the Board of Revenue and the local agents in respect to such Mosque, Temple, or other religious establishment, and to all land, and other property so transferred, except as regards acts done and liabilities incurred by the said Board of Revenue or any local agent previous to such transfer shall cease and determine.

a 3 Madras Reports, 334.

ment. Nor is leave required to file a suit against the heir of a deceased Manager for recovering the property misappropriated by the deceased. The right to bring such suits is a pre-existing right, and is not accorded by the Act. [a]

574. The duty of individuals to submit to, and perform certain religious observances in accordance with the ritual, or conventional practice of their race, or sect is, in the absence of express legal recognition and provision, of imperfect obligation, and of a moral, not a civil, nature. Of such obligations, the present Civil Courts cannot take cognisance. And it is of great importance in this country that the Courts exercising their civil jurisdiction, as now provided, should carefully guard against entertaining suits, in respect of mere

Jurisdiction of the Courts in religious matters.

a 3 Madras Reports, 198.
4 Ibid., 404.
Ibid., 2.
Section 14 says :—Any person or persons interested in any Mosque, Temple or religious establishment or in the performance of the worship or of the service thereof or of the trusts relating thereto may, without joining as plaintiff, any of the other persons interested therein, sue before the Civil Court, the Trustee, Manager or Superintendent of such Mosque, Temple or religious establishment, or the member of any Committee appointed under this Act, for any misfeasance, breach of trust, or neglect of duty committed by such Trustee, Manager, Superintendent or member of such Committee in respect of the trusts vested in or confided to them respectively, and the Civil Court may direct the specific performance of any act by such Trustee, Manager, Superintendent or member of a Committee and may decree damages and costs against such Trustee, Manager, Superintendent, or member of a Committee and may also direct their removal of such Trustee, Manager, Superintendent or member of a Committee.
Section 15 says :—The interest required in order to entitle a person to sue under the last preceding section need not be a pecuniary, or a direct or immediate interest in such an interest

ritual observances, and the conduct of the various kinds of native religious worship and ceremonies, and of what, as incident thereto, may be due to the sacred character, or the religious rank and position of individuals. With such matters the Courts cannot properly deal, and if their jurisdiction extended to interference in them, the law would be made instrumental in upholding and continuing the ceremonials and superstitious observances of idol-worship for the benefit merely of the few who profit by them. [a]

575. So, also in another case which arose in connection with the famous Pagoda of *Srirungam* in the Trichinopoly

as would entitle the person suing to take any part in the management or superintendence of the trusts. Any person having a right of attendance, or having been in the habit of attending at the performance of the worship or service of any Mosque, Temple, or religious establishment, or of partaking in the benefit of any distribution of alms, shall be deemed to be a person interested within the meaning of the last preceding section.

Section 18 provides that no suit shall be entertained under this Act without a preliminary application being first made to the Court for leave to institute such suit. The application may be made upon unstamped paper. The Court, on the perusal of the application, shall determine whether there are sufficient *primâ facie* grounds for the institution of a suit, and, if in the judgment of the Court there are such grounds, leave shall be given for its institution. In calculating the costs at the termination of the suit, the Stamp duty, on the preliminary application, shall be estimated, and shall be added to the costs of the suit. If the Court shall be of opinion that the suit has been for the benefit of the trust, and that no party to the suit is in fault, the Court may order the costs or such portion as it may consider just to be paid out of the estate.

a 1 Madras Reports, 301. This suit was brought by a guroo in the great Temple of Conjeveram to establish his right to certain honors and emoluments which were refused to him from factious feeling.

District, where a suit for enforcing the celebration of certain honors to be paid to the idol was brought by one of the two great Brahman sects (*Thenkalays* and *Vadakalays*) against the other, the Court refused the relief prayed for on similar grounds. And in all cases where the object of the suit is merely to establish ceremonial procedure, the Court will refuse to interfere.

576. Nor will the Courts enforce claims brought by one member of a family against another to compel him to pay his share of expenses, for the maintenance of the worship of the family idols. [a]

577. It must, however, be borne in mind that, though the Courts will not interfere for the purpose of regulating religious ritual, yet cases may arise, and have arisen, in which rights in connection with religious offices have been established by judicial decision. Hence in a suit, which was brought to establish a right to receive certain honors in a temple, as appertaining to the office of priest, and to recover damages for the invasion of this right, the Court held the suit maintainable, saying that there was here no question of the regulation of religious ritual, or of a right to votive offerings, or payment of respect by the wardens and the worshippers of the temple. "The question here relates to a right appertaining to an office in the temple. It is a right claimed in connection with religious worship, which is not a mere matter of religious ceremonial, and which does not

a 5 Sutherland's Weekly Reporter, 29.

trench on the rights of the worshippers at a temple to show to the claimant, or to withhold from him reverence or respect. And in another case the Court said, the claim is for a specific pecuniary benefit, to which plaintiffs declare themselves entitled, on condition of reciting certain hymns. There can exist no doubt that the right to such benefits is a question which the Courts are bound to entertain, and cannot cease to be such a question, because claimed on account of some service connected with religion. If to determine the right to such pecuniary benefit, it becomes necessary to determine incidentally the right to perform certain religious services, we know of no principle which would exonerate the Court from considering and deciding the point.[a]

Religious endowment, cannot be alienated.

578. Property once granted for religious purposes can never, of course, become the subject of partition, or alienation, nor can a religious office be sold.[b]

Powers of Manager of religious endowments.

579. A *shebait*, or manager, is in the position of trustee for the founder, and cannot create permanent encumbrances to the injury of the endowed property. No prescription derived from the trustee can, in such cases, run against the heirs and representatives of the founder.[c]

580. Nor can a manager alienate the whole of the family property, nor even a considerable portion thereof, as a gift

a 4 Madras Reports, 349.

b 7 Ibid., 217.

c Sutherland's Weekly Reporter, 1864, 157.

to an idol; nor can a widow grant property to an idol without the consent of the reversioners. [a]

581. The paid Manager of the affairs of a Pagoda has no power, as such, to encumber the Pagoda property, or to settle large outstanding demands against it. Persons dealing with such Managers are bound to inquire into the extent of their authority. [b]

582. A Manager of property dedicated to religious purposes may borrow money for the worship of the idol, if there is necessity for it, his powers in that respect being similar to those of a manager of an infant heir. [c]

583. Under Hindu law, a permanent alienation by a *shebait* of endowed property is not absolutely null and void. If made under circumstances of necessity, it is valid, such as for the repairs of the temple, idol &c., [d]

584. Ordinarily, a mortgage of *dewattum* property by a *shebait* is *ultra vires.* [e]

Manager of religious endowment in some position as Hindu widows.

585. The case of a person alienating property, which he holds as *shebait* of an idol, is analogous to that of a Hindu widow alienating ancestral property, and the question, as regards the power of a *shebait* to grant a patnee of *dewattur* land is, whether, looking to all the circumstances of the

a 1 Sutherland's Weekly Reporter, 48.

b 1 Madras Reports, 298.

c 2 Indian Appeals, 145.

d 7 Bengal Reports, 621.

e 14 Sutherland's Weekly Reporter, Civil Rulings, 101.

case, the alienation was a prudent and wise act, in respect of the purposes for which he was *shebait*: and in estimating the validity of a purchase of the *patnee* rights, it ought to be considered, whether the purchasers satisfied themselves, as far as they could, that there was a fair and sufficient ground of necessity for the alienation.[a]

Shebait's right cannot be sold in execution of decree.

586. A judgment debtor's right, as *shebait*, to perform the service of an idol cannot be sold in execution of a decree; nor can his right to the surplus profits of the *sheba* be sold, so long as that right is unascertained and uncertain.[b]

CHAPTER XII.

CONTRACTS AND MORTGAGES.

Hindu law of contracts supplanted.

587. The Hindu law of contracts is, to a great extent, supplanted by the Indian Contract Act (Act IX of 1872), and by the Specific Relief Act (Act I of 1877).

Similarity of Hindu law to English.

588. The Hindu law of contracts is somewhat similar in its general principles to that of the English law. Note for instance, the following *dicta* of Hindoo lawyers.

Purchases.

589. As to *purchases*, Nareda thus ordains: "A buyer ought at first to inspect the commodity and ascertain what is good and bad in it; and what after such inspection he

a 12 Sutherland's Weekly Reporter, 299.

b 7 Ibid., Civil Rulings, 266.

has agreed to buy, he shall not return to the seller, *unless it had a concealed blemish.*" [a]

590. As to *duress:* This will include cases of fear and compulsion in which, according to Jagganatha, "the man is not guided by his own will, but solely by the will of another. If terrified by another, he gives his whole estate to any person for relieving him from apprehension, his mind is not in its natural state; but after recovering tranquillity, if he give anything in the form of a recompense, the donation is valid." [b] **Duress.**

591. So also as to *fraud:* Advantage is not to be taken of what was not seriously meant. A true assent, according to Colebrooke, implies "a serious and perfectly free use of power both physical and moral. This essential is wanting to promises made in jest or compliment." [c] **Fraud.**

592. And not only must the parties be in a legal state to contract, but the subject, or cause of their contracting, must be a competent one, according to the apprehension of the law. And wherever money has been paid on an illegal **The consideration of the contract must be legal.**

a 1 Strange's Hindu Law, 306, 307.
W. H. Macnaghten's Hindu Law, 123, 2nd ed.
1 Madras Reports, 390; citing *Johnson* v. *Johnson*, 3 Bos. and Pul., 170.

b 1 Strange's Hindu Law, 273, 274.
W. H. Macnaghten's Hindu Law, 123, 124, 2nd ed., citing Colebrooke on Obligations and Contracts.

c 1 Strange's Hindu Law, 273.
W. H. Macnaghten's Hindu Law, 124, 2nd ed.

consideration, it shall be recovered back again by the party who improperly paid it. [a]

Revocation. 593. Again, as an excessive or illegal gift may be resumed, so may contracts be rescinded, the law in the one case and in the other nearly identifying. [b]

594. He who would disaffirm a contract entered into by mistake must do so within a reasonable time, and will not be allowed to do so, unless both parties can be re-placed in their original position. [c]

The contract need not be in writing. 595. The Hindu law in no instance requires that a contract should be in writing, though it sets upon all occasions a due value upon written evidence. Oral evidence, however, of the discharge of an obligation by writing, is admissible. This is a well known principle of the English law of evidence. [d]

Act XIV of 1840. 596. The Indian Act XIV of 1840 does not apply to contracts between Hindoos. The Act is not part of the

a 1 Strange's Hindu Law, 274, 275.
W. H. Macnaghten's Hindu Law, 128, 2nd ed.
2 Madras Reports, 187, citing *Ward* v. *Lloyd*, 6 Man. and Grang., 785, 189.
Ibid., 243.
Ibid., 128.

b 1 Strange's Hindu Law, 278.
W. H. Macnaghten's Hindu Law, 126, 127, 2nd ed.

c 1 Madras Reports, 390.

d 1 Strange's Hindu Law, 277.
1 Ibid., 101, and Reporter's Note.
2 Madras Reports, 37.
Ibid., 412.

lex fori. It affects the contract itself, and not merely the remedy. It enacts that "no contract shall" be allowed to be good. The contract itself is made void.[a]

597. The law and usages of Hindoos must regulate all matters of contract between Hindoos, subject of course to the provisions of the Contract Acts.[b] Law and usages of Hindoos to regulate contracts between Hindoos.

598. Matters relating to contracts may be considered with reference to bailment, pledge, sale, debt.[c] Heads of contract.

599. According to Hindu law, bailments may be regarded under a triple point of view, *first,* where the object and benefit involved are entirely on the side of the bailor, such as the simple deposit and the commission without reward: *secondly,* loans for use where the bailee or borrower alone is benefited: *thirdly,* mutual trusts, pledges, and the various kinds of hiring in which both parties have an interest.[d] These three divisions include the six sorts of bailments laid down by Lord Holt in *Coggs* v. *Bernard.*[e] Bailments.

600. With regard to the first class of bailments, it may be observed generally that reasonable care as well as perfect fidelity are expected from a gratuitous bailee. Or, as stated by Vrihaspati, "the very thing bailed must be restored to the very man who bailed it, in the very manner in which it

a. 1 Madras Reports, 9.

b Ibid.

c 1 Strange's Hindu Law, 278. On these heads, see further Contract Act.

d Ibid., 280.

e 1 Smith's Leading Cases.

Liability of gratuitous bailee.

was bailed." The bailee will only be liable for gross negligence. What is gross negligence is a question on the facts of each particular case.[a]

Loans for use.

601. With reference to loans for use, in contradistinction to loans of money, or other things for consumption, the bailee is required to exercise extraordinary care, and he is answerable for slight negligence, though not for inevitable accident, or irresistible force.[b]

602. Like all other bailments, the one in question stipulates for the purest good faith; and, therefore, where a special use is in the contemplation of the borrower at the time of borrowing, he should disclose it, if he wishes to be safe.[c]

Mutual trusts.

603. Mutual trusts have the same rules applied to them, only with a reciprocal, instead of a single application.[d]

Provisions of contract Act.

604. According to Section 148 of the Contract Act, a bailment is the delivery of goods by one person to another for some purpose, upon a contract that they shall, when the purpose is accomplished, be returned or otherwise disposed of, according to the directions of the person delivering them.

Explanation.—If a person already in possession of the goods of another, contracts to hold them as a bailee, he thereby becomes bailee, and the owner becomes the bailor

a 1 Strange's Hindu Law, 281—286.
As to liability of a gratuitous bailee, see 2 Madras Reports, 449.

b 1 Strange's Hindu Law, 286.

c Ibid., 287. See section 609 *post*.

d Ibid., 288.

of such goods, although they may not have been delivered by way of bailment.

605. According to section 151 of the Indian Contract Act, however, in all cases of bailments, the bailee is bound to take as much care of the goods bailed to him, as a man of ordinary prudence would, under similar circumstances, take of his own goods of the same bulk, quality and value as the goods bailed.

606. According to Section 154 of the Contract Act, if the bailee makes any use of the goods bailed, which is not according to the conditions of the bailment, he is liable to make compensation to the bailor for any damages arising to the goods, from or during such use of them.

607. A pledge is an accessory contract *(pignus naturâ suâ est tantummodo jus accessorium)*, being a bailment of something to the creditor on a loan of money; which may be for security only, or for security joined with use *(bhog-yadhi, or usufructuary mortgage)*; and in this respect it may be compared with the *vivum radium* and the *mortuum radium*;—the *living* and the *mort*gage in English law. [a] Pledges.

[a] 1 Strange's Hindu Law, 288, 289.
2 Ibid., 463, 464, Colebrooke and Ellis.
The *vivum radium*, or living pledge, is when a man borrows a sum of money of another (suppose 200*l.*) and grants him an estate as of 20*l.* *per annum*, to hold till the rents and profits shall repay the sum borrowed; in this case the land or pledge is said to be *living*; it subsists and survives the debt, and immediately on the discharge of that reverts back to the borrower. (Holth. Law Dic., 2nd ed.) The *mortuum radium*, or dead pledge, is where

Pledge under Contract Act.

608. According to Section 172 of the Contract Act, the bailment of goods as security for payment of a debt, or performance of a promise, is called pledge. The bailor is, in this case, called the pawnor. The bailee is called the pawnee.

Pledge under Hindu law.

609. According to Hindu law, in the case of a pledge for use, the debt and interest being extinguished by the use or otherwise, it reverts to him who made it; on the other hand, any part of the debt remaining upon expiration of the time for payment, the pledgee or creditor may continue to use it, making a demand for payment, and giving notice of his intention to the debtor, or his representative; or if it be a pledge for *security* only, he may, under the like circumstances, begin to use it, if capable of use, without injury to the substance, giving like notice; while an unjustifiable use of one, being a violation of an implied agreement, works a forfeiture of interest.[a]

Pledge assignable.

610. By usage, contrary perhaps to the strict letter of the law, a pledge is assignable; but the assignment (which can only be for an equal or less sum than the sum

lands are conveyed by one to another as a security for money lent, either in fee or for a term, with a condition that if the money be re-paid on a certain day with interest, the lands shall be re-conveyed to the borrower, and with a further proviso, that if default shall be made in re-payment of the money, the person lending the money shall hold the lands without any interruption from the borrower. (Will. Real Pro., 349, *et seq.*, 4th ed., Coote on Mortgages, 4, *et seq.*, 3rd ed). As to pledges, see further Contract Act, Chapter IX.

a 1 Strange's Hindu Law, 289. A summary of Hindu mortgage.

advanced upon it), should correspond with the original contract; from which any variation might embarrass the redemption on the part of the owner by whom it was first pledged.[a]

Pledge of same thing to two different persons improper.

611. A pledge by the owner of the same thing, at the same time, to two different persons, for the full value to each, is fraudulent: and as between the different pledgees, the first prevails, subject to priority of possession; or there may be an equitable adjustment of the right, according to circumstances.[b]

Hypothecation of chattel.

612. There may be a mortgage of a chattel without possession, or hypothecation, as in the case of immovable property.[c]

Hiring.

613. The same rules that apply to the other bailments apply also to hiring of all kinds.[d]

Mortgages.

614. There is a difference between a mortgage and a pledge: the former conveys an absolute interest in the goods, and the latter only a special property in them.

615. As to mortgages, there are three different kinds in India.

Simple mortgage.

616. The first is a *simple* mortgage, in which the mortgagee has a right to sell the property mortgaged to him as

a 1 Strange's Hindu Law, 289.

b Ibid. It would not be fraudulent, if the subject-matter covered both pledges.

c 3 Allahabad Reports, 54.

d 1 Strange's Hindu Law, 292—295.

a collateral security on failure of the mortgagor to pay. In this case, the former is not entitled to anything more than the debt with costs. This form of mortgage is the same as hypothecation under the civil law, and the mortgagor incurs in it a personal liability.

Conditional sale.

617. The second is a *conditional* sale, in which the mortgagee may become the absolute owner of the property, on failure of the mortgagor to pay. In this case the mortgagee gets the property whatever may be its value, the contract executing itself. In this form of mortgage, the mortgagor incurs no personal liability, in the absence of any express agreement to the contrary.[a]

Usufructuary mortgage.

618. The third is a *usufructuary* mortgage, in which the mortgagee enters into possession and repays himself out of the rents and profits. Here also, generally speaking, the mortgagor incurs no personal liability, and the mortgagee must look exclusively to the land for payment.[b]

Equitable mortgage.

619. There is also a kind of mortgage called an *equitable* mortgage more frequent in England than in India, *e.g.*, where money is borrowed upon the deposit of title deeds, the law implies that the property comprised in the deeds is held liable for the money. No particular form of words is necessary to constitute a mortgage.

a 13 Moore's Indian Appeals, 561 ; 7 Select Reports, (Bengal) 92 ; 7 Sutherland's Weekly Reporter, 196.

b See however 2 Moore's Indian Appeals, 487.

620. A mortgagor in possession is not liable to account for the rents and profits. He must not, however, injure the security of the mortgagee, and he must not commit wilful waste. He, however, is bound to account, if he retain possession against the terms of the mortgage, for he will then be liable for mesne profits. He is also liable for the mesne profits from the time of foreclosure.[a]

Mortgagor generally need not account.

621. The mortgagee in possession, (even in a usufructuary mortgage, on payment of the principal by the mortgagor), is always bound to account for the rents and profits.

Mortgagee must account.

622. The mortgagee is however entitled to any outlay made by him for repairs, and interest at the rate given by the mortgage is allowed on the sum so expended. The repairs, however, should be necessary.[b]

Mortgagee entitled to outlay for repairs.

623. So also with regard to improvements, they must be necessary, or made with the consent of the mortgagor. Where a mortgagee in possession has received notice of a puisne mortgage, he must account to the puisne incumbrancer for the surplus rent paid to the mortgagor, if he has no notice, he need not account.[c]

And for improvements, &c.

a 12 Moore's Indian Appeals, 157.
10 Ibid., 340.

b 9 Sutherland's Weekly Reporter, 488.
5 Bombay Reports, 114, 116.

c 2 Moore's Indian Appeals, 487.

Mortgages to same person redeemed together.

624. If a mortgagor mortgage two or more properties to the same person, he will not be allowed to redeem the one without the other.[a]

Prior mortgagee may protect himself against subsequent incumbrancer.

625. A prior mortgagee, having purchased, may still use his mortgage as a shield against the claims of subsequent mortgagees. In this case, the Judges of the Madras High Court, following the Roman law, declined to adhere to the rule of English law, which refuses this privilege to the mortgagee, unless the mortgage is kept alive as a separate security, observing that "the rule of the Civil law is the true rule, and one to which the minds of English Judges are gradually tending."[b]

"Tacking" not applicable to India.

626. The English doctrine of "tacking" as laid down in the leading case of *Marsh* v. *Lee*, by *Lord Hale*, is also not adopted in India.[c] The doctrine is thus stated in the head-note of that case: If a third mortgagee having advanced his money without notice of a second mortgage, afterwards bring in a first mortgage or statute, though it be *pendente lite*, pending a bill brought by the second mortgagee to redeem the first, yet the third mortgage having obtained the first mortgage, or statute and being the law on his side and equal equity, he shall thereby squeeze out and gain priority over the second mortgagee.

a 6 Bombay Reports, 89.

b 7 Madras Reports, 229.

c 11 Sutherland's Weekly Reporter, 310.
1 White and Tudor's Leading Cases.

Rights and duties of mortgagee.

627. If the mortgagor should refuse, or be incapable of delivering the mortgaged property, the mortgagee may sue him at once for the recovery of the money: or if the mortgagee is disturbed in his possession by the mortgagor, or by any claiming through him, he may sue for the balance due to him.[a]

628. A mortgagee can only enforce a power of sale by judicial process, and not, as in England, under the mortgage instrument, without the interference of the Court. It is considered that this power, if granted, would be grossly abused in this country.[b]

629. Generally speaking, a mortgagee is not bound to proceed in the first instance against the property pledged to him. He may proceed against any property in possession of the mortgagor, even although the decree should declare that he should first proceed against the property pledged.[c]

630. A mortgagee has no right to share in proceeds of a Court sale, when the property is sold subject to his mortgage, to the detriment of unsecured creditors. He may perhaps, however, obtain the surplus after they are paid.[d]

a 4 Moore's Indian Appeals, 444.

b Macpherson on Mortgages. This is so in Bengal under Statutory enactments. See Regulation I of 1798, and Regulation XVII, of 1806. This latter Regulation had no retrospective effect upon titles, which had become absolute before it came into force, 5 Sutherland's Weekly Reporter, 88; 1 Prideaux's Precedents.

c 14 Ibid., 209.
24 Ibid., 305.

d See however, 14 Sutherland's Weekly Reporter, 209, 210.

Exception to rule as to indivisibility of mortgage.

631. A mortgage is indivisible, and a part cannot be redeemed without the whole. To this there is one exception viz., where the equity of redemption in a part of the mortgaged estate is vested in the mortgagee, or if more than one, in all the mortgagees.

632. Each of several persons, who may have succeeded to the mortgagor's interest, shall not be entitled to redeem a part of the property on payment of part of the debt, because the whole and every part of the land mortgaged is liable for the whole debt. But it does not follow from this that a mortgagee who, has acquired by purchase a part of the mortgagor's rights and interests, is entitled to throw the whole burden of the mortgaged debt on the remaining portion of the equity of redemption, in the hands of one who has purchased it at a sale, in execution of a decree against the mortgagor. Each has bought subject to a proportionate share of the burden, and must discharge it. [a]

When exception does not apply.

633. Where, however, one of several mortgagees purchases a part of the estate, this principle will not apply, and a purchaser of part must redeem on payment of the whole debt. [b]

Purchasers of mortgaged property entitled to contribution.

634. Where one of several purchasers of portions of the mortgaged estate pays the whole of the mortgage debt, in order to save the particular portion of the mortgaged land purchased by him from being sold by the mortgagee, he

a 2 Agra Reports, 88.

b 5 Allahabad Reports, 149.

is entitled to contribution from the other purchasers, according to the value of the property possessed by each.[a]

Drishtabandhaka, or hypothecation.

635. Though to ensure the efficacy of a pledge, or mortgage, the Hindu law inculcates the necessity of possession, the authorities to this purpose are not applicable to a sort of mortgage termed *Drishtabandhaka* (hypothecation of visible property) common in India, by which the pledge is assigned to the creditor as a security without possession, or intention of possession, till the stipulated time arrive.[b]

English law recognises hypothecations.

636. The English law recognises hypothecations in the vendor's lien for unpaid purchase money.

Definition of hypothecation.

637. The contract of hypothecation is thus defined by a modern jurist: "*Et quia hypotheca constituitur desuper rebus ideo dicitur jus in re, seu jus reale vel actio realis, quia per illam non obligatur persona debitoris sed res et seqitur fundum et datur contra possessionem.*" Its remedies seem to show clearly that when land is the subject of the hypothecation, it is necessarily a contract which gives an interest in immovable property, for it is clear that any subsequent sale must be made subject to it.[c]

638. A creditor suing under such a contract must prove that there was an actual pledge, and that the land was part of the debtor's estate at the time of pledge.[d]

a 12 Sutherland's Weekly Reporter, 291.
1 Story's Equity sections, 477, 484.

b 1 Strange's Hindu Law, 289.

c 2 Madras Reports, 51, citing *Neguzantius*. In connection with hypothecation, see 3 Madras Reports, 241.

d Ibid.

24

Hypothecation to be registered.

639. An instrument of hypothecation is a mortgage instrument, and as such should be registered.[a]

How conditional sales to be regarded.

640. A *drishtabandhaka* which names a time for payment of the money borrowed, and stipulates that, on default, the mortgagee shall be put into exclusive possession and enjoyment of the property, will not be treated strictly as a conditional sale, even though the instrument expressly provide that, on default, the transaction shall be deemed an outright sale; and in a suit by the mortgagee for possession, the Court, in decreeing the right thereto, will give the mortgagor a day for redeeming.[b]

Equity of redemption.

641. Under the common law of England, the mortgagee had not only the possession, but absolute property of the land on the debtor's failing to perform the condition. But equity has always regarded a mortgage as redeemable till foreclosure; and in enforcing a lien, it gives the debtor an opportunity of barring the mortgage, or sale of the property, to which the lien extends, by paying the amount due with interest by a day named by the Court.[c]

642. This principle of equity is now acted on by the Courts with reference to mortgages, and the mortgagor does not lose his equity of redemption though the stipulated time, for payment has been allowed to pass by, and though

a 2 Madras Reports, 108.

b 1 Ibid., 460. See note next page.

c 2 Ibid., 51.

there should be a contemporaneous agreement clogging that right.[a]

643. On a stale claim to redeem a mortgage and dispossess a mortgagee, who had before 1858 acquired an absolute title, there would be strong reasons for adopting the ancient law, as to mortgages by conditional sale. In the case of a security executed since 1858, there would be strong reasons for recognising and giving effect to the Madras authorities, with reference to which the parties might be supposed to have contracted.[b]

Mortgages before and after 1858 how regarded.

a 1 Madras Reports, 460.

2 Ibid., 420; 7 Ibid., 395; 8 Ibid., 31.

With reference to the above decisions of the Indian Courts on mortgages by conditional sale, the Privy Council observe that, up to the year 1858, the Courts in Madras gave effect to such sales: such being in accordance with the ancient law of India: that however subsequently to this, a current of decisions set in, inaugurated by the late Sudder, in which these sales were treated as penalties, and the principles of English Courts of Equity adopted, giving the mortgagor notwithstanding the right to redeem. After reviewing all the cases in Madras and in Bombay, for in Bombay a similar change was effected (vide 9 Bombay Reports, 69,) they held that these decisions were not only unsound and had the effect of usurping the functions of the Legislature, but the change they effected involved very mischievous consequences. Under the law so laid down, persons, who fifty years before had acquired, as the law then stood, an indefeasible title in lands, which they had ever since held and enjoyed *in optima fide*, became liable to be dispossessed and compelled to account for mesne profits, at the suit of the representatives of the mortgagor, against whom the sixty years' rule of limitation had not yet run. And they go on to say this is not an imaginary case, and give an example from 7 Madras Reports, 395, in which the mortgage deed was executed in 1811, the title of the mortgagee becoming absolute in 1816, while the suit was brought just as the limitation was dying out. Other instances are also in the Reports, 2 Indian Appeals, 241.

b 2 Indian Appeals, 255.

Re-purchase.

644. It is quite competent to parties to sell with a condition for re-purchase at a particular time; then, in case of non-payment at the time, there is no equity to relieve against the sale. It is the intention of the parties which governs, and that intention may be shown by the deed itself, by other instruments, or even by oral evidence.[a]

645. It is incorrect to suppose that the condition for re-purchase, with a stipulation for an absolute sale, in case of failure to pay at the time, is a penalty which cannot be enforced.[b]

646. When a *bonâ fide* sale is accompanied by a power to re-purchase, this will not make the transaction a mortgage, if such does not appear to have been the intention of the parties. The best general test of such intention is the existence, or non-existence of a power, in the original purchaser to recover the sum named, as the price for such re-purchase: if there is no such power, there is no mortgage.[c]

a 2 Madras Reports, 420; 7 Ibid., 6. With regard to these decisions, the Privy Council observe that the distinction between sales with a condition for re-purchase and mortgages by conditional sale being made to depend upon the intention of the parties to the original transaction, provable by oral evidence, opens a wide field of litigation, and to leave much to the discretion of the Judge in each particular case; and the inquiry is embarrassed by the circumstance that, the parties whose intention is to be ascertained cannot, in the case of an ancient transaction, have contracted with reference to a state of law, which the Courts of Madras have decided no longer exists. 2 Indian Appeals, 254.

b 2 Madras Reports, 420.

c 1 Ibid., 460, Note.

647. A party mortgaged land to another, the mortgage instrument providing that the mortgagee should be entitled to purchase the land, if it were not redeemed by a specified date. After this date, the mortgagee accepted from the mortgagor a small sum in part-payment of the mortgage-money. It was held that this was a waiver by the mortgagee of his right to purchase.[a]

Waiver of mortgagee's right to purchase.

648. Where a mortgage-bond contained an agreement to re-pay the money with interest by a certain day, and stipulated that if the mortgagor failed to pay the amount, the mortgagee should be put in possession of the land and he might enjoy it; and that when the mortgagor had the means he would redeem the land and pay the debt with interest and take back the bond, it was held that, on the mortgagor's default, the mortgagee might sue for the money, and that he was not bound to accept the land and forego his right of action.[b]

Mortgagee not bound to forego right of action in certain circumstances.

649. The next contract is that of sale. Sale is thus defined in Section 77 of the Contract Act: Sales are the exchange of property for a price. It involves the transfer of the ownership of the thing sold from the seller to the buyer.

Sale and its incidents.

650. Section 78 says:—Sale is effected by offer and acceptance of ascertained goods for a price, or of a price for ascertained goods, together with payment of the first,

a 1 Madras Reports, 69.

b. Ibid., 114.

or delivery of the goods, or with tender, part payment, earnest, or part delivery, or with an agreement, express or implied, that the payment or delivery, or both, shall be postponed.

651. Where there is a contract for the sale of ascertained goods, the property in the goods sold passes to the buyer when the whole or part of the price, or when the earnest is paid, or when the whole or part of the goods is delivered.

652. If the parties agree expressly, or by implication, that the payment or delivery, or both, shall be postponed, the property passes as soon as the proposal for sale is accepted.

653. A thing sold and not delivered (subject to any special agreement) is at the risk of the vendor; so that if, while it remains unduly in his hands, its value sink, he must make it good with an attention to the eventual profit, where it was purchased for exportation; the same obligation attaching by whatever means it may be lost.[a]

654. Where the price has not been stipulated, the law implies a reasonable one *(quantum valuit)* to be settled in case of dispute by merchants.[b]

Damages for breach of contract.

655. If instead of paying down the price, *earnest* be paid, and the buyer afterwards break the agreement, the earnest is forfeited; and if in such case the seller break it, he is liable to re-pay the earnest two-fold; and not only

a 1 Strange's Hindu Law, 303. See however Contract Act, sect. 86. As to sale generally, see Contract Act, Chap. VII.

b 1 Strange's Hindu Law, 303. See Contract Act, sect. 89.

double the earnest money, but also damages for the non-delivery. [a]

656. In an action of damages for non-delivery of goods, it was held that, before the plaintiffs could recover, they must show that they paid, or tendered the amount stipulated, and that the vendor's rights under the contract cannot be controlled by the course of dealing between the parties. [b]

657. Where a vendor contracts to deliver goods within a reasonable time, and payment is to be made on delivery, if, before the lapse of that time, he merely expresses an intention not to perform the contract, the purchaser cannot at once bring his action, unless he exercise his option to treat the contract as rescinded. [c]

658. In a suit for damages for breach of contract to deliver goods, it is not absolutely essential that there should be an allegation in the plaint that plaintiff was willing to pay on delivery. [d]

659. Where the matter rests on the original agreement, and the vendee, upon its being tendered, refuse to accept the commodity he has bought, there is, with regard to him, an end of the contract; and the owner may dispose of the

a 1 Strange's Hindu Law, 303.
1 Madras Reports, 9 applies this principle of Hindu Law.

b 2 Madras Reports, 193.
As to the measure of damages, see 1 Madras Reports, 9, 168.

c 1 Madras Reports, 162. As to the English cases on this point, see Reporter's note to this case.

d 7 Madras Reports, 364.

article as he pleases, the vendee being responsible for any loss resulting from his not having completed his purchase, but he is not entitled to any profit.[a]

Penalty and liquidated damages.

660. Where parties agree that in case of a breach of contract a sum shall be paid, the amount will be regarded as liquidated damages, which the Courts will enforce, and not as a penalty which they will relieve. Act XXVIII of 1855 is a conclusive proof, too, that the intention of the legislature is that, parties shall be left to make, and be compelled to stand by their own bargains.[b]

661. The mere use of the term "penalty," or the term "liquidated damages," does not determine the intention of the parties to a written instrument, but like any other question of construction, it is to be determined by the nature of the provisions, and the language of the whole instrument.[c]

662. One circumstance, however, is of great importance towards the arriving at a conclusion; if the instrument contains many stipulations of varying importance, or relating to objects of small value calculable in money, there is the strongest ground for supposing that a stipulation, applying generally to a breach of all, or any of them, was intended to be a penalty, and not in the way of liquidated damages.[d]

a 1 Strange's Hindu Law, 303. See Contract Act, sect. 107.
b 2 Madras Reports, 451.
Ibid., 205.
c 12 Moore's Indian Appeals, 229.
d Ibid.

663. The rule of construction, therefore, is that, although the stipulation may be held to be a penalty, and therefore not payable upon a breach of any particular stipulation, the resulting damage from which is strictly measurable in money, still the penalty might properly be taken as the amount of damages measured by the parties themselves, in case of an entire non-performance. [a]

664. The contract next to be considered is that of loan, or borrowing for consumption, whether of money, or other thing answering the description. It differs from loan for *use* (which is a bailment), in that the property of the money, or other thing lent for consumption vests in the borrower, (not returned, but) re-placed by him, with an equivalent;—together with such compensation for the loan, as may have been stipulated. [b]

Loans of money.

665. The compensation for the loan of money is *interest;* and for performance of the terms of the contract on the part of the borrower, it is usual to take *security,* consisting in *pledges,* or *sureties,* or both. [c]

Interest.

666. The rule of Hindu law as to interest is that, no greater arrear of interest can be recovered at any one time than what will amount to the principal sum; but if the principal remain outstanding, and the interest be paid in

a 2 Madras Reports, 451.
b 1 Strange's Hindu Law, 296.
Menu, VIII, 151.
c 1 Strange's Hindu Law, 296.

smaller sums than the amount of the principal money, there is no limit to the amount of interest which may be thus received from time to time.[a] Interest however now may be awarded in excess of the principal. Regulation XXXIV of 1802, relating to this subject, has been repealed.[b]

667. In the absence of a demand in writing, interest up to the date of suit cannot be awarded upon sums not payable under a written instrument of which the payment has been illegally delayed. And where a party has offered to pay interest, he should be relieved from interest from the date of such offer.[c]

Sureties.

668. Sureties are for appearance, for the honesty of the debtor, or for payment.[d]

669. In every case, the obligation of the surety becomes absolute, by the failure of the principal.[e]

670. Between the suretyship for payment and the other two kinds, there is this difference, that in the two latter cases, the surety dying, and the principal neglecting to pay, the sons of the surety are not answerable, unless their father was himself indemnified; and then the son is liable, as he

a 1 Strange's Hindu Law, 299.
1 Madras Reports, 5; Reporter's Note, as cited in the Addenda, x.

b 6 Madras Reports, 400.

c 1 Ibid., 369.
Ibid., 124. See Act 32 of 1839 extending to British India, 3 & 4 W. 4, c. 42, s. 28.

d 1 Strange's Hindu Law, 300.

e Ibid., 301. See Contract Act, sect. 128.

is in all cases, subject always to assets, and without interest, where the undertaking was for *payment.*[a]

671. Of sureties, jointly bound, each is answerable for his proportion only of the debt to be fixed, unless it shall have been otherwise agreed.[b]

672. The principal must in all cases be first sued;—the surety having paid has his claim over against his principal for re-payment.[c]

673. Where a judgment was passed against several defendants, jointly and severally, and some of them paid the whole of the judgment-debt, it was held that they might sue the others for contribution.[d]

674. One tortfeasor, however, cannot recover contribution against another.[e]

Maintenance and champerty.

675. As to contracts relating to "maintenance" and "champerty," the law of England as to this offences does not apply to natives of India. In dealing with objections to their contracts on the ground of maintenance, or champerty, the Court must look to the general principles regard-

a 1 Strange's Hindu Law, 301.

b Ibid. So also says the Contract Act sect. 146.

c Ibid., see sects. 140, 141, 148, Contract Act.

d 1 Madras Reports, 411.
As to sureties generally, see Contract Act, sect. 126, *et seq.*
3 Madras Reports, 187.

e 1 Ibid., 411, Note.

ing public policy and the administration of justice upon which that law at present rests.[a]

676. The Privy Council also say that the Mofussil Courts of India, administering justice according to the broad principles of equity and good conscience, will not apply the English law of champerty and maintenance, according to the practice of the English law; but they must consider whether a transaction, impeached on the ground of maintenance is merely the acquisition of an interest in the subject of litigation *bonâ fide* entered into, or whether it is an unfair, or illegitimate transaction, got up merely for the purpose of spoil, or of litigation, and they will not allow a stranger to interfere in family affairs by an agreement between him and the real heirs, that he should be entitled to a share of the estate.[b]

677. Again they say, a fair agreement to supply funds to carry on a suit in consideration of having a share of the property, if recovered, ought not to be regarded, as being *perse* opposed to public policy. But agreements of such a kind ought to be carefully watched, and when extortionate, unconscionable, or made for impropor objects, ought to be held invalid.[c]

a 1 Madras Reports, 153. To constitute "maintenance," improper litigation must have been stirred up with a bad motive, or purpose, contrary to public policy and justice. "Champerty" is a species of maintenauce and of the same character, but with the additional feature of a condition, or bargain providing for a participation in the subject-matter of the litigation.

b 1 Indian Appeals, 241.

c 4 Ibid., 23.

Specific performance.

678. In decreeing specific performance of a contract, the Court has always to consider whether it can enforce the whole of the agreement, and where it cannot do so, this relief will be refused.[a]

679. Under the Specific Relief Act, (Act I of 1877) the following contracts may be specifically enforced:—

(*a.*) When the act agreed to be done is in the performance, wholly or partly, of a trust.

(*b.*) When there exists no standard for ascertaining the actual damage caused by the non-performance of the act agreed to be done.

(*c.*) When the act agreed to be done is such that pecuniary compensation for its non-performance would not afford adequate relief, or

(*d.*) When it is probable that pecuniary compensation cannot be got for the non-performance of the act agreed to be done.

Explanation.—Unless and until the contrary is proved, the Court shall presume that the breach of a contract to transfer immovable property cannot be adequately relieved by compensation in money, and that the breach of a contract to transfer movable property can be thus relieved.

a 1 Madras Reports, 341. See Specific Relief Act, (Act I of 1877) sects. 14, 15.

680. **Contracts which cannot be specifically enforced :—**

(*a.*) A contract for the non-performance of which compensation in money is an adequate relief.

(*b.*) A contract which runs into such minute or numerous details, or which is so dependent on the personal qualifications, or relation of the parties, or otherwise from its nature is such that, the Court cannot enforce specific performance of its material terms.

(*c.*) A contract, the terms of which the Court cannot find with reasonable certainty.

(*d.*) A contract which is in its nature revocable.

(*e.*) A contract made by trustees, either in excess of their powers, or in breach of their trust.

(*f.*) A contract made by, or on behalf of a corporation or public company created for special purposes, or by the promoters of such company, which is in excess of its powers.

(*g.*) A contract, the performance of which wishes the performance of a continuous duty extending over a longer period than three years from its date.

(*h.*) A contract of which a material point of the subject-matters supposed by both parties to exist has, before it has been made, ceased to exist. As to other matters relating to specific performance of contracts, see Specific Relief Act.

681. Specific performance has been decreed of a lease, though the lease formed part of an arrangement whereby as a consideration for the lease the plaintiff was to lend the

defendant money to enable him *inter alia* to commence legal proceedings against the then tenants of the subject-matter of the intended lease.[a]

682. The application of the doctrine of specific performance to partnerships is governed by the same rules as those which govern it in other cases.[b]

683. As to Bills of Exchange, Promissory Notes, &c., Chapter 39 of the new Civil Procedure Code (Act X of 1877) provides a summary remedy for their enforcement.

CHAPTER XIII.

MALABAR LAW.

684. In Malabar and Canara, concubinage is the rule, and the whole law of inheritance is based upon the existence of heritable blood between the mother and son, quite irrespectively of the father. There is there no *agnation* at all.[c] Basis of Malabar law.

685. This system of law is termed *Marumakkatayam* in Malabar, and *Aliya Santana* in Canara. The latter differs from the former in more consistently carrying out Marumakkatayam and Aliya Santana.

a See above decision.

b 1 Madras Reports, 341. See the same case also as to the classes of cases in which specific performance of an agreement to enter into a partnership has been decreed. As to further information on the subject of specific performance, the reader is referred to the admirable work of Mr. (now Sir) Edward Fry on Specific Performance of Contracts.

c 1 Madras Reports, 201.
In Malabar, sons do not inherit. The heirs are sisters, sisters' sons, sisters' daughters, sisters' daughters' sons, &c.

the doctrine that all rights to property are derived from females.[a]

No suit can be brought for division.

686. The whole doctrine of a Malabar family is, that they are all to reside in the family-house and be there supported by the head of the family; and no suit can be brought for division. The same principle is followed in Canara.[b] There may be a division by mutual consent. The principle of division would be according to the *Taverais* or branches of the family, that is according to the number of sisters of the common ancestor.

Origin of *Marumakkatayam.*

687. According to Mr. Strange, the origin of the *Marumakkatayam* Rules is attributable to *Parasooraman,* the first Raja of Malabar. He introduced Brahmins into the District and gave them possessions there. In order to prevent these from being split up, he decreed that they should vest in the elder brothers, whom alone he permitted to contract marriage. The sons of these were to be accounted as sons for the whole family. The junior brothers, being without wives, were allowed to consort with females of lower castes. The offspring of these unions, not being legitimate, could not rank as Brahmins, or inherit from their fathers. Their inheritance was hence made to follow from their mothers. The lower castes fell into the same system of promiscuous

a 2 Madras Reports, 12.
1 Ibid., 380.
Marumakkatayam is the system of inheritance in the female line. *Aliya Santana* implies the same.

b 2 Madras Reports, 12.

intercourse among themselves. The offspring succeed to the estate in the mother's family, it being obvious that parentage cannot be traced out in the line of the male.

688. The castes that follow *Marumakkatayam* are all except Brahmins and *Aka Podnals* a class of pagoda servants, the artisans, viz., carpenters, brassmiths, blacksmiths and goldsmiths and some of the lowest denominations such as the *Cheromars* or slave tribe, the *Malayers* and the *Paniars* with whom the rule of descent is to sons. Some classes in North Malabar follow *Marumakkatayam* while those to the South observe *Makkatayam* or descent to sons. In North Malabar, most of the *Moplahs,* although Mahomedans, follow the former rule in this respect having conformed to Hindu usage in the times of the ascendancy of the Hindoos.[a]

Meaning of term *Taverai.*

689. In Malabar the *Taverai* has several distinct meanings. In the families of the princes all the houses have separate property, and the senior in age of all the houses succeeds to the royalty, with the property specially devoted to it. This mode of succession may be regarded as rather due to public, than to private law. Private families have sometimes adopted the same custom, but there is the strongest presumption against the truth of this in a private family—families becoming very numerous have often split into various branches. In the language of the people there

a. Strange's Manual, § 384.

is *community of purity and impurity but no community of property*. In the only sense of the word *Taverai* with which Courts of Justice are concerned, people so related are not of the same *tarawád*. Where there are several houses bearing the same original *tarawád* name, but with an addition, and there is no evidence of the passing of a member of one house to another, there is the strongest ground for concluding that a separation has taken place. [a]

Law as to self-acquisition in Malabar.

690. By the law of Malabar, all acquisitions of any members of a family which he has not disposed of in his life-time, form part of the family property. [b]

691. The acquirer, however, may during his life-time, hold, alienate at once, and encumber his self-acquisition. [c]

692. The father may give whatever self-acquired property he likes, but no ancestral property, to his children. This, his private property, may be inherited by his children. [d]

In Canara.

693. In Canara, the husband is not permitted to confer even upon his wife any gifts, but the marriage present; if he give more, the family may resume it. [e]

Presumption as to self-acquisition.

694. A *káranavan* of a *tarawád* in possession of the family funds is presumed to have made all acquisitions with

a 6 Madras Reports, 411. A *tarawád* is a family or household.

b Ibid., 162.

c Ibid.

d *Bhútálapándiya cited* in 1 Ibid., 3380

e Ibid., 1 Ibid., 380.

them and for the benefit of the corporate body. But such presumption is not irrebuttable, and his alienation of or charge on such acquisitions made during his life-time may be valid. [a]

695. By Malabar law, the *kárananavan* is the natural guardian of every member within his *tarawád*, and a father can claim no right to the custody of his children. [b] Duties of *káranavan.*

696. A *káranavan* cannot part by contract with the privileges and duties which attach to the position of *káranavan,* so to be unable to resume them. [c]

697. An arrangement whereby the *káranavan* of a *tarawád* delegates the management to two branch *káranavans* is not absolutely irrevocable by himself, or his successors. [d]

698. *A kárnavan* may be superseded for incompetency. The causes which will disqualify the *káranavan* are loss of caste, old age, deafness, blindness, dumbness, madness, disgraceful conduct, and dissipation of the family means. When put aside, whether by the family or by force of legal means, he is to be replaced by the next senior competent male member. [e]

699. An *anandravan* of a *tarawád* governed by the *Marumakkattayam* rule has no right to an account from the Káranavan need not account to anandravan.

a 2 Madras Reports, 162.
A *káranavan* is the senior member of a *tarawád.*

b 7 Madras Reports, 179.

c 6 Ibid., 145.

d 6 Ibid., 401.

e 1 Strange's Manual, § 389.

káranavan. The English doctrine as to the right of a *cestui que trust,* to call for an account, has no application to a case of this sort.[a]

Right of management.

700. Each member of a *tarawád* has a right to succeed by seniority to the management of the family property.[b]

701. The right of the eldest member of a *Nambúdiri* family to manage the *illom* is absolute; and when a junior member has in fact managed it, then this is presumed to have been with the permission of the former, who may at any time take up the actual control.[c]

In Canara.

702. Under the *Aliya Santana* system in Canara, according to *Bhútálapándiya,* "The eldest child of the eldest sister, be it male or female, is to be the *yajamána,* and is to hold the property as such; but it cannot be divided among the family. The remaining members are to act under the authority of such female or male manager.[d] If a disagreement takes place between the sisters, the elder sister is to provide the younger sister with a separate house and its necessary apparatus, retaining the general managership and the performance of ceremonies. But no division of property can be made.

a 2 Madras Reports, 12.

b Ibid.

c Ibid., 110.
A *Nambúdiri* family is a Brahmin family. An *Illom* is a house or family.

d *Bhútálapándiya* cited in; 1 Madras Reports, 380.
Yajamána is a manager.

703. To the dignities of chief families held by the manager of the senior branch, the member of his own *santána* will, on his demise, be entitled to succeed. Those of the junior branch shall have no right. If all the members of the senior branch be extinct, then those of the junior will have a right. [a]

704. Females, before puberty, go through a form of marriage, but in attaining maturity, they cohabit with whom as they please of the same caste. Marriage.

705. There is nothing analogous to the state of widowhood as elsewhere existing. Females whether in alliance with males or not reside in their own families. [b]

706. According to Malabar law an adoption may be made in failure of the sister's children. The adoptee must be a female, but her brother may be adopted with her to manage the property and to perform the family rites. Adoption.

707. In Canara, too, females only are recognized as the proprietors of family property. On failure of collateral descendants, a female of the same *bulli* must be adopted. Males cannot be adopted. [c]

a Bhútálapándiya cited in ; 1 Madras Reports, 380.
Yajamána is a manager.
Santana is offspring or family.

b 1 Strange's Manual, § 400.

c 1 Madras Reports, 380, citing *Bhútálapándiya.*

708. From failure of heirs, *aliya santana* estates cannot be sold nor transferred to the wife's children. The father must adopt a female who is to inherit the property.[a]

709. If a family becomes extinct without such an adoption, the elders of the caste should assemble, and adopt another couple of people from the same lineage, whose offspring then succeeds to the property.[b]

Inalienability of *tarawád* property.

710. It is the unquestionable law of Malabar that *tarawád* property is inalienable except in cases of adequate family necessity. In such cases alienations will be upheld, but it lies upon the purchaser to make out with abundant clearness that the purpose was a proper one. The assent of the senior *anandravan* is some, but rebuttable, evidence that the purpose was proper. Considering the state of Hindu families, a purchaser would be affected with notice by much slighter evidence than a purchaser in other countries.[c]

Property assigned in *Náyar* family for support of females may be taken in execution.

711. Property assigned by the males of a *Náyar* family for the support of their females is still family property, and liable, as such, to be taken in execution of a judgment against the *káranavan*.[d]

Sale of family property when valid.

712. According to Malabar law, a sale of family property is valid when made with the assent, express or

a *Bhútálapándiya* above cite[d]

b Ibid.

c 3 Madras Reports, 294.

d 2 Ibid., 41.

implied, of all the members of the *tarawád,* and when the deed of sale is signed by the *káranavan* and the senior *anandravan,* if *sui juris.* [a]

713. Such signature is *primâ facie* evidence of the assent of the family, and the burden of proving their dissent rests on those who allege it. [b]

714. The assent of the *anandravans* is necessary to a sale of *tarawád* land by a *káranavan.* [c]

715. The chief *anandravan's* signature to the instrument of sale is sufficient, but not indispensable, evidence of such assent. [d]

716. When the *úrálans* of a *dewasvam* are four *tarawáds,* a sale of the *úrálama* right by one *tarawád* without the consent of the others, is altogether invalid. [e] **When invalid.**

717. Debts incurred by a *káranavan* will be presumed to be family debts and are a charge with estate. **Debts.**

718. The share of any member of a *tarawád* is not liable for his debts.

a 1 Madras Reports, 248.
An *anandravan* is one of the members of a *tarawád.*
b 1 Madras Reports, 248.
c Ibid., 359.
d Ibid.
e Ibid., 262.
Urálans are managers. A *dewasvam* is a temple.

Right to maintenance. 719. The right of a member of a Malabar family to maintenance is merely a right to be maintained in the family-house.[a]

Kánam-mortgage. 720. A *kánam-mortgage* cannot be redeemed before the lapse of twelve years from the date of its execution.[b]

Rights of Kánamdár. 721. A *kánamdár's* right to hold for twelve years depends on his acting conformably to usage and the *janmi's* interest, and is lost if he repudiates the *janmi's* title. It can make no difference that this is done for the first time by the *kánamdár* in his answer in the suit, or that on appeal he takes the point, as to non-redemption, within twelve years.[c]

722. A *kánam-mortgagee* does not forfeit his right to hold for twelve years from the date of the *kánam* by allowing the *purappad* fall into arrear.[d]

723. As the land cannot be reclaimed before the lapse of twelve years, it seems only consistent with justice that

a 2 Madras Reports, 12.

b 1 Ibid., 261.

A *kánam* is a deposit of money made upon land leased out for a term of years, the deposit to bear interest which is deducted from the rent. The principal is paid on expiry of the lease which is now renewed.

c 2 Madras Reports, 109.

1 Ibid., 445.

A *kánamdár* is a mortgagee. A *janmi* is a proprietor. As to *jenm* right, see 2 Strange's Hindu Law, 461, 462, Ellis.

d 1 Madras Reports, 112.

Purappad is net-rent.

the money should not be reclaimable until that period has elapsed.[a]

724. Where, however, the demisor is unable to give possession, it is reasonable that the demisee should be allowed to repudiate the contract and recover the amount advanced.[b]

725. Where a first *kánam-holder*, in his answer to a redemption-suit by a second *kánam-holder*, for the first time denied his own *kánam* and alleged an independent *janma* right, it was held that he had not thereby forfeited his right to rely upon the option to make a further advance to which as *kánam-holder* he was entitled, though the denial and allegation were false, and though his documents in support of such allegation were forged.[c]

726. A *melkánamdár* cannot eject a *kánamdár* or his assignee before the expiration of twelve years from the date of the *kánam*.[d]

727. A *káranavan* singly may make an *otti* mortgage.[e] Otti mortgage.

728. An *otti* differs from a *kánam* mortgage, first, in respect of the right of pre-emption which the *otti-holder* possesses; secondly, in being for so large a sum that,

a 2 Madras Reports, 315.
b Ibid.
c 1 Ibid., 13.
d Ibid., 296.
A *melkánamdár* is a second mortgagee.
e 1 Madras Reports, 122.
An *otti* is a species of mortgage.

practically, the *janmi's* right is merely to receive a pepper-corn rent.[a]

729. An *otti,* like a *kánam* mortgage, cannot be redeemed before the lapse of twelve years from its date.[b]

730. During the continuance of a first *otti* mortgage, the *janmi* is in the same position as regards his right to make a second *otti* mortgage to a stranger after, as he was before the lapse of twelve years from the date of the first mortgage.[c]

731. Where a *janmi* made an *otti* mortgage and more than twelve after made a second *otti* mortgage to a stranger without having given notice to the first mortgagees so as to admit of the exercise of their option to advance the further sum required by the *janmi,* it was held that the second mortgagee could not redeem the lands comprised in the first mortgage.[d]

732. An *otti* mortgagee has the option to make the further advance (if any) required by the mortgagor.[e]

733. An *otti-holder,* like a *kánamdár,* forfeits his right to hold for twelve years by denying the *janmi's* title.[f]

a 1 Madras Reports, 261. An *otti* is chiefly a usufructuary mortgage.
b Ibid., 122.
c Ibid., 356.
d Ibid.
e 1 Ibid., 13, note.
f 2 Ibid., 161.

734. There is a species of mortgage which occurs in Canara, termed *iladárawára* mortgage and resembles a Welsh mortgage, the mortgagee being in possession and taking the rents and profits in lieu of interest, and the security carrying a right to redeem but none to foreclose. The *iladárawára* mortgagee pays the Government revenue. [a] **Iladárawára mortgage.**

a 1 Madras Reports, 18, note.

A Welsh mortgage (now fallen into disuse) is one in which there is no condition or proviso for re-payment at any time. The agreement is that the mortgagee to whom the estate is conveyed shall receive the rents till his debt is paid, and in such case the mortgagor and his representatives are at liberty to redeem at any time. 2 Spence, 616.

APPENDIX A.

The Shivagungah Case—involving important questions of Hindu Inheritance.

As an *addendum* to the Chapter on Inheritance, I have thought it would not be out of place to make a few observations in the form of an Appendix on the above case, recently decided in the *Madura* District Court, and now under appeal to the High Court. The case is one of great interest, and involves questions of importance on the subject of Inheritance.

To readers of *Moore's* Indian Appeals, the history of the *Shivagungah* Zemindary must be somewhat familiar. The decision reported in 9 *Moore's* 536, by the late *Lord Justice Turner*, when the succession was last disputed, is very frequently referred to, and is one of the most well-considered judgments in the Reports.

The history of *Shivagungah* and its litigation is briefly this :—

The Zemindary was founded in 1730 by the Nabobs of the Carnatic, having been carved out of the larger estate of *Ramnad*, in the *Madura* country, and was given to one *Sasirverna*, the first and original Zemindar. On his death, he was succeeded by his son who was killed in battle, and who died without issue male. The Zemindary was then nominally held by his widow for a short time. Anarchy and confusion, however, soon followed on the usurpation of the estate by two brothers called *Mundoos*. Shortly afterwards, in 1792 the Zemindary passed into the hands of the *East India Company* with the rest of *Southern India*. The estate was by them considered an escheat for want of heirs, and was thus held till the year 1801 when it was re-granted to the *Istimrar* Zemindar, not from any claims that he had to the property, but by the free choice and will of the Government, as stated in the Proclamation, issued by *Lord Clive* on the occasion.

The *Istimrar* Zemindar thus obtained possession and died in 1829. Not long afterwards commenced a series of law suits for this Estate, which is almost without parallel even in Indian litigation. In the first place, the then Government, in conformity with time-honored traditions, arbitrarily vested the succession in the collateral branch of the family, and enthroned the alleged undivided nephew of the deceased Zemindar upon the *gadi*. He did not, however, long live to enjoy the honor, but died in 1831, and was succeeded by his son, to whom he also left a legacy of law suits. On his death a host of claimants rose in arms, and the *Madura* Court was likely, for at least a score of years, to be employed in the disposal of *Shivagungah* business.

The Zemindar had married seven wives and at his death left three widows. A daughter by one of these wives first filed a suit in 1832, on behalf of her infant son, the elder brother of the present plaintiff. Next in 1833, the eldest widow came into Court. The former of these cases was dismissed by the Sudder in 1837, and in 1844 the latter was eventually decided on a technical ground by the Privy Council against the widow, giving her leave to sue again. She came into Court in 1845, her suit was dismissed, and pending her appeal to the Sudder, in 1850, she died. Her death seemed to give a new *impetus* to *Shivagungah* litigation. The other widows having pre-deceased her, several new claimants now came into the field. The late Rani of Shivagungah, the daughter by the Zemindar's third wife, whose recent death has caused the present litigation, joining with two of her sisters, first applied for leave to prosecute the appeal of the deceased widow. So also did the daughter of the sixth wife, as well as the plaintiff in the very first suit in 1832, already alluded to. After a game of shuttlecock for *six* years with petitions and counter-petitions in the late *Sudder*, between the several parties, the *Sudder* decided that no one had a right to prosecute the appeal, and all were referred to regular suits. In 1856, therefore, the late Rani filed her suit in *formâ pauperis* in the *Madura* Court, and in 1857, the daughter of the sixth wife also filed hers. Both suits were dismissed by the then Civil Judge, *Mr. R. R. Cotton*, in a judgment in which he cut the Gordian knot of *Shivagungah* litigation, at any rate temporarily, by a novel application of the doctrine as to judgments *in rem*. The *Sudder* followed his example. The cases however were appealed to the *Privy Council* through the indefatigable exertions of the late *Mr. G. F. Fischer*, the father of *Mr. Robert Fischer* of Madura, and the Rani was successful. By a decree of the Council dated 1863, she was declared the *Zemindarni* of *Shivagungah*, and the suit of the other daughter was dismissed.

The ground upon which the late Rani based her claims, and which was eventually established, was, that, the estate was her father's self-acquisition, and that whether her father's family was divided, or not, she was, after the deceased widow, the next heir to her father's self-acquisition, in preference to the collaterals.

The late Rani died in 1877, leaving a son and several daughters. Though maiden at the time of her father's death, she had been twice married subsequently, and was married with issue male and female at the time of her succession.

The estate is again in litigation, and the claimant is one *Dorasingah Taver*, the younger brother of the plaintiff in the suit of 1832. He claims it as the eldest surviving grandson of the *Istimrar* Zemindar, in preference to the Rani's son, also a grandson, but junior to the plaintiff in years.

In 1869 the plaintiff had sued for a Declaration of his rights, but, though successful in the Indian Courts, his suit was dismissed by the Privy Council on the ground that the facts could not sustain a declarator. The pleadings in the case shortly were that, the late Rani as a *daughter*, took merely a life-estate from her father, the former Zemindar; that the inheritance is to be traced from the deceased Zemindar, as last full owner, and that according to the Rule of Primogeniture, which it is said prevails in the Zemindary he, as eldest surviving grandson, succeeds to the estate.

The case for the first defendant, the Rani's son was, that, his mother obtained, not a mere life-tenancy, but an absolute estate from her father, that the inheritance is to be traced from her, and was transmitted by her to her son, and that the Rule of Primogeniture does not prevail in the Zemindary. The other defendants, the three daughters of the late Rani submitted that, the estate was their mothers *stridhanum*, and that it descends to them as reversioners.

The fifth defendant was the lessee of the estate, but his case is of no importance in the discussion. The judgment of the District Court was in favor of the plaintiff, as the *eldest* surviving grandson of the Istimrar Zemindar, or in other words he succeeds by *primogeniture*. The other questions as to a daughter's estate and *stridhanum* were not discussed, as the previous judgment of the High Court in the case was considered conclusive on these points. It is proposed, however, to discuss them here. The important questions therefore that are involved in this case are; first, when can the Rule of Primogeniture be said to exist as a mode of descent in an estate? secondly, what kind of an estate does a daughter take who inherits from her father? and thirdly, what kind of property constitutes a woman's *stridhanum?* These two last questions merge into each other and assume the form of the general question as to the *nature* of a woman's estate. They are subjects which perhaps have not received sufficient consideration from Hindu lawyers and text-writers, and the observations, it is hoped that are submitted, will attract more attention than what has been bestowed upon them hitherto. The following considerations, however, are put forward with great diffidence:

First as to Primogeniture.

It may be broadly, at the outset, stated that, primogeniture, as a mode of descent, is quite unknown to the ordinary Hindu law, since it is repugnant to the whole spirit and genius of that law. At one time, no doubt, it did prevail to a certain extent. The eldest son, if possessed of extraordinary merit, was entitled on division to the best chattel, or to the best room in the house. But the "honors of primogeniture" have long been abolished, as being quite uncongenial to the spirit of the law. The most perfect equality exists among sons. In the performance of funeral rites, all perform with equal efficacy, the *manes* of the dead giving no preference, either to the first born, or to the eldest son. As in Roman law, the property of the *propositus* descends to all the heirs, as a universal succession, and primogeniture, as a factor, has vanished from the Hindu *formula* of descent. But though primogeniture has disappeared, as a rule of descent, in *ordinary* Hindu law, it nevertheless prevails as an *exceptional* rule of inheritance in certain classes of estates. Generally speaking, all *impartible* estates descend to the eldest male, since, being impartible, they must of necessity pass to a sole heir, and that heir is almost *always* the eldest male of the family. This mode of descent is attached to the incident of impartibility, the impartible estate being placed by analogy on the same footing as a Sovereign Raj, which invariably descends to the eldest son. The mode of descent of an impartible estate by primogeniture is conceived to be as follows:—It will descend to the eldest son, then to his eldest son and so on *in infinitum*. On failure of male issue, the estate will vest in the next collateral male heir. If there be none, it will escheat to the lord paramount unless there be an adoption.

It must, however, be borne in mind that, since descent by primogeniture is exceptional, it cannot therefore be *assumed* to exist in connection with *all* impartible estates. It must be proved, in each individual case, to exist as a *custom* of descent. In all civilised countries primogeniture is recognised rather as a *custom*, than as a *right*. In *England*, where perhaps primogeniture more largely prevails than elsewhere, it may be traced in the custom of making *strict* family settlements, by which the eldest son becomes the tenant in tail of the fee. Primogeniture, as it exists in *Europe*, is of feudal origin, and it owes its existence in the feudal world and in its present form, to the engrafting of the ideas of the later *Roman* jurisprudents upon the archaic notions which originally held families together. It is in fact, a more perfect development of the normal idea of primogeniture, under the influence of a refined system of jurisprudence. The origin of primogeniture in *Europe*, therefore, is traceable to the archaic form, which appears to have prevailed in the ancient world. In the oldest societies, whenever patriarchal power was not only *domestic*, but *political*, it invariably descended to the eldest *male*. No female was ever entrusted with such a position. Indeed, from the nature of the case she could not be. And the same archaic form of primogeniture exists among the Hindoos. All power and office among them invariably descends to the eldest male, even amongst the pettiest officials of their village communities. Under the gradual development of the feudal system, in Europe, the eldest male there by analogy to the patriarchaic chieftains, obtained a position of power and trust with reference to the family property. And under the full development of that system, from the position of a general manager of the family property, he became to be regarded as the absolute proprietor of the property he managed. The remains of this system are still visible in many parts of *Europe*, particularly in *England*, where it is traceable in the law of entail, as carried out in *strict* family settlements, as also in the general preference given to the eldest son. A good example of primogeniture as it prevailed in Europe is exhibited in the *Salic* law of *France*, under which no female could ever ascend the throne. *a*

Now, from the origin of the *custom* of primogeniture, it is perfectly clear that in a family in which the rule prevailed, no female could ever attain to this position of power and trust. It seems, however, to be a prevalent notion, in some quarters, that where the descent of an estate proceeds according to the rule of primogeniture, a female may enter in the line of heirs, and that primogeniture simply means *seniority by birth,* and is as applicable to *females*, as it is to *males.*

See argument of Counsel, 9 Bengal Reports, 234.

Allusion is also sometime made to the succession of females to landed estate in England, where primogeniture still prevails, in support of the above notion. In the first place, primogeniture, from the nature of the case can have no application to females at all. Primogeniture can only imply the primogeniture of *males.* In *England*, females do not succeed by right of primogeniture. There is no primogeniture amongst them, according to the Common Law, and the only instance in which it applies to females is in the case of the succession to the Crown, because the necessity of a sole and determinate succession is as great in the one sex, as the other and this was passed by special statute. (*Coke* upon *Littleton*, 165). According to English law, landed property vests first in males, who succeed by *right of* primogeniture: on failure of males, it vests in the females *equally,* and they share the estate between them as co-parceners. The only other case, besides the case of the Crown, in which a sole succession is permitted to females under English law, *but not by primogeniture,* is with regard to female dignities and titles of honor. As it is laid down by Littleton, If a man hold an Earldom to him and the heirs of his body and dies, leaving only daughters, the eldest

a See *Sir Henry Maine's* Ancient Law.

shall *not of course* be Countess; but the dignity is in suspense or abeyance, till the king shall declare his pleasure; for he being the fountain of honor, may confer it on which of them he pleases; and the one so selected, and her issue will continue to bear it. If, however, such issue become extinct, the title will again become in *abeyance,* unless there be a failure of issue of all the co-parceners, except one, in which last case, the descendant of that one will be entitled to claim the title (*Coke* upon *Littleton,* 165, *Mr. Hargreave's* note). Hence, it is clear that according to the Common Law of England, generally speaking, females have no connection whatever either with *primogeniture,* or with a *sole* succession. Again though primogeniture has taken deeper root in *England,* than it has in other European countries, it has, nevertheless, been virtually abolished. The *right* exists, and so does the *custom;* but the former may be defeated by will, and the latter is not binding. Primogeniture, as it exists among the landed gentry of *England,* is only a *custom,* and not a *right,* as illustrated by the *strict* settlement. When it is intended to tie up an old family estate, so as to prevent its leaving the family, the practice is to make a *strict* settlement, that is, to limit the estate after the death of the settler, to the first and other sons successively, according to seniority *in tail male,* charged with an annual sum by way of jointure to the wife, if she survives her husband, and with portions for the younger sons and daughters of the marriage. Under such an arrangement, no female can enter, and this is the offspring of that archaic form of primogeniture, by which, under the ancient law, political power descended to the eldest son, and which by analogy was made to apply under the feudal system to the inheritance of property.

This is the state of the case as to primogeniture in the Western world. In India, however, primogeniture has long ceased to be regarded as a *right.* And primogeniture, where it exists, exists only as a *custom,* and that only with reference to *impartible* estates, such as Principalities and ancient Zemindaries. In this mode of descent, the latter have been placed on the same footing as the former. Resembling the former in their *impartible* character and in their descent to a *sole* heir, generally speaking, like the former, they have descended by *custom* according to the rule of primogeniture. And naturally this would be so, for many of these ancient Zemindaries were nothing more than military fiefs, attached to the larger Principalities. But, though it is almost universally the practice for impartible estates so to descend, no *assumption* to that effect can be made even in the case of the larger Principality. In each case, the strictest proof is required of the *custom—a custom* long established and invariable,—and where this *custom* is not proved, the estate will descend according to the general Hindu law of Inheritance.

There are several instances in the Reports of impartible estates descending according to custom by primogeniture. The following are some of them. In 5 *Moore*, p. 169, there is the case of the *Rawutpore Raj.* This case is considered a good example of descent by primogeniture, according to Hindu law. Others appear in 7 *Moore*, 476; 9 *Moore*, 66; 10 *Moore*, 279; 12 *Moore*, 1, &c. Now in each and all of these cases, the *custom* of descent was alleged, and *proved* to have existed for many generations. See the arguments of the eminent counsel in these cases, in which is prominently and frequently urged the fact that, the estate, in each case, has descended according to the *custom of the country;* and according to the *custom of the family,* to the *eldest male by primogeniture.* The estates in these cases were all Ancient Rajs, that in 7 *Moore*, 476, being the well-known case of the *Tanjore Raj* of this Presidency, which was escheated for want of male heirs, when *Sir Charles Trevelyan* was Governor of *Madras.* Now, in each one of these cases, there is no single instance of a female entering into the line of heirs. *Sir Charles Trevelyan's* Minute in the case of the *Tanjore Raj*, is as follows:—

(*Extract from Minute.*)

Para. 4.—The *Rajah* had died leaving no legitimate or adopted son. The only claimant is his senior surviving widow. My first twelve years of public service were passed in the Indian Diplomatic department, and I have as extensive a knowledge of the customs and practice of Native Chiefs as most people. I mention this as my justification for offering a confident opinion, that *the succession of females, forms no part of the constitution of Native States or Chiefships.* It may occasionally have taken place, as in the instance of *Holkar's* widow, *Ashalaya Bhai*, and the *Begum Sumroo*, but the special nature of the circumstances in those cases, shows that it was a deviation from an established rule. No well-informed and impartial native would maintain the right of succession of a female to a Hindu *Raj.*

Para. 5.—I therefore consider that whether regard be had to the customs of the country, or to the public good; this is a true escheat. The so-called *Tanjore Raj* has lapsed to the Government of India. That Government stands in the place of the late *Rajah*. While we are bound to fulfil his just obligations, it is our duty to secure, on behalf of the public, everything belonging to the *Raj* not required for that purpose.

It is alleged, however, that the cases above cited, are examples of a *special* custom of descent and do not apply to the present case. But it is submitted that these are examples of descent by *primogeniture,* and the succession to the *Shivagungah* estate has been determined by the Rule of Primogeniture. Is the rule to be different in one case from one it is in another? The rule of descent is spoken of in the above cases as tho *custom of the country*, that is the general custom. Is there a *special,* as well as a *general* custom of descent by primogeniture? Examples, however, of what may be properly called a *special custom* of descent in these estates also occur in the books. The case of the *Tirhoot Raj,* (6 *Moore,* 164) where the reigning Raja always abdicated shortly before his death in favor of his eldest son is such a case. So is the use of the *Tipperah Raj,* (12 *Moore,* 542) Here a *Jobraj* (*juvenis rex*) and a *Burrah Thakore* were always appointed in the lifetime of the reigning Raja, on whose death the former ascended the *gadi,* and the latter became *Jobraj.* But, even in these cases, no female is allowed to ascend the throne. From these facts it is clear that, in India, where an estate descends according to the Rule of Primogeniture, no female can enter the line of heirs, and where she does, the estate does not descend by primogeniture, but by the general Hindu law of inheritance.

From the books, too, it would appear that there are three kinds of impartible estates. There is first, the real Ancient Raj or Principality proper; secondly, the estate in *the nature* of an Ancient Raj; and thirdly, the estate which is impartible by *consent.* This last kind of estate is, strictly speaking, not impartible, since it becomes divisible at the option of the co-parceners. It is only with the two first, however, that we have to do. The rule of descent in the first class of estates is *almost* invariably by primogeniture; and in the second, it is generally so, but not universally. And it is submitted that the Zemindary *of Shivagungah* (9 *Moore,* 536) is an example of the second class, and that it is a case of an impartible estate descending according to the general Hindu law of Inheritance, and not by primogeniture. The history of this Zemindary has already been recited, and from it, it clearly appears in the first place that it is not an *ancient* Zemindary, and that no rule of descent prevails in it, except that it has always descended to a *sole* heir. As to its antiquity, it was originally created in 1730, under the Carnatic Sovereignty, it is true, but it became an escheat to the East India Company in 1792 for want of heirs. It had, in fact, lost its individuality, and its very existence as a Zemindary. In 1801 it was re-granted by Lord Clive to the first Istimrar Zemindar, who had no claim whatever to the estate, and a new sunnud was granted to him. The terms of the Proclamation declare the hereditary right to the succession to be extinct, and that the Zemindary of *Shivagungah*, upon the principles on which it was erected into a Zemindary, had positively escheated to the State from which it derived protection; from this declaration, *a new order of things has sprung up;* all claims to succession were set aside and it was *optional* with the Government to select or not, as they thought proper, any person for the Zemindary. The *new* creation of the estate as a Zemindary has also been alluded to, at least twice, by the *Privy Council* in their judgments. In 12 *Moore,* 1, a contrast is drawn by them between the state of facts existing in connection with the *Hunsapore Raj* in Northern India, and that connected with the *Shivagungah* Zemindary. The former was declared by them to be an *old* estate, in opposition to the latter which was not. They have likewise done so in their judgment reported in 13 *Moore,* 333. In this latter judgment, the *Shivagungah* Zemindary is expressly called a *new* estate. So far, therefore, as the antiquity of the *Shivagungah* Zemindary is concerned, it is plain that it is not an ancient estate, and there is therefore no presumption which perhaps might arise in the case of an *Ancient* Zemindary, that it descended by the Rule of Primogeniture. As to the descent itself no *custom* of descent is alluded to in the plaint, but a *rule* is spoken of, which is about the same thing. In the previous plaint in the declaration case, a *custom* is expressly mentioned. In the present suit no evidence was given to prove a custom. On the other hand, from the admitted facts, it was quite clear there was no custom of descent by primogeniture, either before the creation of the patent in 1801, or ever after. Afterwards there could not possibly have been a rule established, for the Estate was involved in litigation almost immediately on the death of the Zemindar in 1829. After his death, the Estate was seized by usurpers, who were declared to have had no right whatever to it, and the Zemindary was given to the late Rani, on the ground that it was her father's self-acquisition and she became the second Zemindar of *Shivagungah*. It is difficult, therefore, to see upon what ground the Rule of Primogeniture was made to apply. And the application of the Rule appears the more extraordinary, when it is considered that the rival claimants are grandsons by different mothers. It seems to have been assumed that the *right* of primogeniture prevails under Hindu law, just as it does under English law, and that the eldest grandson succeeds in the same way as an eldest son would succeed to the landed estate of an intestate Englishman. But, for the reasons above submitted, it would appear that this is a misapplication of the Rule, so far at least, as it concerns this country.

It was suggested, as a difficulty, that if this was not the correct interpretation of the Rule the Estate being impartible, and descending to a class of heirs under Hindu law, how was it to go, if it did not go to the eldest of that class? In the first place, it is submitted that, when an impartible estate does not descend by primogeniture, or by any special custom, it is liable under certain circumstances to lose its impartible character, and to become partible. The facts connected with the present succession to the *Shivagungah* Estate would constitute such a set of circumstances. The Estate could be divided, supposing no other questions were involved between the rival grandsons. According to Hindu law, a king might divide his kingdom between his sons, just in the same way as he might, and always does give it to his eldest son. If an impartible estate might escheat altogether, and vest in a stranger, on failure of male heirs, what possible objection can there be to a division, if circumstances demanding it should arise? There are examples of even ancient estates having been divided, and the *Shivagungah* Zemindary therefore, which is by no means an ancient Zemindary, might be divided between the rival claimants, that is, of course, if there were not other grounds, upon which the Rani's son might claim the estate in its entirety. The fact is, in applying the rule of Primogeniture as it has been applied, the English law of real property has been tacitly resorted to. The right of Primogeniture has been assumed to exist under Hindu law, as it does under English law. The *Istimrar* Zemindar is regarded as the last full owner (or as *Benjamin Brown*, the purchaser), the Rani as tenant for life, and the heir is looked for in the same way, as any English Conveyancer would search for the next heir to the landed estate of an intestate Englishman. It is not difficult to see how this has happened. Cases of Hindu law are conducted by English lawyers, and they have insensibly allowed their ideas of Hindu law to run into English grooves. English terms of real property law abound in the Indian Reports. One perpetually stumbles upon such expressions as *estates for life—estates in remainder, vested inheritances*, and *full owners* in reported cases. We have unconsciously imported the principles of our own law into our discussions of Hindu law. It is the tendency of the English mind to make everything English with which it comes in contact. We apply English principles to Hindu mortgages, we have supplanted the Hindu law of Contracts by the Indian Contract Act; and Hindu wills are interpreted according to English rules of construction. We are extending the reform in every direction. The only things we have not touched are Adoption, Marriage, and the *status* of Hindu women—the two former from the nature of the case we are compelled to leave alone, and the last we refrain from improving from a fashion we have of pandering to native prejudices and opinions.

In the present case, the English law of real property has been applied to the *Shivagungah* Zemindary. The Zemindar has been placed in the position of an intestate Englishman, and the Estate has been made to descend according to the *right*, instead of according to the *custom* of primogeniture. The *right* of primogeniture does not exist in India, and the *custom* in this particular case has not been proved. The Estate has, therefore, been illegally decreed to the plaintiff.

As to the next question, namely, the nature of the estate taken by a *daughter* inheriting from her *father*, and which merges into the more general question as to the kind of property which constitutes *Stridhanum*, or woman's property, the following observations are submitted :—

The Zemindary descended to the Rani from her father, and in so devolving it either still retained its character as *ancestral* estate, or in the devolution, it became the *Stridhanum* of the late Rani. If it was the former, it would descend to her son, if there was no other claimant, if the latter, it would pass to her daughters, as her next heirs. The question of *Stridhanum* will be presently discussed, but we have now to see, supposing the property to be ancestral, whether the late Rani took an absolute estate according to Hindu law, so as to enable her to transmit the same to her son, the first defendant, in preference to the plaintiff, and thus to override the right of primogeniture. Or, in other words, are the rights of the plaintiff and the first defendant so evenly balanced that the right of primogeniture can be made to apply, and turn the scale in favor of the plaintiff? If they were both grandsons by the same mother, their rights would be *primâ facie* equal, and, if the right of primogeniture existed, there would be no doubt that the plaintiff would be entitled to succeed. But they are grandsons by different mothers, and the Zemindary having never vested in the plaintiff's mother, from whom alone he could derive his title, the *status* of the rival claimants is not the same, and the right of primogeniture cannot apply.

This involves the question of the rights of the daughter's son. The statement that the title of the plaintiff should be traced from his *mother*, and not from his grandfather, will no doubt be controverted, but the following observations on the subject are submitted.

Before however considering the rights of the daughter's son, let us discuss the nature of the estate taken by a daughter, inheriting from her father. Supposing the property in its descent to her still to retain its ancestral character, and not to become *Stridhanum*, does she, when she inherits, take a limited estate, like the widow, or does she take an estate, as absolute as that taken by a son under Hindu law? In reply it may at once be stated that, supposing the property not to become *Stridhanum* in its descent, a daughter inheriting from her father takes an estate similar to that of a son, and that she transmits the same by representation to *her* son, just as the son's estate is transmitted by him to *his* son.

It is submitted that there is ample authority to support this proposition. *Vrihaspati* says: As a son, so does the daughter of a man proceed from his several limbs. How then should any other person take her father's wealth? Again *Devala* says: To an unmarried daughter a nuptial portion must be given out of the estate of the father; and his own daughter lawfully begotten shall take like a son, the estate of him who leaves no male issue. So *Nareda:* If there be no son, the daughter is *heiress* by parity of reason: for she keeps up the progeny, since a son and a daughter both continue the race of their fathers. So *Menu:* The son of a man is even as himself, and the daughter is equal to the son: how then can any other inherit his property but his daughter, who is, as it were, himself? And *Misra* in his commentary on these texts says: It should not be argued that all this relates to the daughter who has been appointed to raise up issue for her father, and that the term "not appointed" in the text of *Vrihaspati* relates to her who is selected by an implied intention without a formal declaration. It is ordained by *Menu* that if a son exist, such a daughter shall have an equal share with him. Upon this *Jagannatha* remarks, Consequently, a daughter, though not appointed to raise up issue to her father, shall inherit, as appears from the terms "him who left no male issue." Are not those terms employed to show that she takes the whole estate of him who leaves no son born in lawful wedlock; for the texts relating to the succession of a daughter, and of her son are delivered by *Menu* among precepts relative to an appointed daughter? Since he has propounded no separate law concerning the claim of a daughter, these texts must be taken as intending by implication the succession of daughters *in general.* It should not be objected that their right of inheritance is not ordained by codes of law. The text of *Yajnawalkya* expressing "this rule concerning the heritage of him who has gone to heaven leaving no male issue extends to all classes," declares the succession of a daughter to the estate of him who leaves no son, begotten or adopted, neither one born in lawful wedlock, nor an appointed daughter or the like; and the text of *Vishnu* conveys the same implied sense. According to the opinion of those who contend that the son of the appointed daughter becomes the adoptive son of her father, there is no difference whatever between an appointed daughter and any other female offspring. As the producer also of a son who presents the funeral cake with equal efficacy with the son's son, she has a title to the inheritance, although the *Mitakshara* controverts this idea and urges that she takes in her own right and without reference to her son. From all the texts it is apparent therefore, that she is placed by the sages on the same footing as a son. She obtains ownership in the property, like the son, by *birth.* Against this array of texts of the ancient lawyers is placed a passage in the *Dayabhaga,* Chapter II, Section 2, para. 30, to the effect that since it had been shown that, on the decease of the widow in whom the succession had vested, the legal heirs of the former owner, who would regularly inherit his property, if there were no widow, in whom the succession vested, namely, the daughters and the rest, succeed to the wealth; therefore the same rule (concerning the succession of the former possessor's next heirs) is inferred *à fortiori,* in the case of the daughter and grandson, whose pretensions are *inferior* to the wife's. This text, *Jagannatha* admits, is *not* supported by any legislator, or commentators, but it appears, he says, to have met with the approval of many lawyers—a very vague and ambiguous statement, for nothing further is said as to who these lawyers are, or where their approval is to be found. On the strength of this isolated and dubious text in the *Dayabhaga,* the exponent of the Bengal School, the rights of the daughters, so highly respected by Hindu sages, have been annihilated with one fell swoop. Further, this text has been made applicable to the case of daughters in Southern India as well, and it appears to have received the sanction of the very highest Court of Appeal, (see 2, Indian Appeals, 113). The arbitrary statement at the close of the text, as to the inferiority of the daughter's position to that of the widows is nowhere supported by a single *sloka.* It is a pure assumption of *Jimuta Vahana's,* quite in accordance with his Mahomedan notions of women's rights. *Mr. Norton,* too, in his *Leading Cases,* Vol. II, has shown that this inferiority is simply imaginary, and is based on the fact that the daughter stands *next* in the order of heirs after the widow, there being no son. It is submitted, therefore, that there is ample authority for the position that, the daughter takes as a son, and that therefore, like the son, she is capable of transmitting the estate to *her* son, who like her presents with efficacy the funeral cake. The analogy drawn by Hindu lawyers between the daughter and the son is very striking. And it is only by a strained commentary on these texts, that their meaning has been simply tortured and twisted into something diametrically opposite, in order to suit the particular views of the commentator's school.

With regard to the daughter's son also, his position is defined with equal clearness by the sages. *Menu* says in the well known texts. By that male child whom a daughter, whether formally appointed or not, shall produce for a husband of an equal class, the maternal grandfather becomes the grandsire of a son's son: let that son give the funeral oblation and possess the inheritance. So also *Vishnu:* If a man leave neither son, nor son's son (nor wife, nor female issue), the daughters, son shall take his wealth. For in regard to the obsequies of ancestor's, daughter's sons are considered as son's sons. And as son's sons inherit by right of *representation,* so also do daughters' sons inherit from their mothers by the same right. The proposition, therefore, that is contended for, and which shall be stated at the outset is, that daughters' sons take *per stirpes* and not *per capita,* and that the only case in which daughters' sons take *per capita,* is when their mothers have *pre-deceased* their grandfather. There are authorities of weight on each side of the question. Among the writers who support the former doctrine are *Sir Thomas Strange, Mr. Justice Strange,* and Messrs. *West* and *Buhler.* This is no mean array. The principal authority on the other side is *Sir W. H. Macnaghten,* a Bengal writer. And he maintains this view apparently from the alleged fact that *Jagannatha,* whom *Sir Thomas Strange* cites in support of the former, really maintains the latter view. Now it is only due to the memory of *Sir Thomas Strange* to say that, he is a singularly accurate author, and, up to the present time, no one, except *Sir W. H. Macnaghten,* (and, very recently, *Mr. Sham Churn Sirkar* of Bengal) has ever found any errors in his work. It is curious, therefore, that in this particular instance the late Chief Justice should be found nodding.

The passage in question occurs in *Colebrooke's Digest*, vol. 2, 549, 3rd edition, in the commentary to *Sloka* CCCCXXII of *Vrihaspati*: "On failure of them (sons of daughters) uterine brothers and sons of brothers, kinsmen bearing the same family name, pupils, and learned priests are entitled to possess the estate." It runs thus: "Again if daughter's sons be numerous, a distribution must be made. In that case, if there be two sons of one daughter, and three of another, five equal shares must be allotted: they shall not first divide the estate into two parts and afterwards allot one share to each son; *for such a mode of distribution is only ordained in partition among the sons of sons, and the reasoning is not equal for a son's son, whose own father is dead, receives a share from his uncle; but the daughter's son whose mother is deceased, does not receive a share from his mother's sister.*" Now, it is submitted that, this applies to the sole case, where the daughters (the sons' mothers) have pre-deceased their father, that is, the sons' grandfather. This is evident from the context, and the commentary itself. The preceding *Sloka* CCCCXXI thus runs: VISHNU.—"On failure of sons, and of their male issue, *the sons of daughters* shall obtain the property, for the male offspring of a son and of a daughter are equally qualified to perform obsequies for men of all classes." The *Sloka* previous to this relates to the inheritance of daughters, and is as follows; DEVALA.—"To unmarried daughters, a nuptial portion must be given out of the estate of the father: and his own daughter lawfully begotten shall take, *like a son*, the estate of him who leaves no male issue." This clearly shows that *Jagannatha* was discussing the right of daughter's sons to succeed sons in the *absence* of daughters, at the time of the devolution of the ancestral estate, as for instance, where the latter had all pre-deceased their father. This is further evident from the commentary on p. 548, on *Sloka* CCCCXXII, where he says: "Consequently on *failure* of the givers of a principal funeral cake, namely, the son, the son's son, and the son of such a grandson, *the daughter's son*, who gives a secondary funeral cake in the double set of oblations is heir; that is propounded as confirmed by the reason of the law." Again, from the portion in italics of the commentary under discussion, this is still further evident. For a comparison is drawn by *Jagannatha* between a partition among son's sons and daughter's sons. And he says that there is a slight difference between the position of son's sons and that of daughter's sons. He urges that so thoroughly does the right of representation exist among sons and son's sons, that when the sons die even before the vesting of the inheritance, the son's sons stand in their places, and obtain their shares from their uncles on partition; therefore they take *per stirpes* and not *per capita.* But this right of representation he argues does not exist *to that extent* among daughters and their sons, unless the inheritance has actually vested in the daughters. But, if the inheritance has vested in the daughters, then the son represents his mother, and inherits her share in preference to her sister. It is the inference that fairly follows from *Jaggannatha's* commentary, and it is clear that *Sir Thomas Strange* was right in citing the commentary in support of this doctrine that daughter's sons ordinarily take *per stirpes,* and not *per capita.*

This will also become the more apparent if it is remembered, as laid down in *Jagannatha's* previous commentary to *Sloka* CCCCXX, p. 547, already cited, to the effect that "if the daughters be numerous, a distribution is made. Such is their succession." Now, if this is read with the commentary under discussion, it will become still clearer that *Sir Thomas Strange* is right, and *Sir W. H. Macnaghten* wrong. For if the daughters having inherited, can divide, surely in the name of common sense, the sons of each will succeed to the share of their mother's estate, that is, they will inherit *per stirpes* and not *per capita.* To prove still further that succession *per capita* is the exception, and not the rule with regard to the inheritance of daughter's sons, let us take a *reductio ad absurdum* case. Say A. B. and C. are daughters (each having sons), who have inherited ancestral estate, and have divided. After division, we will suppose that A. B. and C. have gone to live in different parts of the country which, of course, it is quite open to them to do. Let us say A. goes to Poona, B. to Calcutta, and C. remains in Madras, where the division took place. A dies, and according to *Sir W. H. Macnaghten,* her property will go by *survivorship* to her sisters, supposing them to be equally qualified. Her son does not inherit. Then B. dies, and her property instead of going to her son, vests in C.; C. then dies. Now of course a division takes place *per capita* amongst the sons. How is this division to be effected, the sons living so far apart? Surely in reason after daughters have divided, which they have a right to do, their respective shares descend to the sons of each. And, doubtless, *Sir Thomas Strange* had not only the particular commentary in dispute in view, but the commentary on the preceding *Slokas* as well, when he made the statement that daughters' sons ordinarily succeed *per stirpes* and not *per capita.* And it is submitted that this doctrine is correct, supported as it is in addition by such names as *Mr. Justice Strange* and *Messrs. West* and *Buhler.* *

The right of daughters to divide however may be disputed. But it is difficult though to see how it can be, when *Jagannatha* the great commentator of the *Bengal* School admits it—the school that is generally so much opposed to the freedom of women. The *Vyavahara Mayukha* (*Stokes'* edition, p. 86) also maintains the same, and the *Mayukha* is more or less an interpretation of the *Mitakshara.* In the *Mitakshara* there is nothing at all said about it, but it is a proposition that is almost self-evident. For if daughters by analogy are placed on the footing of sons, and sons unquestionably can divide, so can daughters; otherwise what would become of the analogy?

With regard to the sisters of daughters taking before the sons of the latter, when the estate has vested in them, there do not appear to be many decisions. The Privy Council in a judgment (2 Indian Appeals 113,) which will presently be noticed, allude to but one Bengal case on the subject. That was the case of *Boidyanath Sett* v. *Durga Churn Barak.* This case, however, does not show whether the daughter, whose estate passed to her surviving childless sister, had or had not sons. It would appear she had none. If so, the case is no authority at all upon the question. It is admitted, however, on all hands, that there is one case in Bengal, in which survivorship does not exist among daughters, but that the inheritance goes to the *son* instead. That is the case in which a daughter, who is unmarried at the time she succeeds to the inheritance, afterwards marries and has

* *Sir Thomas Strange* repeats the same doctrine again at p. 145. It is curious he should have made the blunder *twice.*

a son, the son succeeds in preference to his mother's sister. This is said to be an *exception*, and an exception which proves the general rule alleged to be otherwise. It is submitted, however, that this is not an exception, but is rather an *illustration* of the rule that daughters' sons take *per stirpes*, and not *per capita*. In the first place there seems to be no direct authority for the position that daughters' sons ordinarily take *per capita*, except the disputed commentary of *Jagannatha*, said to be misquoted by *Sir Thomas Strange*. *Mr. Justice Strange*, too, in noticing the various points of difference between the *Mitakshara* and the *Dayabhaga*, does not mention that in Bengal daughters' son's take *per capita*, and not *per stirpes*. Indeed, on the other hand, some Bengal text writers lay it down absolutely that daughters' sons succeed, *jure representationis*, to the inheritance of their mothers, in preference to their mother's sisters.

The exception above referred to is supported, it is said, by a passage in the *Dayakrama Sangraha*, Section 3, para. 3. Para. 2 says that the unmarried daughter is first entitled to the succession. *Parasara* declares: "Let a maiden daughter take the heritage of one, who dies leaving no male issue; or if there be no such daughter, a married one shall inherit." Then Para. 3 says: The following *special* rule must be here observed, namely, that, if a *maiden* daughter in whom the succession *had once vested*, and who was *subsequently married*, should die without having borne issue, the married sister, who has, and the sister who is likely to have male issue, inherit together the estate which had so vested in her. It does not become the property of her husband, or others, *for their right is exclusively to a woman's separate property* (*Stridhanum.*) But if she bear a son, then, according to the analogy of the appointed daughter, as laid down by *Jagannatha*, though that son die, the estates passes to her *husband*, and not to her sisters. That is to say, the birth of a son prevents the property passing to her sisters after her death, and even if that son should die, instead of the property going to her sisters, it goes to her husband, as if it were her *Stridhanum*. There does not appear to be any authority stating in direct terms that the property will pass to her son, and not to the sisters, according to the ordinary rule, but that is the inference drawn, and from this inference it is argued that this is an exception to the ordinary rule, and that the ordinary rule is otherwise. The basis, therefore, for this forming an exception and not an illustration of the rule, as contended for, is exceedingly slender. It is submitted that the object of the special, or rule of importance in the mind of the writer was, to show that such property does not descend as *Stridhanum*, that is to say, that it does not constitute woman's peculiar property. The independence of women is the great bugbear of the Bengal School, and the author fearing that this might be considered *Stridhanum* is anxious to show that it is not. The reason is not far to seek. For the woman receives the property *from her father in his house before her marriage, and when she marries it passes with her to her husband.* There would be a likelihood therefore that such property would be regarded as her *Stridhanum*, and pass on her death without issue to her husband as heir. To prevent this misapprehension seems to have been the anxiety of the writer, and hence the *special* rule to which he draws attention. He does not say that the property would pass to her *son* if he lived, which he would have done, if he wanted to show that such a descent formed an exception to the ordinary rule of descent of property from a daughter. He only takes care to say that it does not pass as *Stridhanum* to the *husband.* There is a precisely similar provision with regard to the *widow* in the same author. *Dayakrama Sangraha*, Chapter I, Section 2, para. 1, says: In default of the grandson and great-grandson, the widow succeeds to the estate, in conformity with the text of *Yajnawalkya.* The wife and the daughters, also both parents, brothers likewise, and their sons, gentiles, cognates, a pupil, and a fellow student. On failure of the first among these, the next in order is indeed heir to the estate of one, who departed for heaven, leaving no male issue. This rule extends to all classes.

Para. 2.—*Here however a particular rule is to be observed, viz.:*

Para. 3.—The wife is only to *enjoy* the estate of her deceased husband. She must not make a gift, mortgage, or sale of it. So *Katyayana* declares let the childless widow, preserving unsullied the bed of her lord, and abiding with her venerable protector, enjoy with moderation the property until her death. After her, let the *heirs* take it. Here also the anxiety exhibits itself to limit the woman's estate, which is the favorite pastime of the writers of the Bengal School.

Further another idea suggests itself. It is very curious that the Bengal School should in the case of the descent of property be so partial to *survivorship* as represented. The Bengal law rather favours the doctrine of *representation* than that of *survivorship.* In this respect it goes further than the law in Madras. For it permits a widow in an undivided family to inherit the estate of her husband, dying without male issue, in preference to the male co-parceners. Here the widow's right of inheritance is made to override that of *survivorship* among males. It is anomalous therefore, to say the least, that, it should tolerate it among daughters, when such daughters have sons, whose claim to their mother's property is quite as strong, in fact stronger than that of a widow to her husband's. Again, in Bengal the daughter is of less account than her son. She confers less spiritual benefits than he does. She succeeds *because* she produces a son, who confers spiritual benefits superior to hers, and equal to those of a son's son. Yet, according to the popular theory although that son is born, her property does not descend to him, but to his mother's sister, who is considerably inferior to him. Surely this entirely conflicts with the idea which pervades the whole Bengal law of inheritance, namely, that it is the efficacy of the funeral cake which decides the right to inherit. It is curious too that all the authorities cited in connection with the rights of the daughter's son are from Bengal, that is, with regard to the supersession of his rights in favour of his mother's sisters. There is not a syllable in the *Mitakshara,* that favours the doctrine. In Chapter II, Section 2, para. 6, occurs this passage: By the import of the particle "also" (Section 7, para. 2) the daughter's son succeeds to the estate *on failure of daughters.* Thus *Vishnu* says: If a man leave neither son, nor son's son nor (wife nor female) issue, the son (daughter's son) shall take his wealth. For in regard to the obsequies of ancestors, daughters' sons are considered as son's sons. *Menu* likewise declares. By that male child whom a daughter, whether formally appointed or not, shall produce from a husband of an equal class, the maternal grandfather becomes the grandsire of a son's son: let that son give the funeral oblation and possess the inheritance. The Bengal authorities are the *Dayabhaga*, Chapter XI, Section 2, and the *Dayakrama Sangraha,* Section 4. Paras. 23 to 25 of the former are as follows:—But *Govinda Raja,* in his commentary on *Menu,* states the claim of the daughter's son, as preferable to that of the married daughter on the grounds of the following passage of *Vishnu:* If one die leaving neither son, nor grandson, the daughter's son shall inherit the estate, by consent of all, the son's son, and the daughter's son are alike in respect of the celebration of obsequies.

Para. 24.—This does not appear to us satisfactory, for it contradicts the text above cited, (para. 8.)

Para. 25.—But *in default* of a married daughter, such as above described, the succession assuredly devolves on the daughter's son notwithstanding the existence of the father and other kinsmen.

The *Dayakrama Sangraha*, Section 4, is to the same effect. Para. 1, says: *In default of all daughters* (who are entitled to succeed) the daughter's son takes the inheritance, according to the text. Let the daughter's son take the whole estate of his own father who leaves no (other) son, and let him offer two funeral oblations—one to his own father, the other to his maternal grandfather, and other texts of alike import: "Of his own father" here means his mother's father. Seeing "no (other) sons" is here used indefinitely *to signify a failure of heirs* including the daughter, otherwise it would contradict the text of *Yajnawalkya*.

The text of *Yajnawalkya* is in Section 2, para. 1, namely, the wife and the daughters also with parents, brothers, likewise other sons, gentiles, cognates, a pupil and a fellow student. *On failure of the first among these, the next in order* is indeed heir to the estate of one who departed for heaven leaving no male issue. This will extend to all classes.

Para. 2, says: The opinion maintained by *Govinda Raja*, namely, that on failure of a son, (grandson and great-grandson) the daughter's son is entitled to the inheritance notwithstanding the existence of the daughter, is consequently refuted by the text above quoted.

Upon these texts *Sir Thomas Strange* remarks:—Where there are sons, their right of succession is postponed to that of other daughters of the deceased, and where such sons are numerous, when they do take, they take *per stirpes* and not *per capita*.

Now it is submitted that these texts are no authority for the doctrine that survivorship subsists among daughters when they have sons, that is, that the estate goes to the sisters in preference to the daughter's sons. The texts simply give the *order* of heirs. First, the daughters unmarried or married, then on failure of them, the daughter's sons succeed. That is to say, if at the time of the death of the father, a daughter and the son of a deceased daughter happen to exist, the former would inherit before the latter; on failure of the one, the other succeeds. They are no authority for the position that the son of a daughter, in whose mother, a portion of the inheritance has vested, will, on his mother's death, have his right to his mother's share postponed, and that his mother's share will pass to his mother's sister. If this be the meaning of the authorities, then the passage above cited from *Sir Thomas Strange* would be simply contradictory. For the daughter's, sons could not be said to take *per stirpes* if their mothers' shares passed to their mothers' sisters, instead of to them in the first instance. It is hardly possible that so astute and accurate a writer, as the late Chief Justice, would place such contradictory statements side by side. This view of the case is further confirmed by the fact that there is also an analogous case in the succession of brother's sons, who, when they take through their fathers, take *per stirpes*, but who, when the inheritance devolves upon them alone as *nephews* take *per capita* as daughters' sons do when their mothers have predeceased their grandfather. (*Macnaghten*, 27, *2nd edition*; see also *Strange* 145). The proposition contended for therefore is that, if a man die leaving daughters and sons by each, the share of each daughter will vest in her sons, in preference to her sister, that is in other words that her sons take *per stirpes*, or by right of representation. And this proposition is inevitable, if it be admitted, that the daughters have the power to divide the inheritance, and this power they undoubtedly have, according to the very authorities upon which the Courts have proceeded, in deciding upon the rights of their sons.

There is no doubt that there is a great weight of authority against this proposition, owing doubtless to the fact that *Sir W. H. Macnaghten's* statement has been taken unquestioned. Very recently there has been a decision of the Privy Council (2 *Indian Appeals*, 113) to the effect that, a daughter's son is not entitled by Hindu law to succeed as heir to his maternal grand-father's estate, so long as any daughters not disqualified, or in whom a right of inheritance has once vested, survives. And that although a daughter who is a childless widow is incompetent, according to the *Bengal* School, to take by inheritance from her father, yet where two daughters have already succeeded jointly by inheritance to their father's estate, and at the death of one of them, the survivor is a childless widow, the latter will nevertheless take by *survivorship* the whole estate. Her disqualification to inherit existing at the death of her sister, does not destroy the heritable right which has once vested, nor the right of succession by survivorship to her sister which is incident thereto. And their Lordships observe that there is a great analogy between the case of widows and that of daughters taking by inheritance, *though the pretension of daughters is inferior to that of widows.**

With the greatest possible deference to their Lordships, it is submitted that there is no analogy between the case of the widow and that of the daughter. Under the *Mitakshara*, doubtless, in its breadth of view, as to the rights of women, no distinction has been drawn between widows and other women, as to the inheritance of property. This will presently be referred to under the question of *Stridhanum*. But since the Courts have to a great extent if not totally, ignored the view of the *Mitakshara*, as to a woman's inheritance, and have indulged in wire-drawn speculations, as to the grounds upon which women inherit at all, it will be necessary in this argument to show that a daughter inherits upon grounds quite different from those of the widow. The alleged inferiority of the daughter to the widow has already been disposed of.

Now the key to the right of the woman's inheritance, according to judicial apprehension, may be discovered in 11 *Moore's Indian Appeals*, 487, in the judgment in the case of *Bugwandeen Debia* v. *Myna Boye*. In the course of that judgment, their Lordships observe that, the estate of two widows who take their husbands' property by inheritance is one estate. The right of survivorship is so strong that the survivor takes the whole property, even to the exclusion of daughters of the deceased widow. They are, therefore, in the strictest sense co-parceners, and one widow cannot alienate any portion of the estate, without the consent of the other. And this principle has been applied to daughters. But it is submitted

* This case proceeds entirely upon Bengal law.

however, that though this condition may exist with regard to the widow, from the texts already cited as to the daughter, and from the analogy she bears to the son, it is clear that she takes as a son, *in her own right*, and not on the principle of survivorship. Survivorship is a creature of the English law, and although it has been very generally recognised, as the rule of succession among Hindu co-parceners, yet according to *Dr. Burnell*, it is a principle entirely foreign to the Hindu law. However this may be, it seems certain that it does not regulate the succession among daughters. Indeed, the application of the term co-parceners, even to widows, is inappropriate. And it only shows the random manner in which English law terms have been employed to describe Hindu estates, and Hindu persons. Now it is held that generally speaking under Hindu law, widows have not the right to divide. And yet they are declared in the strictest sense to be co-parceners. But it is an incident of co-parcenery under English law that co-parceners have the right to divide without mutual consent, that is the peculiarity of their position. How comes the term then to be applied to widows at all? Where a man leaves several widows they are said to succeed him as joint tenants, and as one heir, with rights of survivorship. But even joint tenants may sever their estate. The application of these terms therefore to Hindu estates conveys very inaccurately the actual condition of things. And there is no doubt that the application, or rather misapplication of these terms has led to mischief. The term co-parceners having been applied to widows succeeding their husbands, the right of survivorship followed, and the extension of the terms to daughters became at once easy and natural. The males are co-parceners with rights of survivorship, so by analogy must be the females. The amount of injury we have been inflicting upon the natives of this country by unconsciously, perhaps, engrafting upon their jurisprudence, ideas borrowed from English law, must be considerable. Of course, as we have removed women from the position they had under the ancient law, we have been obliged to make a law of our own for them. This law seems to consist of the feudal law of real property, more or less engrafted on the Hindu law. We call widows co-parceners, but then co-parceners may divide, whereas women can never possess property as their own by inheritance, so they must not be allowed to divide. But what text of Hindu law is there prohibiting widows from dividing? This however brings us back to the fact that the Courts have determined to carry out in its literal sense the text of *Menu*, that women are never fit for independence, and have therefore ignored the provisions of the *Mitakshara* on the inheritance of women.

But supposing the mischief to have been done with regard to the rights of widows, this is no reason for spreading it further by extending the analogy to daughters. It has not yet been laid down by the Privy Council that widows and daughters of Hindoos in Southern India are on the same footing. There arises therefore the opportunity for accurately deciding upon their relative rights. Does the Hindu law place daughters in the position of sons is the only question for decision. The texts on this subject are explicit. Let these texts be decided upon on their merits without any forced analogies drawn from other sources, and without the aid of dubious commentaries. If the daughter takes as a son then, like the son she transmits the estate to *her* son by representation, which principle will and must override any imaginary rule of survivorship, supposed to exist from the analogy to widows. The point is simple, and materials exist in abundance for its decision. There seems no reason, therefore, why a strictly accurate decision may not be formed upon such materials. If the view contended for be correct, the Shivagungah Zemindary will then descend to the first defendant, as the son of the late Rani, in preference to the plaintiff, the son of her deceased sister and in whose mother the estate never vested. As to the next question, whether or not the estate taken by a daughter inheriting from her father, in its devolution becomes the daughter's *Stridhanum*, or peculiar property, the following observations are submitted :—

There can be no doubt in the first place that, there is a strong tendency in the Courts to circumscribe, rather than enlarge the estate possessed by a woman. One of the most important decisions on the subject is that of the *Privy Council*, reported in 11 *Moore*, 487, in which it is categorically laid down in a case that arose in Bengal under the *Benares* law, that no property movable or immovable inherited by a woman from her husband forms her *Stridhanum*. She may alienate the *movable* during her lifetime, but not the immovable property, and both descend to the reversioners after her death. In nearly all the cases indeed in which the estate inherited by a woman has been declared not to be her *Stridhanum*, the person inheriting has been a widow. Her case has been selected as a sort of model for the decision of the others. In Bengal, of course, where a woman seems to be in a position little better than a slave, and where the greatest restrictions are placed upon her powers of alienation, and so forth, it has long been held that no estate inherited by any woman forms her *Stridhanum*. In Bombay, the Courts are more liberal, and in their interpretation of the *Mitakshara*, they hold that all property *inherited* by a woman, with certain limitations as to alienation, forms her *Stridhanum*. The Madras Courts, however, seem inclined to follow the Bengal School and rigidly to limit the *quantum* of a woman's estate to a mere life-tenancy.

The position of Hindu women in these modern times does not seem to improve; they are still kept in a comparatively abject condition. And while Hindu males have reaped largely the benefits of Western civilisation, Hindu females are kept deplorably in the background, not only with regard to education, but with regard to their rights to property, and their position generally. If *Sanscrit* scholars have not misled us, Hindu women were in a much better position in the old *Vedic* period. *Mr. Monier Williams*, writing to the *London Times*, observes :—" No one can read the *Vedic* hymns, without coming to the conclusion that, when the songs of the *Rishis* were current in Northern India, (fourteen or fifteen centuries B. C.), women enjoyed considerable independence. Monogamy has probably the rule, though polygamy existed, and even polygamy was not unknown." In *Rig-Veda*, 1, 62, 11, it is said " our hymns touch thee, O strong god, as loving wives a loving husband." The *Assus* had only one wife between them (1, 119, 5,) women were allowed to marry a second time (*Atharwa-veda*, 9, 5, 27.) Widows might marry their deceased husband's brother (*Rig-veda*, 10, 40, 2.) There were even allusions to a woman's choosing her own husband (*Swagam-vara*), which was a common practice among the daughters of *Kshatryas* in the heroic period. * * * The condition of women, as represented in the laws of *Menu*, several centuries later (perhaps about 500 B. C.) was one of less liberty. But, the contradictions in the code show that no settled social organisation unfavourable to women prevailed at that epoch. * * * As time went on, the jealousy of the opposite sex imposed various restraints, restrictions, and prohibitions. A more settled conviction as to some inherent inferiority, and weakness in the constitution of women took possession of men's minds. Yet through the whole heroic period of Indian history, and up to the commencement of the Christian era, women had many rights and immunities, from which they were subsequently debarred. * * * In India, mothers have always been treated with the greatest reverence. We may note, too, that something of the spirit of chivalry was displayed in the tournaments of Indian warriors, who contended for the possession of the heroine of the *Swagam-vara.* Women were certainly not yet incarcerated. They were not yet shut out from the light of heaven behind the *Purdah,* or within the four walls of the *Zenana.* It is even clear from the dramas that the better classes had received some sort of education, or could, at least read and write; and it is noteworthy that, although they spoke the provincial dialects, they understood the learned language, Sanskrit. They often appeared unveiled in public. They were not confined to intercourse with their own families. *Sita* showed herself to the army. *Sakuntala* appeared in the Court of king *Dushyante. Dumayunte* travelled about by herself. The mother of *Rama* came to the hermitage of *Valmiki. Rama* says in reference to his wife, neither houses, nor vestments, nor enclosing walls are the screen of a woman. Her own virtue alone protects her. All those characters may be more mythical and ideal than historical, but they are true reflections of social and domestic life, in the heroic age of India.

After speaking of the gradual decline of the *status* of women, *Mr. Monier Williams* goes on to say that in the time of *Warren Hastings* an assembly of the best *Pundits* was formed in Calcutta for the purpose of drawing up an authoritative summary of Hindu law, and he gives a specimen from this summary taken from the Chapter on Women. Here it is: "A man both night and day must keep his wife so much in subjection that she by no means be mistress of her own actions. If the wife have her own free will, she will behave amiss. A woman must never go out of the house, without the consent of her husband. She must never hold converse with a strange man. She must not stand at the door. She must never look out at the window. She must not eat till she has served her husband and his guests with food. She may, however, take *physic* before they eat. It is proper for a woman after her husband's death to burn herself in the fire with his corpse." These are still Bengal ideas as to women, and it is not difficult to trace herein the effect of the Mahomedan conquest upon the Hindu mind. These notions as to women are purely of Mahomedan origin. Continuing his observations *Mr. Monier Williams* asks, what is the present position of the women in India? and thus describes the climax. A little study of the Indian Office Statistics reveals a condition of prostration which even the most sanguine might pronounce hopelessly irremediable. One hundred millions of women supposed to be actual subjects of the British empire are, with few exceptions, sunk in absolute ignorance. They are unable to read a syllable of their mother-tongue, they are never taught the rules of life and health, the laws of God, or the most rudimentary truths of science. In fact, a feeling exists in most Hindu families that a girl, who has learnt to read and write, has committed a sin which is sure to bring down a judgment upon herself and her husband. She will probably have to atone for her crime by early widowhood. And to be a young widow, is believed to be the greatest misfortune that can possibly befal her. This is a true picture of woman's social and domestic *status*. There has been also a corresponding diminution of her legal rights as has been already alluded to. Let us hear what the late *Mr. Horace Hayman Wilson*, Boden Professor of Sanskrit, at Oxford says in regard to her ancient rights. In Vol. V, of his Works containing a *critique* on *Sir Francis Macnaghten's* Considerations of Hindu law, speaking of the widow, p. 17 he says :—Originally the duty of the widow was only pointed out to her, and she was left in law, as she was in reason, free agent to do what she pleased with that which was her own, but that in later times attempts of an indefinite nature have been made to limit her powers. The eagerness with which the latter doctrine is regarded by the scholiasts of the present day is ascribable in all probability to that contempt for the female sex which they have learned from their Mahomedan masters.

At page 21 he says :—There being no law against the validity of her donation, it follows that she has absolute power over the property—at least such was the case till a new race of lawgivers, with *Jimuta Vahana* at their head, chose to alter it, but they only tampered with the law of inheritance, and the law respecting legal alienation being untouched, remains to bear testimony against their interpretation of a different branch of the law. And at page 22: The ancient lawgivers were too wise to attempt impossibilities, they gave the widow good advice but abstained from legislating what it was impossible to enforce. And he makes many other observations to a similar effect.

The great conflict of authority at the present day in connection with the rights of women relates to the question, whether or not, property *inherited* by a woman constitutes her *Stridhanum*. All are agreed, more or less, as to the different kinds of property which constitute it, as laid down in the books, except as to this one kind, namely, property *inherited*, about which they differ. The text which has given rise to the discussion occurs in the *Mitakshara*, Chapter XI, Section 2, para. 2, which after describing other kinds of woman's property, ends by saying, "and also property which she may have acquired by *inheritance*, purchase, partition, seizure, or finding, are denominated by *Menu* and the rest woman's property." Writers of the *Bengal* school ignore this *dictum* altogether, it being by many regarded as an interpolation. But *Sanscrit* scholars affirm that it is not, but that it is simply the conclusion arrived at in accordance with the previous reasoning of the author. (See *Messrs. West* and *Buhler's Digest*, Vol. II, *Appendix*, where the whole question is elaborately discussed with much learning.)

It has been already observed that the Bengal school whether in imitation of their Mahomedan conquerors, or from motives of expediency, or otherwise, have placed the utmost restrictions upon the power of a woman over her property. The latest decision of the Bengal High Court on the subject is by *Couch, C.J.*, reported in 14, Bengal Reports. In this, the learned Chief Justice reviews all the cases, and after dissenting from the views of the Bombay High Court, more than ever establishes the law as to *Stridhanum* peculiar to Bengal. This was a case of a daughter inheriting from her father. The Madras High Court in its decisions on the question has followed in the wake of the Bengal Courts and has decided the point upon Bengal authorities. The two leading cases of the Madras Courts as to *Stridhanum* are, 2 Madras Reports, 402 ; and 3 Madras Reports, 312, (see also 8 Madras Reports, 88)—the former decided by *Sir Adam Bittleston*, the latter by *Sir Colley Scotland.* The latter seems simply to follow the former and coincides entirely with the reasons therein stated. One ground which appears to have induced the former learned Judge to follow Bengal authorities is the alleged fact that *Sir Thomas Strange* himself seems to have changed his views as to the prevalence of the doctrine of the *Mitakshara* as to *Stridhanum* in Southern India. *Sir Thomas Strange,* it is said, omitted in his edition of 1830 the distinction between the Bengal and the Madras schools, as to the inheritance of a woman constituting *Stridhanum.* He is also stated to have decided that a mother inheriting from a son would not take the property as *Stridhanum* (2 Notes of Cases, 211, decided in 1813). But it is clear that the alleged omission is not an omission of the kind stated. In the edition of 1830 at page 31, *Sir Thomas Strange* gives a list of property constituting *Stridhanum* and in this list he classes as *Stridhanum* property acquired by women by inheritance and the doctrine of the Southern school is alluded to in opposition to that of the Eastern or Bengal school. It is again spoken of by him at pp. 248, 249 of the same edition and is also cited by him as the opinion of *Colebrooke* (2 Strange's Hindu Law, 22) that the doctrine in question is a peculiarity of Southern India. The decision of *Sir Thomas Strange* above spoken of was passed in 1813, long prior to the 2nd edition of his work (1830). The statement in this decision as to the kind of estate which a mother takes from her son is a mere *obiter dictum* and had nothing to do with the merits of that case. Further the foot notes clearly show that the Chief Justice was referring to *Jagannatha* at the time. It is respectfully submitted therefore that the grounds upon which the learned Judge proceeded as the reason for abandoning the Madras doctrine are of a shadowy nature.

In Bombay, however, the Judges have adopted more liberal views as to a woman's inheritance. Various have been the cases there decided on this question. The earliest case of authority there is reported in 1 Bombay Reports, 130, known as *Devkoorabai's* case in which it was decided on the authority of the *Vyavahara Mayukha* and the *Mitakshara*, that *daughters* inheriting immovable estate from a *father* take absolutely. The decision by *Sausse, C.J.*, seems to have been passed after much deliberation, and after consultation with the *Pundits.** The next case is reported in 1 Bombay Reports, 117, in which it was held citing with approval the last case, that *sisters* inheriting to a *brother* take an absolute estate in immovable property by analogy to daughters. All the authorities are cited and reviewed in this case also. The next is in 1 Bombay Reports, 209, in which it is held that immovable property inherited by a *married woman* from her *father*, whether or not it be strictly entitled to the name of *Stridhanum*, descends on her death to her own heirs, and not to her father's ascendants. An inheritance thus descending to a *married woman* from her *father*, *classes* as *Stridhanum* and descends accordingly. The next of importance is in 6 Bombay Reports 1, a well considered judgment passed by *Sir Joseph Arnould*, in which it was decided that a *sister* inheriting to her *brother*, takes his property as *Stridhanum* with an *absolute power of disposition over it*, and such property upon her death passes in the first instance to her daughters. And further that property acquired by a married woman by inheritance *with the exception of property inherited by a woman from her husband*, classes as *Stridhanum*, and descends accordingly.

The last and most important of all the decisions is that of *Mr. Justice West* reported in 8 Bombay Reports, 244. This judgment derives importance not only from the fact of its being the judgment of one well versed in Hindu law and literature, but it elaborately reviews the whole law upon the subject. It holds that the *Mitakshara* recognises only one class of *Stridhanum* and includes in that class *all* property *acquired by a woman by inheritance*. It

* This case seems to have been approved by the Privy Council. See 9 *Moore*, 528.

decides that over *Stridhanum* acquired by inheritance, so far as it consists of *immovable* property, a woman's power of alienation is limited, that the *Vyavahara Mayuka* considers property acquired by a woman by inheritance to be *Stridhanum*, but classes *Stridhanum* under two heads:—*Stridhanum* in a narrower sense, embracing particular species for which a peculiar mode of devolution is prescribed, and *Stridhanum* generally, including *Stridhanum* acquired by inheritance, which descends in the same line as if the woman had been a male, that is, to her sons and the rest, and this notwithstanding her having left daughters.

From these cases of the Bombay Courts it will be observed that the decisions gradually proceed from the qualified statement that some women, under given circumstances, take an absolute estate by inheritance to the broad and unmistakable doctrine laid down by *Mr. Justice West*, that all women by inheritance obtain the estate as *Stridhanum.* But this last decision, though it may be regarded, in one sense, as an advance upon the ordinary Bombay doctrine up to that time received, nevertheless seems to make a sort of compromise of the matter in dispute; for while it classes all the property a woman inherits as *Stridhanum*, it at the same time places a restriction upon a woman's power of alienating immovables. That is to say they will not be allowed to alienate them at mere caprice, but will be in that respect subject to the control of their male relatives.

The whole subject has been reviewed by the learned Judge with great learning and ability, and the judgment is well worth perusal. With reference to the disputed doctrine of the *Mitakshara*, *Mr. Justice West* remarks that *Vijianeswara* in his argument regards the term *Stridhanum* in its *etymological* sense, (Chapter 2, Section 11, para. 3.) This sense will include all property, which a woman gets by inheritance, or by any other mode of acquisition as *Stridhanum.* The refinements, therefore, that arise in the Eastern school as to what does and what does not constitute *Stridhanum* do not appear under the *Mitakshara.* And in this respect, no light matter, this definition of *Stridhanum* has the advantage of simplicity. The learned Judge therefore adopts the doctrine of the *Mitakshara* as applicable to Western India with the qualification attached to it, that as regards the alienation of immovable property inherited,—she shall be subject to control, as this seems in accordance with the spirit of the ancient law. This decision appears to state accurately the law on the subject of *Stridhanum.* Although it does not give the woman the power of absolute disposal over immovable property inherited it must be remembered that according to Hindu law there is no such thing as an absolute estate. Even among males, landed property, though it be self-acquisition, is not alienable without the consent of the co-heirs. And even with regard to *Stridhanum* proper, where it consists of immovable property, it has been held by the Madras High Court (5 Madras Reports) that it is not alienable without the consent of the woman's daughters, who are the reversioners. Under the judgment of *Mr. Justice West* the female is placed in a position analogous to that of the male.

As to the division of *Stridhanum* into two kinds adopted by *Nilakantha,* the author of the *Vyavahara Mayukha,* this has been approved of by some text writers. *Sir W. Macnaghten,* page 38, seems to consider that a woman's estate may be so divided. First, there is what may be called a woman's general estate, and secondly, her *peculium* or *Stridhanum* proper. This division appears to have received some countenance from the Privy Council, for in their judgment above referred to (11 Moore's Indian Appeals, 487) they refer to it as a plausible statement of the law. It is also considered by *Mr. Norton* (1 *Leading Cases,*) as a not improbable solution of the *Stridhanum* question—a solution which in all probability will be attempted by the Privy Council in their decision in the *Shivagungah* case. Up to the present time the judgments of their Lordships on this subject have chiefly had regard to the widow. And the doctrine of the *Mitakshare,* as contained in the disputed text, has been declared by them to be ambiguous. But the question will doubtless receive fuller discussion than it has hitherto done, in connection with the present case. We may therefore expect in course of time a judgment from the Council which, either one way or the other, will finally set at rest the doubts and difficulties which beset the subject of *Stridhanum.**

* See also another decision, 9 Bombay Reports, 3. As to *stridhanum* (Bride Price) see too *Sir Henry Main's* Early History of Institutions.

Independently however of the legal aspect of the question, it seems almost ludicrous in these days to deny to Hindu women at any rate in Southern India rights which they undoubtedly possess as to property. It is dangerous, if not presumptuous, considering the general ignorance of *Sanskrit* that prevails, to assert that the law books on the subject are interpolated. Those who know *Sanskrit* assure us that they are not. The difference between the *Mitakshara* and the *Dayabhaga* is easily accounted for, and the reason of it has been frequently insisted on in these pages. Let Bengalees, however, please themselves, but it is hardly fair to thrust upon Southerners the peculiar tenets of a school which has adopted Mahomedan notions as to the *status* of women. Morally speaking, in thus treating the women of this country we are doing them a cruel injustice. We are in fact encouraging a system among the Hindoos, which, if it had been tolerated in Europe, would have been the means of securing us in a state of comparative bondage and semi-barbarism. There is no reason on earth why Hindu women should be placed in a position inferior to Hindu men. Generally speaking, they are not much inferior to men in point even of education, for the whole race, as a mass, is comparatively speaking uneducated. It is said they are more likely to be imposed upon. But this is to beg the question, and to assume their mental inferiority. There are myriads of male Hindoos uneducated, superstitious, in no better condition than the females, who still are allowed the fullest rights as to property, so far as they are consistent with the Hindu law. It seems anomalous, therefore, that women should not have similar privileges, particularly when those privileges are granted to them by their law. Belonging as we do to the civilized nations of the West, it comes with an ill-grace from us to seek to circumscribe their liberties. The position of Hindu women is one of comparative bondage. Nothing, it is submitted, will tend more to perpetuate this condition than depriving them of legitimate rights over property. Up to the present time the decisions of the Courts have dealt chiefly with the *status* of the widow. Her rights have been restricted, and the position of the other female members of the family have been to some extent, placed upon an analogy to it. In all conscience, the position of the widow in Hindu society is miserable enough, and needs no aggravation. Probably, if a widow were allowed more freedom in the use of property, she might be able to emancipate herself from this forlorn condition. There must be thousands of women who fully appreciate the inhuman and helpless position they are placed in by an antique code of laws or rather by the interpretation of an antique code of law, and who must be only too willing to improve that condition, if they had the means at their disposal. Mammon is a god who commands respect in all societies. A woman of fortune, with the power to use it, would be just as much an object of respect and of adoration in India as well as elsewhere. The example of one strong-minded Hindu female in the matter of re-marriage, for instance, or of the education of her children would be catching. Thousands, perhaps, would emulate her. And the general elevation of the whole race might thus become a problem far more easy of solution than what it is now generally conceived to be. If the reports of *Zenana* missions be true, Hindu women seem far more amenable to instruction, and more open to conviction than the males of that race. If the Courts were to supplement the efforts of educationists by establishing the legal rights of the female, so as to raise her in the social scale, and enable her to regain the position she seems to have fallen from, it is impossible to calculate the beneficial results which would accrue to the country. It is submitted that so important a case as the present would be a fitting opportunity for the highest Court of Appeal to go exhaustively into the question of women's rights to property. And if it be true, as such scholars as *Dr. Burnell* of Tanjore, *Dr. Buhler* of Bombay, and *Mr. Justice West* assure us it is, that at any rate, under the *Mitakshara*, Hindu women, according to the law as at present administered, have the full enjoyment of their rights curtailed, let the truth be finally ascertained, and the matter settled once and for ever in the judgment of this case. It is submitted, therefore, with all respect that, since according to the opinion of eminent *Sanskrit* scholars, women under the *Mitakshara* acquire *Stridhanum* by *inheritance*, that therefore on this ground the *Shivagungah* estate passes as the *Stridhanum* of the late Rani to her daughters, the second, third and fourth defendants in this case.

There are other points of interest connected with the case which perhaps it would be out of place to consider here—points involving

32

nice questions of equity. There is also the consideration that this Estate might be regarded as the *Stridhanam* of the late Rani, on the ground that she acquired it by her own unaided exertions, as the whole record of the Shivagungah litigation only too plainly proves. But these are facts which speak more eloquently for themselves. One point however deserves notice. It was decided in this case that houses purchased by the late *Istimrar* Zemindar, situated out of the Zemindary, and granted by the Rani to her daughters were nevertheless *appurtenant* to the Zemindary, and descended with it. So that upon this principle, if the Zemindar had bought a hovel in Whitechapel, or a wigwam in America, and these had passed to third parties after his death, they would have to deliver them up as being *appurtenant* to the Estate,—another misapplication, it is submitted, of an English term of Real Property.

I cannot conclude these observations without saying that it is a matter for regret that the learned Judge (*P. P. Hutchins, Esq.*,) who tried the case in the District Court, had not, from uncontrollable circumstances, the opportunity of writing an exhaustive judgment in the case, otherwise, from his experience and well known ability, we should have had an able exposition of the views of the other side.

APPENDIX B.

ACT NO. XXI OF 1870.

PASSED BY THE GOVERNOR-GENERAL OF INDIA IN COUNCIL.

(Received the assent of the Governor-General on the 19th July 1870.)

An Act to regulate the Wills of Hindús, Jainas, Sikhs and Buddhists in the Lower Provinces of Bengal and in the towns of Madras and Bombay.

Preamble.

WHEREAS it is expedient to provide rules for the execution, attestation, revocation, revival, interpretation and probate of the wills of Hindús, Jainas, Sikhs and Buddhists in the territories subject to the Lieutenant-Governor of Bengal and in the towns of Madras and Bombay; It is hereby enacted as follows:—

Short Title.

1. This Act may be called "The Hindú Wills' Act, 1870."

2. The following portions of the Indian Succession Act, 1865, namely,—

so much of Parts XXX and XXXI as relates to grants of probate and letters of administration with the will annexed, and

Parts XXXIII to XL, (both inclusive), so far as they relate to an executor and an administrator with the will annexed,

shall, notwithstanding anything contained in section three hundred and thirty-one of the said Act, apply—

Extent of Act.

(*a*) to all wills and codicils made by any Hindú, Jaina, Sikh or Buddhist, on or after the first day of September one thousand eight hundred and seventy, within the said territories of the local limits of the ordinary original civil jurisdiction of the High Courts of Judicature at Madras and Bombay; and

(*b*) to all such wills and codicils made outside those territories and limits, so far as relates to immoveable property situate within those territories or limits:

Provisos.

3. Provided that marriage shall not revoke any such will or codicil:

And that nothing herein contained shall authorise a testator to bequeath property which he could not have alienated *inter vivos*, or to deprive any persons of any right of maintenance of which, but for section two of this Act, he could not deprive them by will:

And that nothing herein contained shall vest in the executor or administrator with the will annexed of a deceased person any property which such person could not have alienated *inter vivos:*

And that nothing herein contained shall affect any law of adoption or intestate succession:

And that nothing herein contained shall authorise any Hindú, Jaina, Sikh or Buddhist to create in property any interest which he could not have created before the first day of September one thousand eight hundred and seventy.

Partial repeal of Bengal Regulation V of 1799, section 2.

4. On and from that day section two of Bengal Regulation V of 1799 shall be repealed so far as relates to the executors of persons who are not Muhammadans, but are subject to the jurisdiction of a District Court in the territories subject to the Lieutenant-Governor of Bengal.

Saving of rights of Administrator-General.

5. Nothing contained in this Act shall affect the rights, duties and privileges of the Administrators-General of Bengal, Madras and Bombay, respectively.

Interpretation-clause.

6. In this Act and in the said sections and Parts of the Indian Succession Act all words defined in section three of the same Act shall, unless there be something repugnant in the subject or context, be deemed to have the same meaning as the said section three has attached to such words respectively:

And in applying sections sixty-two, sixty-three, ninety-two, ninety-six, ninety-eight, ninety-nine, one hundred, one hundred and one, one hundred and two, one hundred and three and one hundred and eighty-two of the said Succession Act, to wills and codicils made under this Act, the words "son," "sons," "child" and "children" shall be deemed to include an adopted child; and the word "grand-children" shall be deemed to include the children, whether adopted or natural-born, of a child whether adopted or natural-born; and the expression "daughter-in-law" shall be deemed to include the wife of an adopted son:

And in making grants under this Act of letters of administration with the will annexed, or with a copy of the will annexed, section one hundred and ninety-five of the said Succession Act shall be construed as if the words "and in case the Hindú Wills' Act had not been passed" were added thereto; and section one hundred and ninety-eight of the said Succession Act shall be construed as if, after the word "intestate," the words "and the Hindú Wills' Act had not been passed" were inserted; and sections two hundred and thirty and two hundred and thirty-one of the said Succession Act shall be construed as if the words "if the Hindú Wills' Act had not been passed" were added thereto, respectively.

The following are the principal sections of the Indian Succession Act (Act X of 1865) above referred to.

PART VII.

OF WILLS AND CODICILS.

Persons capable of making Wills.

46. Every person of sound mind and not a minor may dispose of his property by Will.

Explanation 1.—A married woman may dispose by Will of any property which she could alienate by her own act during her life.

Explanation 2.—Persons who are deaf, or dumb, or blind are not thereby incapacitated for making a Will if they are able to know what they do by it.

Explanation 3.—One who is ordinarily insane may make a Will during an interval in which he is of sound mind.

Explanation 4.—No person can make a Will while he is in such a state of mind, whether arising from drunkenness, or from illness, or from any other cause, that he does not know what he is doing.

Will obtained by fraud, coercion or importunity.

48. A Will or any part of a Will, the making of which has been caused by fraud or coercion, or by such importunity as takes away the free agency of the testator, is void.

Will may be revoked or altered.

49. A Will is liable to be revoked or altered by the maker of it at any time when he is competent to dispose of his property by Will.

PART VIII.

OF THE EXECUTION OF UNPRIVILEGED WILLS.

Execution of unprivileged Wills.

50. Every testator, not being a soldier employed in an expedition, or engaged in actual warfare, or a mariner at sea, must execute his Will according to the following rules :—

First.—The testator shall sign or shall affix his mark to the Will, or it shall be signed by some other person in his presence and by his direction.

Second.—The signature or mark of the testator or the signature of the person signing for him shall be so placed that it shall appear that it was intended thereby to give effect to the writing as a Will.

Third.—The Will shall be attested by two or more witnesses, each of whom must have seen the testator sign or affix his mark to the Will, or have seen some other person sign the Will in the presence and by the direction of the testator, or have received from the testator a personal acknowledgment of his signature or mark, or of the signature of such other person ; and each of the witnesses must sign the Will in the presence of the testator, but it shall not be necessary that more than one witness be present at the same time, and no particular form of attestation shall be necessary.

51. If a testator, in a Will or Codicil duly attested, refers to any other document then actually written, as expressing any part of his intentions, such document shall be considered as forming a part of the Will or Codicil in which it is referred to.

Incorporation of papers by reference.

PART X.

OF THE ATTESTATION, REVOCATION, ALTERATION AND REVIVAL OF WILLS.

Witness not disqualified by interest or by being executor.

55. No person, by reason of interest in or of his being an executor of a Will, is disqualified as a witness to prove the execution of the Will or to prove the validity or invalidity thereof.

Revocation of unprivileged Will or Codicil.

57. No unprivileged Will or Codicil, nor any part thereof, shall be revoked otherwise than by marriage, or by another Will or Codicil, or by some writing declaring an intention to revoke the same, and executed in the manner in which an unprivileged Will is hereinbefore required to be executed, or by the burning, tearing, or otherwise destroying the same by the testator, or by some person in his presence and by his direction, with the intention of revoking the same.

Effect of obliteration, interlineation, or alteration in unprivileged Will.

58. No obliteration, interlineation, or other alteration made in any unprivileged Will after the execution thereof shall have any effect, except so far as the words or meaning of the Will shall have been thereby rendered illegible or undiscernible, unless such alteration shall be executed in like manner as hereinbefore is required for the execution of the Will; save that the Will, as so altered, shall be deemed to be duly executed if the signature of the testator and the subscription of the witnesses be made in the margin or on some other part of the Will opposite or near to such alteration, or at the foot or end of, or opposite to, a memorandum referring to such alteration, and written at the end or some other part of the Will.

59. A privileged Will or Codicil may be revoked by the testator, by an unprivileged Will or Codicil, or by any act expressing an intention to revoke it, and accompanied with such formalities as would be sufficient to give validity to a privileged Will, or by the burning, tearing, or otherwise destroying the same by the testator, or by some person in his presence and by his direction, with the intention of revoking the same.

Revocation of privileged Will or Codicil.

Explanation.—In order to the revocation of a privileged Will or Codicil by an act accompanied with such formalities as would be sufficient to give validity to a privileged Will, it is not necessary that the testator should at the time of doing that act be in a situation which entitles him to make a privileged Will.

60. No unprivileged Will or Codicil, nor any part thereof, which shall be in any manner revoked, shall be revived otherwise than by the re-execution thereof, or by a Codicil executed in manner herein before required, and showing an intention to revive the same; and when any Will or Codicil which shall be partly revoked, and afterwards wholly revoked, shall be revived, such revival shall not extend to so much thereof as shall have been revoked before the revocation of the whole thereof, unless an intention to the contrary shall be shown by the Will or Codicil.

Revival of unprivileged Will.

Extent of revival of Will or Codicil partly revoked and afterwards wholly revoked.

PART XI.

OF THE CONSTRUCTION OF WILLS.

61. It is not necessary that any technical words or terms of art shall be used in a Will, but only that the wording shall be such that the intentions of the testator can be known therefrom.

Wording of Will.

62. For the purpose of determining questions as to what person or what property is denoted by any words used in a Will, a Court must inquire into every material fact relating to the persons who claim to be interested under such Will, the property which is

Enquiries to determine questions as to object or subject of Will.

claimed as the subject of disposition, the circumstances of the testator and of his family, and into every fact a knowledge of which may conduce to the right application of the words which the testator has used.

Misnomer or misdescription of object.

63. Where the words used in the Will to designate or describe a legatee, or a class of legatees, sufficiently show what is meant, an error in the name or description shall not prevent the legacy from taking effect. A mistake in the name of a legatee may be corrected by a description of him, and a mistake in the description of a legatee may be corrected by the name.

When words may be supplied.

64. Where any word material to the full expression of the meaning has been omitted, it may be supplied by the context.

Rejection of erroneous particulars in description of subject.

65. If the thing which the testator intended to bequeath can be sufficiently identified from the description of it given in the Will, but some parts of the description do not apply, such parts of the description shall be rejected as erroneous, and the bequest shall take effect.

When part of description may not be rejected as erroneous.

66. If the Will mentions several circumstances as descriptive of the thing which the testator intends to bequeath, and there is any property of his in respect of which all those circumstances exist, the bequest shall be considered as limited to such property, and it shall not be lawful to reject any part of the description as erroneous, because the testator had other property to which such part of the description does not apply.

Explanation.—In judging whether a case falls within the meaning of this section, any words which would be liable to rejection under the sixty-fifth Section are to be considered as struck out of the Will.

Extrinsic evidence admissible in case of latent ambiguity.

67. Where the words of the Will are unambiguous, but it is found by extrinsic evidence that they admit of applications, one only of which can have been intended by the testator, extrinsic evidence may be taken to show which of these applications was intended.

Extrinsic evidence inadmissible in cases of patent ambiguity or deficiency.

68. Where there is an ambiguity or deficiency on the face of the Will, no extrinsic evidence as to the intentions of the testator shall be admitted.

Meaning of any clause to be collected from entire Will.

69. The meaning of any clause in a Will is to be collected from the entire instrument, and all its parts are to be construed with reference to each other; and for this purpose a Codicil is to be considered as part of the Will.

When words may be understood in a restricted sense, and when in a sense wider than usual.

70. General words may be understood in a restricted sense where it may be collected from the Will that the testator meant to use them in a restricted sense; and words may be understood in a wider sense than that which they usually bear, where it may be collected from the other words of the Will that the testator meant to use them in such wider sense.

Where a clause is open to two constructions, that which has some effect is to be preferred.

71. Where a clause is susceptible of two meanings, according to one of which it has some effect, and according to the other it can have none, the former is to be preferred.

No part of Will to be rejected, if reasonable constructions can be put on it.

72. No part of a Will is to be rejected as destitute of meaning if it is possible to put a reasonable construction upon it.

Interpretation of words repeated in different parts of Will.

73. If the same words occur in different parts of the same Will, they must be taken to have used everywhere in the same sense, unless there appears an intention to the contrary.

Testator's intention to be effectuated as far as possible.

74. The intention of the testator is not to be set aside because it cannot take effect to the full extent, but effect is to be given to it as far as possible.

The last of two inconsistent clauses prevails.

75. Where two clauses or gifts in a Will are irreconcilable, so that they cannot possibly stand together, the last shall prevail.

Will or bequest void for uncertainty.

76. A Will or bequest not expressive of any definite intention is void for uncertainty.

Words describing subject refer to property answering that description at testator's death.

77. The description contained in a Will, of property the subject of gift, shall, unless a contrary intention appear by the Will, be deemed to refer to and comprise the property answering that description at the death of the testator.

Bequest without words of limitation.

82. Where property is bequeathed to any person, he is entitled to the whole interest of the testator therein, unless it appears from the Will that only a restricted interest was intended for him.

Bequest in the alternative.

83. Where property is bequeathed to a person, with a bequest in the alternative to another person or to a class of persons;—if a contrary intention does not appear by the Will, the legatee first named shall be entitled to the legacy, if he be alive at the time when it takes effect; but if he be then dead, the person or class of persons named in the second branch of the alternative shall take the legacy.

Bequest to a class of persons under a general description only.

85. Where a bequest is made to a class of persons under a general description only, no one to whom the words of the description are not in their ordinary sense applicable shall take the legacy.

Rules of construction where a Will purports to make two bequests to the same person.

88. Where a Will purports to make two bequests to the same person, and a question arises whether the testator intended to make the second bequest instead of or in addition to the first; if there is nothing in the Will to show what he intended, the following rules shall prevail in determining the construction to be put upon the Will:—

First.—If the same specific thing is bequeathed twice to the same legatee in the same Will, or in the Will and again in a Codicil, he is entitled to receive that specific thing only.

Second.—Where one and the same Will or one and the same Codicil purports to make in two places a bequest to the same person of the same quantity or amount of anything, he shall be entitled to one such legacy only.

Third.—Where two legacies of unequal amount are given to the same person in the same Will, or in the same Codicil, the legatee is entitled to both.

Fourth.—Where two legacies, whether equal or unequal in amount, are given to the same legatee, one by a Will and the other by a Codicil, or each by a different Codicil, the legatee is entitled to both legacies.

Explanation.—In the four last rules, the word Will does not include a Codicil.

Constitution of residuary legatee.

89. A residuary legatee may be constituted by any words that show an intention on the part of the testator that the person designated shall take the surplus or residue of his property.

Property to which a residuary legatee is entitled.

90. Under a residuary bequest, the legatee is entitled to all property belonging to the testator at the time of his death, of which he has not made any other testamentary disposition which is capable of taking effect.

Time of vesting of legacy in general terms.

91. If a legacy be given in general terms without specifying the time, when it is to be paid, the legatee has a vested interest in it from the day of the death of the testator, and if he dies without having received it, it shall pass to his representatives.

In what case a legacy lapses.

92. If the legatee does not survive the testator, the legacy cannot take effect, but shall lapse and form part of the residue of the testator's property unless it appear by the Will that the testator intended that it should go to some other person. In order to entitle the representatives of the legatee to receive the legacy, it must be proved that he survived the testator.

A legacy does not lapse if one of two joint legatees die before the testator.

93. If a legacy be given to two persons jointly, and one of them die before the testator, the other legatee takes the whole.

Effect in such a case, of words showing testator's intention that the shares should be distinct.

94. But where a legacy is given to legatees in words which show that the testator intended to give them distinct shares of it, then if any legatee die before the testator, so much of the legacy as was intended for him shall fall into the residue of the testator's property.

When lapsed share goes as undisposed of.

95. Where the share that lapses is a part of the general residue bequeathed by the Will, that share shall go as undisposed of.

When a bequest to testator's child or lineal descendant does not lapse on his death in testator's lifetime.

96. Where a bequest shall have been made to any child or other lineal descendant of the testator, and the legatee shall die in the lifetime of the testator, but any lineal descendant of his shall survive the testator, the bequest shall not lapse, but shall take effect as if the death of the legatee had happened immediately after the death of the testator, unless a contrary intention shall appear by the Will.

Bequest to A for the benefit of B does not lapse by A's death in testator's lifetime.

97. Where a bequest is made to one person for the benefit of another, the legacy does not lapse by the death, in the testator's lifetime, of the person to whom the bequest is made.

Survivorship in case of bequest to a described class.

98. Where a bequest is made simply to a described class of persons, the thing bequeathed shall go only to such as shall be alive at the testator's death.

Exception.—If property is bequeathed to a class of persons described as standing in a particular degree of kindred to a specified individual, but their possession of it is deferred until a time later than the death of the testator, by reason of a prior bequest or otherwise, the property shall at that time go to such of them as shall be then alive, and to the representatives of any of them who have died since the death of the testator.

PART XII.

OF VOID BEQUESTS.

Bequest to a person by a particular description, who is not in existence at the testator's death.

99. Where a bequest is made to a person by a particular description, and there is no person in existence at the testator's death who answers the description, the bequest is void.

Exception.—If property is bequeathed to a person described as standing in a particular degree of kindred to a specified individual, but his possession of it is deferred until a time later than the death of the testator, by reason of a prior bequest, or otherwise; and if a person answering the description is alive at the death of the testator, or comes into existence between that event and such later time, the property shall, at such later time, go to that person, or if he be dead, to his representatives.

Bequest to a person not in existence at the testator's death, subject to a prior bequest.

100. Where a bequest is made to a person not in existence at the time of the testator's death, subject to a prior bequest contained in the Will, the later bequest shall be void, unless it comprises the whole of the remaining interest of the testator in the thing bequeathed.

Rule against perpetuity.

101. No bequest is valid whereby the vesting of the thing bequeathed may be delayed beyond the lifetime of one or more persons living at the testator's decease, and the minority of some person who shall be in existence at the expiration of that period, and to whom, if he attains full age, the thing bequeathed is to belong.

Bequests to a class, some of whom may come under the rules in the Section 100, 101.

102. If a bequest is made to a class of persons, with regard to some of whom it is inoperative by reason of the rules contained in the two last preceding Sections, or either of them, such bequest shall be wholly void.

Bequest to take effect on failure of bequest void under Sections 100, 101, or 102.

103. Where a bequest is void by reason of any of the rules contained in the three last preceding Sections, any bequest contained in the same Will, and intended to take effect after or upon failure of such prior bequest, is also void.

PART XXIX.

OF GRANT OF PROBATE AND LETTERS OF ADMINISTRATION.

Character and property of executor or administrator as such.

179. The executor or administrator, as the case may be, of a deceased person, is his legal representative for all purposes, and all the property of the deceased person vests in him as such.

Administration with copy annexed of authenticated copy of Will proved abroad.

180. When a Will has been proved and deposited in a Court of competent jurisdiction, situated beyond the limits of the province, whether in the British dominions or in a foreign country, and a properly authenticated copy of the Will is produced, letters of administration may be granted with a copy of such copy annexed.

Probate to be granted to executor appointed by Will.

181. Probate can be granted only to an executor appointed by the Will.

Appointment express or implied.

182. The appointment may be express or by necessary implication.

Persons to whom probate cannot be granted.

183. Probate cannot be granted to any person who is a minor or is of unsound mind, nor to a married woman without the previous consent of her husband.

Grant of probate to several executors simultaneously or at different times.

184. When several executors are appointed, probate may be granted to them all simultaneously or at different times.

Separate probate of Codicil discovered after grant of probate.

Procedure when different executors are appointed by the Codicil.

185. If a Codicil be discovered after the grant of probate, a separate probate of that Codicil may be granted to the executor, if it in no way repeals the appointment of executors made by the Will. If different executors are appointed by the Codicil, the probate of the Will must be revoked, and a new probate granted of the Will and the Codicil together.

Accrual of representation to surviving executor.

186. When probate has been granted to several executors, and one of them dies, the entire representation of the testator accrues to the surviving executor or executors.

No right as executor or legatee can be established, unless probate or letters of administration shall have been granted by a competent Court.

187. No right as executor or legatee can be established in any Court of Justice, unless a Court of competent jurisdiction within the Province shall have granted probate of the Will under which the right is claimed, or shall have granted letters of administration under the one hundred and eightieth Section.

Probate establishes the Will from testator's death.

188. Probate of a Will when granted establishes the Will from the death of the testator, and renders valid all intermediate acts of the executor as such.

Persons to whom letters of administration may not be granted.

189. Letters of administration cannot be granted to any person who is a minor or is of unsound mind, nor to a married woman without the previous consent of her husband.

From what period letters of administration entitle administrator to intestate's rights.

191. Letters of administration entitle the administrator to all rights belonging to the intestate as effectually as if the administration had been granted at the moment after his death.

Acts of administrator not validated by letters of administration.

192. Letters of administration do not render valid any intermediate acts of the administrator, tending to the diminution or damage of the intestate's estate.

Grant of administration where executor has not renounced.

193. When a person appointed an executor has not renounced the executorship, letters of administration shall not be granted to any other person until a citation has been issued, calling upon the executor to accept or renounce his executorship; except that when one or more of several executors have proved a Will, the Court may, on the death of the survivor of those who have proved, grant letters of administration without citing those who have not proved.

Exception.

Form and effect of renunciation of executorship.

194. The renunciation may be made orally in the presence of the Judge, or by a writing signed by the person renouncing, and when made shall preclude him from ever thereafter applying for probate of the Will appointing him executor.

Procedure where executor renounces or fails to accept within the time limited.

195. If the executor renounce, or fail to accept the executorship within the time limited for the acceptance or refusal thereof, the Will may be proved and letters of administration, with a copy of the Will annexed, may be granted to the person who would be entitled to administration in case of intestacy.

Grant of administration to universal of residuary legatee.

196. When the deceased has made a Will, but has not appointed an executor, or when he has appointed an executor who is legally incapable or refuses to act, or has died before the testator, or before he has proved the Will, or when the executor dies after having proved the Will but before he has administered all the estate of the deceased; an universal or a residuary legatee may be admitted to prove the Will, and letters of administration with the Will annexed may be granted to him of the whole estate, or of so much thereof as may be unadministered.

Right to administration of representative of deceased residuary legatee.

197. When a residuary legatee who has a beneficial interest survives the testator, but dies before the estate has been fully administered, his representative has the same right to administration with the Will annexed as such residuary legatee.

Grant of administration when there is no executor, nor residuary legatee, nor representative of such legatee.

198. When there is no executor and no residuary legatee or representative of a residuary legatee, or he declines or is incapable to act, or cannot be found, the person or persons who would be entitled to the administration of the estate of the deceased if he had died intestate, or any other legatee having a beneficial interest, or a creditor, may be admitted to prove the Will, and letters of administration may be granted to him or them accordingly.

Citation to be issued before grant of administration to any legatee other than universal or residuary.

199. Letters of administration with the Will annexed shall not be granted to any legatee other than an universal or a residuary legatee, until a citation has been issued and published in the manner hereinafter mentioned, calling on the next of kin to accept or refuse letters of administration.